INHERITING THE CROWN IN JEWISH LAW

INHERITING THE CROWN IN JEWISH LAW

The Struggle for Rabbinic Compensation, Tenure, and Inheritance Rights

JEFFREY I. ROTH

University of South Carolina Press

© 2006 University of South Carolina

Published in Columbia, South Carolina,
by the University of South Carolina Press

Manufactured in the United States of America

10 09 08 07 06   5 4 3 2 1

Library of Congress Cataloging-in-Publication Data

Roth, Jeffrey I., 1947–
   Inheriting the crown in Jewish law : the struggle for rabbinic compensation, tenure, and inheritance rights / Jeffrey I. Roth.
     p. cm.
   Includes bibliographical references and index.
   ISBN 1-57003-608-X (cloth : alk. paper)
   1. Rabbis—Legal status, laws, etc. (Jewish law) 2. Rabbis—Selection and appointment. 3. Rabbis—Salaries, etc. 4. Inheritance and succession (Jewish law) I. Title.
   KBM2614.R33R68 2006
   296.6'1—dc22

2005025950

Portions of this volume were published previously as "Three Aspects of the Rabbinate: Compensation, Competition and Tenure," in *Drake Law Review* 45 (1997): 569–624, and "Inheriting the Crown in Jewish Law: The Question of Rabbinic Succession," in *Jewish Law Association Studies 10: The London Conference Volume,* edited by E. A. Goldman (Atlanta, Ga.: Scholars Press, 1997). Permission is gratefully acknowledged.

To
Beatrice, Barbara, Alex and Cam, Frank and Natalie
Sources of inspiration
Sources of love

CONTENTS

Acknowledgments ix

Prologue 1

PART 1 COMPENSATION
1 "A Spade for Digging" 5
2 "The Way of Torah Is Bread with Salt" 10
3 The Throne of Honor 15
4 "Nowadays the Prince of Forgetfulness Reigns" 23
5 The Variety of Rabbinic Emoluments 27

PART 2 COMPETITION
6 "These Fees Embarrass Us" 37
7 The Residence Right and the Residence Ban 41
8 "The Envy of Scholars Increases Wisdom" 45
9 "No Better Than an Outright Thief" 49
10 Rabbis and Schoolteachers: Two Competitive Regimes 52

PART 3 TENURE
11 "All the Same, Go and Consult Them" 59
12 Justifications for Tenure 63
13 Tenure and Merit 68
14 Alternatives to Tenure 72
15 The Community versus the Tenured Rabbi 77

PART 4 SUCCESSION
16 "When Will These Two Old Men Die?" 85
17 The Case against Inheritance: Part One 89
18 The Case against Inheritance: Part Two 94
19 Forging a New Consensus for Inheritance 103
20 Explaining the New Consensus: Rabbinic Posts as Property 112
21 Inheritance in the Modern Era 116

Epilogue 122

Notes 125
Bibliography 155
Index 165

ACKNOWLEDGMENTS

The road we travel in this volume is not a well-trodden path. Studies that address the legal history of the rabbinic profession are few and far between. At the same time, rabbinic literature itself is a vast and churning sea of codes, responsa, treatises, periodicals, and encyclopedias. I was fortunate to have access to the impressive Judaica collections at two institutions of higher learning, Hebrew Union College–Jewish Institute of Religion in New York and Spertus Institute of Jewish Studies in Chicago.

A mentor once defined scholarship as a dialogue. A portion of this study was presented at the Jewish Law Association conference in London in June 1996. In addition, many colleagues read portions of the work, including Arnold Enker, Mayer G. Freed, David M. Cobin, Richard D. Klein, and Yale L. Rosenberg. I am grateful for their comments. Research for the study was supported in part by Touro College Law Center of Huntington, New York. I would like to thank Dean Howard A. Glickstein for his support.

The Jewish Historical Institute (Zydowski Instytut Historyczny) of Warsaw, Poland, is a major cultural resource for the Jews of Central Europe and for interested visitors from abroad. The Torah crown, dating from 1853, that appears on the cover of this volume is displayed in the Institute's Gallery of Jewish Art dedicated to the memory of Jack Burton Weissman, M.D. The permission of Dr. Feliks Tych, the Institute's director, to use this image is gratefully acknowledged.

Finally, at the University of South Carolina Press I found supportive partners to help give this study tangible form. To Barry Blose and his colleagues, I express appreciation for their attention to detail that never lost sight of broader perspectives.

INHERITING
THE CROWN IN
JEWISH LAW

PROLOGUE

Who is the ideal religious leader? In the Jewish tradition, religion, history, and law combine to provide an unequivocal answer. The ideal religious leader is a scholar motivated solely by love of God who is devoted to studying and teaching the Torah for its own sake, expecting no compensation in this world but surely receiving a reward in the world to come. This selfless ideal, divorcing communal leadership from material gain and coupling it with devotion to study, has evident religious appeal. It posits that the persons best qualified to exercise spiritual authority over the community as rabbis, teachers, and judges are those persons who are least concerned with matters of material advancement, including their own. But the ideal also entails a practical problem, for the individual called to service must still somehow support himself and his family.

This volume traces the history of this principle in Jewish law and documents a striking departure from the classic ideal. In the end, accepting compensation became the norm for rabbis, scholars, and judges. For, while calling upon its sages to study and teach the Torah without compensation, at the same time Jewish law never endorsed asceticism as a way of life even for them. The law never permitted the sages to withdraw from the world, shun its concerns, choose to live in poverty, and renounce family obligations. It never sanctioned the establishment of monastic orders that would have made this possible. Instead, Jewish law created for its scholars, with their consuming passion for the Torah, a deep conflict between their desire to meditate on the Law day and night, on the one hand, and the mundane necessities of seeking a livelihood and supporting a family, on the other.

This study of legal history assesses how the authorities of Jewish law adjusted these two compelling needs, in the process defining the material contours of the rabbinate. Part 1 presents the controversy between those authorities who wished to uphold the classic ideal of uncompensated service and those who held the times demanded a change, arguing that a full-time salaried rabbinate was urgently required to minister to the needs of the Jewish people. Parts 2, 3, and 4 explore the ways this rabbinate, once salaries were sanctioned, insulated its material gains from competitors, strove to secure the benefits of rabbinic office for life, and claimed the right to pass their posts to their qualified heirs at death. Together these developments tell a story of legal ingenuity and religious courage, of flexibility in Jewish law and of changes responsive to historical circumstances that ultimately, although sometimes reluctantly, laid the foundation for the modern professional rabbinate.

PART I

Compensation

Chapter 1

"A SPADE FOR DIGGING"

The rabbinate is both ancient and new. Jewish tradition regards Moses as a rabbi for he occupied himself with learning the Torah and teaching it to others, judging the people according to its laws, and guiding the nation in accordance with its spirit. In Jewish eyes, when Moses laid his hands on Joshua and made him his successor, he ordained him as a rabbi.[1] But the Hebrew Bible is not peopled with rabbis. They do not walk among its patriarchs and prophets, warriors and priests, psalmists and kings. Centuries after the close of the biblical era, "rabbi" will appear as a title for learned sages in Judea who are ordained as judges by their peers.[2] Another millennium must pass before the modern profession begins to take shape. In Europe, seasoned scholars who have matured in their studies will be awarded a type of ordination, allowing them to judge cases according to Jewish law and to minister as rabbis to the religious needs of the continent's growing Jewish communities.[3] The nineteenth century will be well underway before a rabbinical seminary of the modern type opens its doors.[4]

Still, in every generation there were those who, like Moses, occupied themselves with study and teaching of the Torah and judging their neighbors' cases. The people naturally directed questions about their ancestral traditions to these scholars, whom they knew in earliest times as elders (*zeḳanim*), scribes (*soferim*), and sages (*haḳhamim*).[5] These learned individuals shared a religious outlook that valued piety, scholarship, continuity, and tradition. They taught that the world is based on three principles: Torah study, worship, and acts of kindness.[6] In their teachings they stressed observance of God's commandments, service to the Jewish nation, and, above all, love of Torah. If they were not rabbis, they were the profession's able precursors.

The sages recommended making one's house a meeting place for scholars and absorbing their words, preferably in silence.[7] When they advised everyone to acquire a teacher, they used the Hebrew word for master (*rav*).[8] This suggests they likened the student-teacher relationship to that of the master and his disciple, or the craftsman and his apprentice. When *rav* becomes *rabbi*, it means "my master" in the sense of teacher, mentor, and spiritual and practical guide through life.

The early teachers believed it was their duty to place their knowledge of the Torah at the nation's disposal free of charge, to serve as the people's judges and teachers without accepting compensation from them. The Mishnah ruled, "If one takes a fee for judging, his judgments are void."[9] Commentators noted the plural "judgments" in the Mishnah's formulation of the rule. To them this signified that a judge who took a fee to decide a case invalidated not just his verdict in the specific case but all his verdicts, for accepting compensation marked him as an unworthy jurist in general.[10]

Scholars of the Talmudic era held it was inappropriate to use their Torah knowledge to derive worldly benefits like status or wealth. Rabbi Zadok gave this principle its classic formulation when he admonished colleagues never to use the Torah "as a crown for self-glorification nor as a spade for digging."[11] Both tangible and intangible benefits are forbidden. A learned person may neither display his Torah knowledge as one might wear a crown, seeking honor and acclaim for his learning, nor use his Torah knowledge as a spade—a tool to extract material profits and amass wealth. Hillel added a cautionary addendum to Rabbi Zadok's maxim: a scholar who makes a worldly profit from his knowledge of the Torah will perish from the world.[12]

That it is proper for scholars to divorce their Torah knowledge from material gain has an unimpeachable biblical source in Moses. In his farewell address to the Israelites, Moses said, "Behold, I have taught you statutes and ordinances, even as the Lord my God commanded me" (Deut. 4:5). Rabbinic commentators focused on the phrase "even as the Lord my God commanded me," asking why Moses included it in his address. Surely he could not have been seeking to reassure the people regarding either the source of his teachings or their accuracy, for the Israelites would never have suspected Moses of teaching them incorrect laws or laws he had received from any source other than God.[13] Instead, the phrase was meant to convey something about the manner in which they should transmit the law to future generations. As Moses was privileged to learn the Torah directly from God free of charge, so he instructed the nation and so they must instruct future generations. At Mount Sinai, Moses learned by example from God that teaching Torah to others must be performed without asking for or receiving compensation.[14]

The Talmud is replete with stories of the hardships endured by learned men who sought their livelihoods apart from their calling as scholar, teacher, and judge. These sages engaged in a wide variety of secular trades and occupations as farmers, woodchoppers, tanners, laundrymen, sandal makers, carpenters, wine tasters, water carriers, and tailors.[15] In part, their dual status reflected the nature of their ancient society in which roles were not specialized and functions overlapped. It also reflected the stratum of society from which the sages primarily were drawn. Their strain of Judaism was a popular movement that attracted both adherents and leaders largely from the ranks of the common folk. But their situation can also be attributed at least in part to their taking to heart the admonition against using one's knowledge of Torah for material gain.

There were, however, darker sides to the matter. A gap developed between scholars who were well-to-do and those who were not. The Talmud tells of an occasion on which Rabban Gamaliel, the distinguished leader of the assembly of scholars in Yavneh (Jamnia) at the end of the first century C.E., visited Rabbi Joshua to apologize for a wrong. Upon seeing that the walls of Rabbi Joshua's house were black,

Rabban Gamaliel said, "It is apparent you are a smith." Rabbi Joshua replied, "Alas for the generation of which you are the leader, seeing that you know nothing of the troubles of the scholars, their struggles to support and sustain themselves."[16] In subsequent generations, Rabban Gamaliel's successors, the patriarchs (*nesi'im*) of the Jews in the Roman period, supported poor scholars in their vocations.[17]

Some indigent scholars were forced by their circumstances to consider extreme measures to support themselves and their families. The Talmud relates the case of a poor scholar who considered divorcing his wife for the sole purpose of enabling her to collect her marriage settlement from its guarantor, her father. He then intended to remarry her and live off the proceeds of the settlement while continuing his studies. He was dissuaded from this course of conduct only upon learning that as a descendant of priests, he would be prohibited from remarrying his former wife once she became a divorcée.[18]

In addition, the prohibition on earning a living from the Torah impeded the development of a full-time professional rabbinate. By definition, the sage who was true to his calling could spend only part of the day studying Torah, for the rest of the day he would have to spend earning a living. Later, Maimonides would embrace this concept as an ideal, recommending that one work three hours a day and study Torah for nine.[19] Further, it seemed to some that only those blessed with wealth who employed workers to earn a living for them were entitled to become scholars. In this vein, the School of Shammai held that one may teach only the student who is wise, meek, of distinguished ancestry, and rich.[20] The School of Hillel countered that one may teach everyone.[21]

It became clear even in Talmudic times that some accommodation would have to be made for the material needs of the scholar, or the position of Shammai's school, that only the wealthy should be taught, would become the norm by default. The result was a patchwork of preferences and exemptions for the sage that, while falling short of a steady salary, tended to improve his material situation. The scholar was exempt from communal taxation.[22] If he engaged in trade, he was entitled to priority in the marketplace.[23] He opened his stall first and other merchants selling similar wares could not open until he sold out his stock. This ensured him the best price for his merchandise and also permitted him to return to his scholarly pursuits early in the day. Returning a scholar's lost articles of property was a priority.[24] Disciples were required to perform personal services for their teacher, relieving him to that extent of the need to hire servants.[25] If a sage became engaged in litigation, his case was moved to the head of the court's docket and tried first.[26] The scholar called away from his work to judge a case might ask the litigants to supply someone to continue his labor while he was involved in their litigation.[27] Wealthy merchants were encouraged to take on scholars as silent partners in their businesses, to invest their assets and share the profits with them.[28] Their reward would be to share by association in the scholar's honor and prestige, for "whoever casts merchandise into the pockets of scholars will be privileged to sit in the Heavenly Academy."[29] And a scholar might always marry into a wealthy family. Fathers were encouraged to marry off their daughters to worthy scholars, provide them with large dowries, and augment the settlement with generous bequests.[30] The sages taught: "Let a man always sell all he has and marry the daughter of a scholar, and marry his daughter to a scholar."[31]

Was the scholar who took advantage of these preferences using the Torah as a spade for digging? Any scholar who felt this way was at liberty to decline the preferences, and doing so was considered a mark of personal piety.[32] But at the same time, in each case a basis for the preference was found that allowed the scholar to accept the benefit without violating the letter—if not the spirit—of Rabbi Zadok's maxim. Scholars were exempt from taxation just as priests were exempt from the yearly half-shekel contribution all other Jews were required to donate to the Temple.[33] Some of the sages argued that, after the destruction of the Temple, the people should give their tithes to them, rather than to the priests.[34] Regarding the market priority, this was a custom that ordinary merchants sometimes extended to each other out of honor and respect, even when the honoree was not a learned individual. Why then should it not be available as a matter of course to the scholar-merchant?[35] Accepting household help and personal service from one's disciples was a way of teaching them humility and fear of Heaven.[36] Furthermore, the Torah commands all Jews to "cleave unto the Lord" (Deut. 4:4). Yet how is this possible, for the Torah states that "the Lord your God is a devouring fire" (Deut. 4:24)? The answer is to cleave unto the Lord's scholars by marrying off one's daughters to them, engaging in trade on their behalf, and generally putting one's assets at their disposal.[37]

In addition, justifications were found that permitted elementary school teachers to be paid. They could receive a fee for "babysitting" their charges, that is, guarding their students of tender years against harm during school hours, totally apart from any services performed in teaching them.[38] Also, they could accept a stipend for teaching aspects of the Jewish heritage that were not part of the revelation at Sinai, such as the accentuation of the biblical text.[39]

Harder to reconcile with the ideal of uncompensated service was the practice of a judge named Karna, who collected a coin of equal value from each litigant and then pronounced his verdict.[40] In the Talmud's discussion of this practice there follows a string of objections, each of which is surmounted in turn: Was Karna violating the prohibition on judges' taking bribes? No, for he had no intention of perverting justice by rendering an unjust verdict. But is it not prohibited for a judge to receive a gift even when he renders a righteous judgment? Karna was not receiving a gift but compensation. How then was his verdict valid, for is it not the rule that the verdict of a judge who receives compensation for judging is invalid? Karna did not receive compensation for his judging but rather to replace the earnings he lost from his secular profession during the hours he was engaged as a judge. But have we not learned that a judge who accepts such compensation is contemptible? That epithet does not apply to Karna, but only to the judge who accepts such compensation where the losses from his secular occupation are not proven. In Karna's case, the losses he incurred from suspending his secular occupation were proven. Karna was engaged by the wine merchants in his locality as a quality control expert. He could determine by smelling the vats of wine which would age well and should be held back for sale at a later date and which would age poorly and should be sold at once. He was very much in demand in his profession and had employment every day, so that whenever he was called upon to act as a judge he incurred a *proven* monetary loss.[41] The Talmud depicts Karna as a very discerning individual with a nose for truth as well as a nose for wine; hence the heavy demands on his time.

Later commentators saw in Karna's example the solution to a vexing problem in the Talmud. One passage tells of certain judges in Jerusalem who received salaries from the Temple treasury. If the amounts were insufficient to cover their living expenses, they were given an increase even if they objected.[42] Another passage mentions learned men who tutored priests in the rules of ritual procedure. They too received fees from the Temple treasury.[43] The payments appeared to violate two legal norms, the one against taking a fee for judging[44] and the other against using one's Torah knowledge to derive material benefits.[45] Commentators explained why in fact no violation had occurred in either case. Like Karna, these men were awarded a "suspension fee" (*sekhar battalah*),[46] a payment to recoup the earnings they lost when they suspended their regular secular trades in order to have the time to judge cases or to teach the priests, as the case might be.[47] Thus their salaries were not impermissible payments for judging or teaching per se but rather compensation for their inability to earn their livelihoods from their usual employment while so engaged.

A related concept was the "fee for trouble" (*sekhar tirha*). This permitted a scholar to accept a fee, not for performing a religious duty, but for the physical toil and trouble involved in preparing to do so, such as handling large animals before inspecting them for blemishes that would disqualify them as altar sacrifices in the Temple.[48]

However deft the verbal formulations used to justify the scholar's preferences, exemptions, and fees, by the end of the Talmudic period Rabbi Zadok's ideal of uncompensated Torah service was very much attenuated, much like a common law rule riddled with exceptions. In fact, virtually all of the principles that in the coming centuries were to work a complete reversal of the ideal were already in place.

Chapter 2

"THE WAY OF TORAH IS BREAD WITH SALT"

In the aftermath of the Muslim conquest, the Jewish communities in Babylonia found themselves in the midst of an expanding empire that came to encompass half the known world and a majority of the world's Jews. When the Abbasid caliph Abu Jafar (al Mansur) established his seat in Baghdad in 762, Jews in Baghdad occupied a position at the very center of the empire. As People of the Book, the Jews were a protected community within the new empire, and they obtained from the regime the right to establish an indigenous religious competence.[1] In the vicinity of Baghdad, rabbinical colleges (*yeshivot*) in Sura and Pumbeditha, with predecessors in the Talmudic era, revived as major academic, administrative, and judicial centers for the Jews of Babylonia and other parts of the Arab world. The schools, possessed of both the text of the Talmud and the oral traditions needed to interpret it, applied Talmudic law to contemporary conditions.[2] Through the collective wisdom of their scholars, they answered legal inquiries received by post from Jewish communities in Eretz Israel, Egypt, North Africa, and Spain. In the process, they established the Talmud as the basic source of postbiblical Jewish law and ingrained in the Jewish public the habit of turning to the yeshivah and its head (*rosh yeshivah*) to render rulings in novel legal situations.[3]

Although the scholars in the schools deliberated collectively to arrive at legal conclusions, the final rulings always issued in the principal's name only. He alone had the right to represent the institution and to speak in its name.[4] The principals known during this period by the title "Excellency" (*gaon,* pl. *geonim*)[5] were drawn from a small number of distinguished families that provided candidates for four hundred years.[6] They were accorded extraordinary honors, maintained courts of oriental splendor, wore robes of gold on ceremonial occasions, and administered the Jews under their jurisdiction with a cadre of salaried officials and judges whom they appointed.

To support the enterprise, agents of the geonim collected levies from Jews at home and solicited donations from coreligionists living abroad. The two geonim and a third Jewish official, the exilarch (Aram. *resh galuta,* "head of the Exile"), divided the Jewish communities of Babylonia (roughly present-day Iraq and Iran) into three jurisdictions, one for each, with the exclusive right to farm their territory for revenues. The gaon received a salary for his personal use that may have amounted to one-half of the contributions received from abroad.[7] To support the network of colleges, judges, and local officials, the geonim adopted a managerial style described as "the maintenance of a retinue of scholars at public expense by relentless importuning for contributions."[8] Through frequent correspondence with local notables and the visits of their personal emissaries, the geonim provided the Jews of the Muslim empire with religious guidance and received in return allegiance and financial support.

In the course of centuries, Jewish communities that were distant from the Babylonian center, particularly in North Africa and Europe, achieved religious independence from the geonim. They developed their own ranks of rabbinic scholars who settled among them, opened academies, judged their controversies according to Jewish law, and ministered to their religious needs. We have a vivid account of how this happened in Spain in the tenth century in *The Book of Tradition* by Abraham ibn Daud.[9] He relates how Rabbi Moses ben Hanokh, together with his son and three prominent scholars, were aboard a ship en route to a rabbinic assembly in Babylonia (the semiannual month of public study known as the *kallah*) when pirates took them hostage. The captain sold Moses and his son in Cordova, where the townsfolk redeemed them from slavery. At first Rabbi Moses did not reveal his scholarship. One day, he attended a lecture by the local judge, Rabbi Nathan. Although Spanish scholars at the time were not completely learned in Jewish lore, they had some knowledge of it and were able to teach it more or less accurately. At a certain point in the lecture, Rabbi Moses raised an objection. As he explained his reasoning and answered questions, the listeners came to recognize his erudition. Rabbi Nathan abdicated his post in favor of Rabbi Moses, and the townsfolk appointed him as their judge. Ibn Daud writes, "The community then assigned him a large stipend and honored him with costly garments and a carriage."[10] From that date forward, Spanish Jewry looked to him for religious guidance rather than to the geonim in Babylonia.

Ibn Daud depicts a clean break with the geonim, but the decline of the Babylonian academies and their influence abroad was a protracted process of decentralization and shifting centers of gravity in Jewish life.[11] Still, the middle of the tenth century, when Rabbi Moses arrived in Spain (whether in the manner legend recounts or in another manner), was a pivotal time in the development of Spanish Jewry. Its close ties with the geonim had been in place for two centuries, ever since the Babylonian Talmud was introduced to Spain, and were fostered by the unifying culture of the Islamic empire, centered in Baghdad with Spain at its western extremity.[12] Despite the distance and the fact that Spain was ruled by rival emirs and caliphs, for centuries the Babylonian geonim maintained closer ties to Spanish Jewry than to the Jews of any other European land.[13] Now the presence of prominent rabbinic scholars, like Rabbi Moses ben Hanokh, and the opening of their academies on Spanish soil brought a loosening of links to the ancient Babylonian center. By the time the ties were severed, the Jewish communities of Muslim Spain had been conditioned by the geonim, through frequent appeals and even occasional threats, to support Torah scholars generously with their wealth.[14] This ingrained habit did not cease in the middle of the tenth century, but the recipients shifted. It was natural for Spanish communities to transfer their financial support from distant academies to local institutions and scholars, just as Ibn Daud relates. Local scholars became the beneficiaries of the community chest.[15]

It was against this background of expensive religious pomp and circumstance, and perhaps in reaction to it, that Moses Maimonides, who was born in Cordova in 1135, reaffirmed the classic ideal of uncompensated devotion to Torah for its own sake. Viewing the situation with the hindsight of more than a century, Maimonides observed not just the lavish material aspect of the geonic enterprise and its offshoots but also the noticeable decline over time in the quality of its academic and literary output, especially in contrast to the preceding epoch that had produced the two Talmuds, Bavli and Yerushalmi. Maimonides concluded the two factors were related.

In the broad panorama of Jewish history, the geonic era was a necessary period of consolidation after the brilliant Talmudic age. The tasks were to study, preserve, and promulgate the vast and intricate corpus of Talmudic jurisprudence, to promote the Babylonian version of the rabbinic tradition, and to defend Talmud and tradition against attacks from the Karaites, efforts in which the geonim were largely successful. But Maimonides saw only decline. In his writings, he is uncompromising in his condemnation of Torah scholars molded in the geonic model, who were able to earn a living by labor but instead chose to support themselves with donations from the public. In Maimonides' view, such individuals profane the name of God, despise the Torah, extinguish the light of faith, cause harm to themselves, and remove their lives from the world to come, for it is forbidden to profit materially from words of Torah in this world.[16]

Maimonides himself was the foremost exemplar of his own philosophy. During the early decades of his life, he migrated with his family through Spain and North Africa, fleeing persecution, eventually settling in Egypt. At first he lived as a silent partner off the earnings of the family's business in precious gems conducted by his brother David.[17] After David was lost at sea, Maimonides employed his extensive knowledge of medicine to earn his living as a physician. His skill in the healing arts and his friendship with the vizier led to his appointment as a physician to the sultan's court in Egypt.[18] All the while, he ministered to the religious needs of the Jewish community in Egypt without receiving compensation for this service.

Maimonides extolled as paradigms of virtue his scholarly forebears of the Talmudic era, the choppers of wood and drawers of water, who, despite material hardship and physical disability, combined the study of Torah with labor.[19] Their decision to engage in labor to support themselves was not undertaken in the face of an indifferent public unconcerned about their material well-being, for had the sages asked for communal support for themselves and their schools, the public would have responded generously, filling their coffers with gold and precious stones.[20] But the sages of old refrained from asking, for they had concluded correctly that deriving material gain from knowledge of the Torah is prohibited by the Torah.

For Maimonides, earning one's living by ordinary labor is a mark of excellence in every man, including the sage.[21] Ideally his study of the Torah should occur at fixed times, while the pursuit of his trade should occupy only the remaining hours of the day, for accumulating great wealth is inconsistent with a life dedicated to Torah.[22] The way of Torah is to eat bread with salt, drink water in small measures, sleep on the ground, and endure the hardships of life while toiling to perfect one's knowledge of the Torah.[23] Rewards are sure to follow, but in the world to come.[24]

In Maimonides' view, those who had succeeded in convincing the public that it was their duty to support Torah scholars with donations made a fundamental error. They took isolated exceptions to the rule—the cases of scholars who were too ill or too old to work at a secular trade and hence forced to accept charity to survive—and turned them into a permissive norm for all to follow.[25] This is error, for a scholar who is able to work and earn a living apart from the Torah must do so.[26] In imposing this obligation from his perch of financial independence, Maimonides sought both to remain faithful to ancient traditions and to safeguard the rabbinate's freedom in decision making. He feared that the rabbis' growing economic dependence on their communities for their livelihoods would jeopardize their autonomy as free and impartial judges and arbitrators.

Although inconsistent with his overall view of the matter, Maimonides nonetheless endorsed the scholar's priorities and exemptions that had solid roots in Talmudic jurisprudence, each with its own justification.[27] He ruled that scholars were exempt from taxes and from communal work obligations, entitled to priority in the marketplace and the courthouse, and should have their lost articles restored first.[28] Where it is the custom of the country to pay elementary school teachers a salary, they may accept it, but only for teaching youngsters the Bible, not the oral law.[29] He approved of the arrangement whereby a scholar placed his assets with an individual who utilized them on the scholar's behalf.[30] But these preferences and their rationales never coalesced in Maimonides' writing into a broad justification for rabbinic compensation in general.

Maimonides also failed to endorse the suspension fee as a way to compensate rabbis, scholars, and teachers. In his commentary on the Mishnah, Maimonides discusses Karna's case,[31] but interestingly, he recites the facts differently from the way they are presented in the Talmud.[32] In his rendition of the facts, Maimonides cites Karna as offering the litigants who requested his services as judge two options, only one of which involved paying him a fee. According to Maimonides, Karna asked the litigants either to supply someone to do his work while he was judging their case or to pay him the earnings he would forgo.[33] By contrast, in the Talmud, Karna requests the suspension fee, while another sage, Rav Huna, asks litigants to provide someone to irrigate his fields while he is trying their case.[34] Now it is extremely unlikely that Karna would have or could have requested someone to perform his work for him because his profession, as we saw in the preceding chapter, as a quality control expert for wine merchants, was highly specialized, unlike irrigating fields, a task that any fit individual could perform. Hence it was unlikely that a suitable replacement with Karna's expertise in wine testing could ever be found, which also explains why Karna himself was so much in demand that he had work every day.[35] Either Maimonides melded the two Talmudic cases, or he felt Rav Huna's practice implicitly would have been acceptable to Karna.[36] In any case, Maimonides weakens the force of Karna's example as a precedent by stating an acceptable alternative that does not involve paying him a fee. In his code of Jewish law, Maimonides cites his version of Karna's practice in his treatise on courts and judges as a practice acceptable for judges,[37] but there is no mention of the suspension fee in his treatise on Torah scholars and teachers.[38]

Maimonides anticipated that the majority, or perhaps even all, of his colleagues would find fault with his position condemning rabbinic compensation.[39] In this he was correct. We turn to the critique of Maimonides' position in the following chapters.

Chapter 3

THE THRONE OF HONOR

In the generation following Maimonides' death, the tension between the classic ideal that he championed and the hard realities facing the Jewish communities in Europe was already evident. Early in the thirteenth century, Rabbi Eliezer of Bohemia sent a letter to a colleague, Rabbi Judah ben Samuel Hahasid (d. 1217), concerning a practice certain Jewish communities had instituted to collect funds for the town's cantor.[1] Collections were undertaken on the holidays of Purim and Simhat Torah, and the communities also collected a fee from the guests at wedding banquets for the fund to compensate the cantor. Rabbi Judah Hahasid, espousing the traditional view of the matter, opposed the practice as a form of imposition that lacked a proper legal foundation. Beyond that, his opposition was rooted in a social and religious current coursing through Ashkenazic Jewry at the time. Among their many ethical, mystical, and social teachings, the "pietists of Ashkenaz" (Hasidei Ashkenaz) believed that wealth was an implement for serving God, bestowed on some for a religious purpose—to support the less fortunate.[2] In their view, communal assessments that fell upon rich and poor alike were an economic abuse and a religious error that interfered with the divine will for the distribution and utilization of wealth. They should be opposed, as Rabbi Judah Hahasid did here.

Rabbi Eliezer wrote his colleague to try to persuade him to withdraw his opposition before knowledge of his views led to communal harm. Rabbi Judah Hahasid was a pivotal figure in the world of Hasidei Ashkenaz, with a wide circle of disciples, students, and followers. If his opposition to the collections became widely known, Rabbi Eliezer feared that some members of the public would rely on it as grounds for refusing to contribute their share of the assessments. This would deprive many communities of the means to compensate their cantors, for they had no other source of funds, and no one was going to serve as a cantor without the prospect of adequate compensation. Rabbi Eliezer wrote:

> If you eliminate the collections at wedding feasts, Purim, and Simhat Torah, then in most places in Poland, Russia, and Hungary, where, because of their poverty, they lack Torah scholars and have to engage whatever intelligent individual they may find as their cantor, preacher, and teacher, and make assurances to him based on these [collections]—if you eliminate them, their compensation will be inadequate and they will vacate their posts, leaving the communities without Torah, without prayer, and without a teacher of righteousness.[3]

Rabbi Eliezer viewed the collections as a continuation of the half-shekel levy ordained by the Bible for the upkeep of the Temple.[4] But what authorized religious functionaries such as cantors to accept compensation? Rabbi Eliezer suggested a biblical antecedent to justify their fees. "From Zion our Creator fixed compensation for the caretakers of His sanctuary," he wrote.[5] For although priestly service in the Holy Temple in Jerusalem was beloved in the eyes of all, the priests and Levites were not commanded to serve gratuitously. On the contrary, the Torah ordained an elaborate system of tithes and gifts for Levites and priests, portions of sacred things they were entitled to consume, for, according to the Torah, "it is your reward for your service in the Tabernacle" (Num. 18:31).

In our days, Rabbi Eliezer wrote, we offer prayers in synagogues in the place of sacrifices in the Temple. Prayer requires a quorum of ten, and a quorum requires the services of a cantor, for without a cantor prayer lacks the beauty that is pleasing to the Creator. Since no one will serve as a cantor in our day without compensation, and communal collections are needed to raise funds for this purpose, it follows that such collections should not be condemned. He urged his colleague to withdraw his objections before they led to communal harm.

Rabbi Eliezer's brief letter is an important contribution to the debate over compensation. That the synagogue service stands in place of the Temple cult is a well-accepted notion in Judaism. The citation of biblically ordained Levitical tithes and priestly gifts as precedents for compensating synagogue personnel is therefore strong and compelling. At the same time, he refrained from mentioning any of the traditional arguments against compensation. Further, he extended the discussion beyond the matter at hand—fees for cantors—and applied his analysis to all necessary religious functionaries, including teachers and preachers. Most significantly, he grounded his reversal of the traditional approach on the pressing needs of the Jewish community of his day, a time when no one would come forward to serve in a religious capacity without adequate compensation.

From Rabbi Eliezer's letter we learn that opposition to compensation for religious personnel might emanate from two sources in Ashkenazic Jewry: a segment of the rabbinate that remained faithful to traditional inhibitions, like Rabbi Judah ben Samuel Hahasid, and a segment of the public that was all too willing to follow their lead and resist contributing their assessments. We know that the situation could be radically different in Spain. There, large, grateful, well-to-do congregations were likely to endow the rabbinic scholars in their midst with generous stipends, costly garments, and carriages.[6]

The comfortable circumstances enjoyed by the leader of a large Jewish community in Spain are confirmed in a letter of Judah ben Asher, who served as rabbi of Toledo, Spain, from the death of his father, Rabbenu Asher ben Yehiel, in 1328, until his own death in 1349. Judah wrote his letter, which he calls a "Letter of Admonitions" (*iggeret tokhahot*),[7] as an ethical will for his children, commanding them to read it once a month and mend their ways in accordance with his views. The letter is equal parts autobiography and family chronicle, ethical tract, financial report, last will and testament, and trust indenture. In the fashion of the time, it contains Rabbi Judah's moral teachings for his offspring, interspersed with reflections on his life, his family's history, an accounting of his finances, and directions for the distribution of his estate.

Judah recounts many parts of the story relating how his father's family came to reside in Spain.[8] His father, Rabbenu Asher, was one of the principal rabbinical scholars in Germany during the latter half of the twelfth century and the beginning of the thirteenth. When government authorities imprisoned the community's foremost religious authority, the renowned Rabbi Meir of Rothenburg, and held him for ransom, German Jewry looked to Rabbenu Asher for leadership. But he feared that he would suffer the same fate as Rabbi Meir and left Germany with his family.[9] They settled first in France and then in Barcelona. When a vacancy occurred in Toledo's rabbinic chair, one of Barcelona's scholars, Rabbi Solomon ibn Adret, recommended Asher for the post. He was installed in 1305. During an illustrious tenure lasting more than two decades, the Ashkenazic scholar served as the revered shepherd of the prominent Sephardic community. He authored halakhic works of lasting importance, introduced the German style of Talmud study to Spain, and produced learned sons. One of them, Jacob (d. 1340), wrote an important Jewish legal code, *Arba'ah Turim*. He never held a rabbinic post. Another son, Judah (d. 1349), was elevated to the rabbinate of Toledo at his father's death.

In his letter, Judah states categorically that his own merit played no role in his selection to be Toledo's rabbi. He regards himself as the least of Asher's sons.[10] At the time of his father's death, there were others in the town who were more learned and more deserving of the post. He had no experience that would suit him for high office, and his scholarship was lacking. Yet the Lord in His grace inclined the inhabitants to view him favorably. Judah attributes his selection as Toledo's rabbi to God's providence, the community's generosity, and their love for his father.[11] Judah writes movingly of Divine Providence guiding him through life: "He directed me in a strange land, made me to find favor and love and mercy in the eyes of its people, and set me upon a throne of honor."[12] From what the author recounts, his rabbinate was conducted in an exemplary fashion, with mutual respect and affection between the community and their leader, ample time for Torah study, no undue communal burdens, nor any hint of communal strife. Litigants, including government officials, readily accepted his decisions as judge, not because of his wisdom but because God disposed them kindly toward Judah and they regarded him as a capable and impartial judge.[13]

The throne of honor Judah occupied provided him and his family with an undeniably comfortable existence. When, toward the middle of the tract, he turns from ethical teaching to financial accounting, Judah surveys, in a precise and methodical manner, seven categories of financial assets and how he fared in each category —inheritance, marriage settlements, gifts, loans, investments, salary, and pension.

From his father he had inherited next to nothing. Rabbenu Asher's estate was not large enough to satisfy all of the bequests in his will, and Judah's sole inheritance was a share of his father's library.[14] From his two marriages Judah netted only enough to pay for the wedding celebrations. He never accepted gifts from well-wishers except on one occasion. When he sought a loan for his sister's marriage from three individuals, they insisted on tendering the sum he requested as a gift. Because they were prominent personages, Judah felt unable to refuse.[15]

Judah borrowed large sums of capital from wealthy individuals. He then placed the capital with agents to invest on his behalf. He could not manage the investments himself because that would detract from the time he devoted to his Torah studies. It was his intention to live off the profits his investments earned and to repay his creditors. But Judah was disappointed as an investor. The agents deducted commissions, risked capital, lost large parts of it, earned meager profits, and paid these tardily and only after being pressured. As a result, both to support his family and repay his debts, Judah felt compelled to accept a salary from the *kahal* (Toledo's Jewish community), but he regretted having to do so. He hoped that once he repaid his creditors, he would be able to forego his salary. He even entertained the notion that he might one day refund his salary through the gift of his library to the kahal and the sale of some of his assets.[16]

Fortunately, the community was generous in providing ample compensation. Although his salary began rather modestly, it was increased substantially over the years. Judah relates that during the first two years and four months after his father's death, he received from the kahal, under the terms of the contract, a total of 1,290 gold pieces.[17] There seems to have been a gap in time after the first contract expired. When, however, the congregation learned that their religious leader was thinking of relocating to another city, they entered into a new contract that stipulated an annual salary of 1,500 gold pieces. This arrangement continued for close to a decade. At that point, upon learning of Judah's investment losses and his intention to emigrate to Seville, the heads of the kahal increased his salary to 3,000 gold pieces annually. In addition, each of Judah's sons whose occupation was Torah study was granted a stipend of 300 gold pieces per year. Also, the community awarded its rabbi a pension of 1,000 gold pieces annually for his wife and children payable for ten years after his death.

With ample provision for his family's material well-being, Judah was able to devote a substantial portion of his wealth to charitable purposes. He tithed for charity 10 percent of his income from all sources. In his tithing, Judah continued a practice his father imported from Germany to Spain while, at the same time, expanding its scope beyond what Rabbenu Asher required. Judah quotes the original agreement in Rabbenu Asher's handwriting that obligated the parties to tithe "all business profits, whether interest on investments or trade transactions."[18] Judah and his brothers went further. They agreed to tithe, in addition to business income, "whatever is or shall be in the hand of any of us, whether it consists of money, legacies, gifts, marriage settlements, or any other property."[19] Judah incorporates the terms of this agreement in his letter, recommending that his younger children, who were not yet signatories, sign the agreement after his death, and hoping that others in the community would follow their example.

Judah next turns to his will and gives his testamentary instructions. He directs that two thousand gold pieces be invested and the profits accumulated to create a dowry for his daughter Dona's marriage.[20] He bequeaths the token amount of one hundred gold pieces to each of his sons. He places the balance of his estate in a trust fund under the control of his wife during her life and names, to direct the trust after her death, five treasurers (trustees)—two sons, his brother, Rabbi Eleazar, and two town notables. He directs them to disburse the income of the trust fund and, where necessary, the principal to support his sons and sons-in-law who were engaged in Torah study as their occupation. The payments were to be based on each family's needs. Sons not engaged in Torah study but who are God fearing and assist their learned brothers are also eligible to receive support from the trust. With any surplus funds, the trustees might support members of his father's family who needed financial assistance. Finally, he authorizes the trustees to devote remaining funds to support any needy Torah students.

Judah concludes his ethical tract with three heartfelt prayers.[21] The first is for the congregation as a body and those individuals who assisted him, that God might requite their generosity. The second is a prayer that the congregation would treat his descendants as they had his father and himself, with kindness after kindness. The final prayer is that God's bounty and his fathers' merit might cause that there never fail from among his offspring someone to fill Rabbenu Asher's rabbinic chair in Toledo. This prayer for a rabbinic dynasty should be read alongside Judah's repeated requests for his sons to make Torah their main object, to teach Torah daily to others, and to engage in Torah studies as their sole occupation.[22] In essence, he wanted all of his sons to be rabbis and one of them to be elevated to Toledo's rabbinic chair.[23]

To the modern eye there is something striking about Judah's financial accounting. It is not the appearance of the data in the midst of a religious and ethical tract, for the document is also his will, and the financial data serve as the predicate for his bequests. It is, rather, the specificity of the information Judah conveys about his finances. We read the exact amounts he earned, down to the last gold piece, during each contract period, and the total he received from the kahal as salary to the time of his writing (37,240 gold pieces), the exact amount he tithed to charity (3,724 gold pieces), the amounts of his loans and his investments (various amounts such as 3,000, 7,000, and 8,500 gold pieces),[24] the precise amount of his outlays for his sons (18,090 gold pieces), the size and duration of his wife's pension (1,000 gold pieces annually for ten years), and the amount of his sons' stipends for Torah study (300 gold pieces annually per son). It is clear that he wanted his readers—primarily his wife and sons—to have the specifics of his financial history and not just a general understanding of the matter. In memorializing for them the details of his agreements with the kahal, his purposes would appear to have been twofold. First, he was providing a road map to their entitlements, particularly those that would accrue after his death, such as his wife's pension and his sons' stipends. He wanted them to know the specific terms of the congregation's undertakings so that they could enforce them after his death and collect their due. He referred them to a variety of materials that would help them—his account books, an appraisal of his library, a letter from the congregation that he had retained for years.[25] Second, he was educating his descendants about the business of being a rabbi. Using his own experiences to enlighten his offspring, he provided a detailed account of his rabbinic career and its emoluments to both guide and temper their expectations. From studying his letter they would learn how to conduct their relationships with the kahal and with other possible financial benefactors and what they could reasonably anticipate as compensation and benefits. Reading about his experiences, perhaps they would learn to be cautious when taking loans and placing their assets with agents for investment.[26]

Given his dual objectives—ethical training and financial education—in the same tract, Judah's endeavor to portray himself as a traditional Torah sage, remote from financial matters, was destined never to succeed. If at one point he wrote that he never made contract demands of the congregation,[27] at another point he blessed the kahal for "granting all of my requests."[28] Judah was a frequent borrower and wrote that God put it in the hearts of men to lend him capital,[29] but it cannot be the case that potential creditors simply approached and offered loans. Judah must have spent some time and effort cultivating his relationships with wealthy individuals, soliciting loans from them and creating the conditions under which they would treat his requests for capital favorably. From the detailed accounting of his lifetime's finances, it is clear he was a meticulous record keeper. A good portion of each week must have been spent tallying items of income and expenditure, updating account books, and filing important documents for future reference. He budgeted his sons' expenses and kept track of the modest demands his daughters-in-law made on their husbands.[30] He must have done the same for his own household. He engaged three individuals to appraise the contents of his library and two to witness his will.[31] In the will, through the combination of outright bequests in token amounts to his sons, coupled with a generous trust fund should they elect to make Torah study their occupation, he used financial incentives effectively to channel his sons' behavior in a direction he desired. If his financial house was in order, it was not by happenstance but by dint of Judah's efforts, a combination of negotiating, borrowing, investing, budgeting, and saving supported by proficient record keeping, filing, appraisal, and estate planning.

Judah's attitude toward his wealth was noticeably ambivalent. He employed an impressive array of rhetorical strategies to explain and justify it. He wrote, "He fed me with my allotted bread, and I had no impulse to run after money; but He thought differently, and God caused it to come into my hand."[32] Judah did not pursue wealth and made no demands on the congregation. He deemed himself unworthy of receiving emoluments even from the smallest community, all the more so from the great congregation of Toledo.[33] The generous compensation he received was due not to Judah's merit or efforts but to God's bounty, the merit of Judah's forefathers, the generosity of the community, and their affection for his father, Rabbenu Asher.[34] God causes men to lend him their capital. They force gifts upon him and he cannot refuse. He has no alternative but to accept, having inherited nothing from his father and earning little as an investor. The salary irks him and he would rather have done without it, but engaging in business would interfere with his Torah studies. Further, he requires funds to repay his creditors.

At the same time, Judah's prosperity filled him with happiness and gratitude. He wrote, "Wealth, too, the Lord, blessed be He, hath bestowed on me beyond the ordinary, in that He hath provided me with the measure of mine allotted bread. I rejoice in my portion."[35] His gratitude toward the congregation and his individual benefactors knew no bounds. Too numerous to count are the occasions on which he thanked them for the mercies they showered upon him, like manna from heaven. Judah never used this metaphor in relation to himself, but he did employ it in relation to his children: "And if the Law was given to those who ate the manna, surely ye are in [a] similar case."[36]

And what of Rabbi Zadok's maxim never to use the Torah as a spade for digging? Judah reads a chapter from *Avot* (Ethics of the Fathers) daily and recommends the same course for his children.[37] We would expect an ethical will to draw heavily on this work, and Judah does not disappoint us. While his letter is studded with moral teachings derived from *Avot*,[38] it does not mention Rabbi Zadok's maxim.[39] Judah's objection to accepting a salary from the kahal was not "using the Torah as a spade for digging." His objection was to being forced to eat from other men's tables, that is, becoming beholden to others for his livelihood.[40] At the same time, Rabbi Zadok's teaching is present implicitly in Judah's conflicted attitude toward his salary. He was uncomfortable taking it, would have preferred to do without it, felt compelled by circumstances to accept it, took less than the kahal offered, hoped in the future to forego it, and wanted to refund it should circumstances permit. All of these sentiments can be traced to the traditional teaching against using the Torah as a spade for digging. Yet Judah's salary is the lynchpin of his economic existence. Aside from his salary, all other sources of income—inheritance, marriage settlements, gifts, loans, and investments—yielded him little or nothing. He reminds his children, "All that you possess comes from the congregation and the trust fund."[41] The result is profound ambivalence.

In an interesting passage, Judah flexes his financial muscles. He considered and decided against returning to the congregation any surplus in his salary not needed for his family's maintenance.[42] Since the congregation contributed the money to him for a religious purpose, he reasoned, he would not return it to them to use for secular purposes. Instead, he would use it to support deserving Torah students, and surely he was in a better position than the congregation to decide who was deserving. Further, if a question in this regard arose between his sons and other students, he would select his sons, whose method of Torah study was known to him, rather than others whose methods were unknown. In any event, the congregation would get the credit for this good deed, "for I and mine are theirs."[43] In this passage Judah acknowledges his economic clout in relation to the congregation and displays self-confidence in his ability to deploy assets correctly.

In Judah we see a rabbi growing accustomed to having adequate financial resources and learning what he could do with them. He could provide daily sustenance for his family's table, a library for his sons,[44] a generous dowry for his daughter, and a pension for his wife. He could contribute 10 percent of his income to charity. After his death, his sons and sons-in-law would have stipends for Torah study. There would be a trust fund to support needy members of his father's family and all deserving students of Torah. Surely Judah must have felt that life in these comfortable circumstances, with his ample capacity to provide for his family, do good in the community, and promote Torah study near and far, was undeniably better than a life of privation and hardship, possessing little, eking out a meager income through occasional trade, and, most importantly, losing in pursuit of his living precious hours that could have been spent studying Torah.

Judah's situation marks an intermediate stage on the way to a salaried rabbinate.[45] In the Toledo of his day we find the availability of salary, offered by a grateful, well-to-do congregation, and a rabbi who is prepared to accept it, however reluctantly, and use it as he sees fit. What is missing to complete the transformation is a religious rationale for the salary, a cogent, well-reasoned halakhic justification that would permit rabbis to accept their compensation without reservations. There is no hint of this in Judah's letter. He did not mention arguments like those of Rabbi Eliezer of Bohemia[46] or propose any new rationales for accepting a salary, other than to state the traditional complaint that having to engage in commerce for his livelihood would detract from his time to study the Torah. But the ancients were aware of this dilemma, and even so they advised part-time secular employment and modest living, not accepting compensation in exchange for one's Torah knowledge.

A new approach to rabbinic compensation must await the appointment of Rabbi Simon ben Zemah Duran as chief rabbi of Algiers. We turn in the next chapter to the far-reaching arguments he developed to justify his rabbinic salary.

Chapter 4

"NOWADAYS THE PRINCE OF FORGETFULNESS REIGNS"

Maimonides' attack on rabbinic compensation was a rearguard action that failed to persuade his colleagues or dissuade them from taking fees. While most of his critics simply overruled him sub rosa, relying on the scholar's traditional exemptions and priorities as a way to make the rabbinate their profession and to receive compensation for their endeavors, others penned point-by-point refutations of his sources and reasoning.

Among Maimonides' major disputants on this point was the chief rabbi of Algiers, Rabbi Simon ben Zemah Duran.[1] In some respects, their lives and careers paralleled each other with surprising symmetry, but in other respects their circumstances veered in opposite directions. Like Maimonides a century earlier, Duran was forced to flee with his family from anti-Jewish persecution in Spain and settled in North Africa. Also like his predecessor, Duran was schooled in both rabbinics and secular knowledge, including medicine. But in Algiers, Duran found an impoverished Jewish community much different from the Jewish community in Egypt. Unlike Maimonides, he was unable to earn a living as a physician, for the populace relied on folk remedies for healing rather than on doctors.[2]

At the same time, the Jewish community recognized Duran's learning. They were anxious to engage him as their rabbi and to compensate him for his service. Here, Maimonides' rulings created an impasse for Duran. Algerian Jewry regarded the Rambam (Maimonides) as their foremost authority. The Rambam's uncompromising position on rabbinic compensation seemed to bar Duran's engagement.[3] Nor was there any support to be found in Maimonides' code for the notion that Duran could be compensated for his lost earnings as a physician, earnings he would surely be unable to recoup if he were engaged full time as the chief rabbi of Algiers. In the end, though, the community adopted this rationale as the basis for paying him a salary. Duran's salary was collected from each Jewish household by special assessment on a weekly or monthly basis and paid monthly according to the lunar calendar, so that in leap years he received a thirteenth payment.[4]

In part to justify receiving a salary, Duran published an extensive tract disputing Maimonides' position on rabbinic compensation.[5] But the scope of his argument extended well beyond his own arrangement in Algiers. Duran developed and presented a series of legal and policy rationales that, in his view, would permit Jewish communities to pay salaries to their rabbis and permit the rabbis in good conscience to accept them. He clearly perceived, as Maimonides did not, that Israel now required the services of a full-time professional rabbinate and that this would not be possible without compensation for practitioners.

Duran's arguments had a large and durable impact and, in an indirect way, infiltrated Maimonides' code, *Mishneh Torah*. Rabbi Joseph Karo, author of the foremost commentary on the code, adopted Duran's views on this issue. In his comments on the passage in which Maimonides condemns scholars who accept compensation, Karo engages in an energetic refutation of Maimonides' position that tracks Duran's arguments closely.[6] This is a striking departure for Karo, who in most instances supports Maimonides' legal rulings and details the sources on which they are based. Since Karo's commentary is printed in all standard editions of *Mishneh Torah,* Duran's arguments are available in the margins to anyone who consults Maimonides' code on this point.

For his critics, Maimonides idealized the ancient sages, painting an inaccurate portrait of their times to accord with his view that compensation was forbidden. If the Talmud depicts the great sages of yore as performing menial labor, such as Hillel as a chopper of wood, then surely the depiction can apply only to their early days before their merit as scholars became apparent.[7] But it was impossible for Maimonides' critics to believe that once a sage such as Hillel had acquired the full measure of his wisdom and begun teaching Israel, he continued to earn his living as a woodchopper.[8]

Rather, they held, it had always been the case, even in Talmudic times, that the community supported its scholars with funds to ensure their livelihoods. It is a positive commandment, a mitzvah, imposed on the community as a whole to honor the scholars and students in its midst and to maintain them at a comfortable level of support.[9] This certainty of communal support for life comprises one of the glories of Torah above all other professions, for while the ability to perform labor wanes with old age and leaves the laborer destitute, the Torah provides an honorable living to its practitioners even in their declining years.[10]

The Talmud stipulates that the high priest must exceed his fellows in splendor, strength, wisdom, and riches; and if he is lacking in riches, his fellow priests must endow him with their wealth.[11] From this, Duran drew an analogy: just as fellow priests were required to enrich a high priest, so too are all Israel obligated to endow the needy scholar in their midst.[12] Duran buttressed his conclusion by citing a Talmudic dictum that equates giving gifts to scholars with offering first fruits in the Temple.[13]

From the fact that the Talmud permits the teachers of young children to be paid, Duran constructed an a fortiori argument. If elementary school teachers merit a stipend from the community, then how much more so do the learned sages who teach Torah to seasoned scholars at the highest level.[14] The admonition against accepting fees for teaching, attributed in the Talmud to Moses,[15] Duran regarded as merely a midrash, not a clear-cut halakhic pronouncement, and thus possessing less authority as a legal norm.[16]

That students and scholars were maintained by the public in the Talmudic era is substantiated in the Talmud itself. It mentions a certain *shipura* whose custody passed from one college principal (rosh yeshivah) to his successor.[17] The meaning of the term is uncertain. Rav Sherira Gaon (10th c.) explained it as a community collection box for donations to support students at the academy.[18] Rashi cites a second explanation that it was a ram's horn (shofar) used to sound the end of the Sabbath.[19] Duran preferred the first explanation, for Babylonian sages such as Rav Sherira had traditions from their predecessors concerning the meaning of unfamiliar terms in the Talmud.[20] This then was a clear indication that scholars in the Talmudic age were maintained with public donations.

In the era after the close of the Talmud, as we have seen, the geonim employed a widespread network of agents to obtain contributions to support their schools. For Maimonides this practice constituted a serious breach of law and tradition that needed to be remedied. By contrast, for Duran the long usage legitimated the practice as a custom that had taken on the force of law. Custom is particularly effective in establishing the law in a case such as this where the halakhah is, at best, uncertain.[21]

If in days of yore the sages declined compensation and engaged in secular labor, they did so as an act of piety to fulfill the scriptural verse "By the sweat of your brow shall you get bread to eat" (Gen. 3:19). In those days the nation received competent religious guidance from part-time scholars because the ancients had the ability to perform labor and study Torah and to succeed at both. But not all generations are alike in this ability. Nowadays the prince of forgetfulness reigns, even among great scholars, and anyone who tries to occupy himself with both scholarship and a secular occupation succeeds at neither.[22] For this reason today's sages must guide their conduct by the commands of a different verse, the one that requires them to meditate on the Torah "day and night" (Josh. 1:8), that is, full time. They must forgo all secular employment and accept compensation from the community to make the Torah their sole profession.[23]

Further, the functions the Torah sage is called upon to perform had changed over the course of time. While retaining the roles of teacher and religious authority, he had in many locations acquired the functions of a community administrator, sharing responsibility with town councilors to dispense and oversee community-wide services as diverse as charity, education, discipline, rule making, and relations with government officials. The rabbi's new role had two implications bearing on his compensation. First, a rabbi was entitled to compensation for his communal service on the same basis as anyone who renders a service that benefits the community as a whole, such as the learned men in the Temple who tutored the priests in the laws governing the sacrificial rites.[24] Second, the rabbi should receive compensation at a generous level that exceeds his mere subsistence requirements. As a leader of the Jewish community, he must present himself in public with the stature and dignity that befit his high communal position, appearing more like a grandee than a simple laborer, both to represent the Jews appropriately vis-à-vis the Gentile population and to elicit respect from the ordinary Jews who must obey his edicts.[25]

Maimonides' opponents also took issue with him over the tenor of public opinion on the matter. He believed that the sight of Torah sages receiving fees for their services would debase Torah in the public's eyes, making Torah appear like all other occupations, merely a way to earn a living.[26] For his critics, it was more degrading for Torah sages to appear before the public as menial laborers or ordinary tradesmen. If the public observed them in the marketplace struggling to earn a living, they would not respect them as communal leaders or obey their religious admonitions.[27]

Maimonides' critics acknowledged a small kernel of truth remaining in his position, a pious sentiment firmly rooted in Jewish tradition to which all could agree. No one should embark upon a career as a teacher or scholar with the deliberate purpose of earning a living from their Torah knowledge.[28] This would be using the Torah as a spade for digging, condemned by Rabbi Zadok in the Mishnah.[29] When, however, one has commenced his studies with all the proper motivations and pursued Torah knowledge for its own sake, then rewards are sure to follow and there is no impropriety in accepting them.[30] This is what the Talmud meant when it admonished, "One should not say, I will read Scripture that I may be called a Sage; I will study, that I may be called Rabbi . . . but learn out of love, and honour will come in the end."[31]

Duran and Karo argued that the sage who accepts compensation has no cause to believe that he is acting in a manner that is less than completely pious, for in their view the very definition of piety had changed in the course of time. If in former times declining compensation as rabbi or scholar and working at a trade were considered pious, at present a life devoted solely to Torah is considered a righteous life.[32] The times demand it. This generation is governed by the biblical verse that is the clarion call to radical change in Jewish law: "It is a time to act for the Lord, for they have violated Your teaching" (Ps. 119:126). Thus even if the sages, both before Maimonides and after, who accepted compensation to make the Torah their profession were annulling one principle of Jewish law, they were justified in doing so, for they acted to preserve the rest, lest the Torah be forgotten in Israel.[33]

Chapter 5

THE VARIETY OF RABBINIC EMOLUMENTS

With a full complement of arguments on behalf of compensation, Duran and others laid a solid legal foundation for the economic well-being of the rabbinate. By the fifteenth century it was the norm for Ashkenazic Jewry to compensate their rabbis,[1] and by then the practice was already well established in Sephardic communities.[2] Still, rabbis continued to feel the need to justify their salaries well into the sixteenth and seventeenth centuries.[3] At the very least, a community could pay its rabbi a salary, and he could accept it as long as the parties regarded the payments as a suspension fee, that is, compensation for wages the scholar lost from not pursuing a secular occupation.

This suspension fee differed in material respects from its Talmudic antecedent. In the Talmud, the wage earner who was also a scholar received a suspension fee on the occasions when litigants called him away from his everyday trade to judge their legal cases. He was allowed to recoup his proven lost wages. The judge in the Talmudic era who took a suspension fee without demonstrating his actual losses was considered contemptible. By contrast, the suspension fee that underlay the professional rabbi's salary was paid to someone who had no other employment to suspend and hence no lost earnings. Now it is true that if the individual had avoided the rabbinate as his profession and engaged in some secular trade instead, he surely would have received wages, but that amount was entirely a matter of speculation and could not possibly be proven. These unprovable wages could not be the basis of a suspension fee in the Talmudic sense.[4]

Fees for services performed on Sabbaths and festivals, such as delivering a sermon, were also difficult to justify as suspension fees based on the Talmudic precedents.[5] On these holy days the rabbi or preacher, who would have refrained from working at a secular trade, would not have had any gainful employment to suspend and hence no lost earnings to recoup.

Despite its theoretical shortcomings, the suspension fee rationale was applied to rabbinic salaries. As a justification for rabbinic compensation, halakhic authorities preferred it to the broad "change of circumstances" argument that Duran had so methodically articulated in his responsa. There were compelling reasons for this preference. Given the great distance in time between the Talmudic era and the modern era, arguing that "times have changed" could jeopardize the entire corpus of Talmudic jurisprudence. Further, a change-of-circumstances argument seems at odds with a revealed legal system claimed to be divinely inspired and formulated for all times. By contrast, the *sekhar battalah* (suspension fee) had a basis in the Talmud itself and permitted rabbis to argue that they were not receiving a salary but something else. At the same time, everyone understood that the suspension fee was in reality a salary. Its availability as a matter of course made it possible to enter the rabbinate directly as a career without first engaging in or even preparing for any other profession. In short, the suspension fee was transformed from the Talmud's measure of actual economic loss into an acceptable legal fiction used to justify rabbinic salaries whose propriety remained subject to question.

Despite the stated justification for his salary, in most locales the incumbent was still free to engage in a secular trade while maintaining his position as rabbi. This was sometimes a necessity, for salary payments were liable to be interrupted when community elders found themselves short of funds.[6] Further, in all but the largest Jewish communities, rabbinic salaries were low.[7] A synod representing the Jewish communities of Castile, meeting in Valladolid in 1432, found it necessary to decree that every community of forty households or more pay its rabbi a *living* wage in order to prevent him from begging.[8]

How rabbis dealt with salaries that were less than generous differed from time to time and place to place. A study of the Italian rabbinate during the Renaissance found that Italian rabbis had other employments and sources of income, so that the small rabbinic salaries they received were in fact suspension fees, intended as payments to cover the income they lost during the short periods of time when they suspended their gainful employment to execute their communal duties.[9] By contrast, a study of the Lithuanian rabbinate three centuries later found that when rabbis were not involved in community affairs, they engaged in nonremunerative study of Torah for its own sake. They had no secular employment and no income apart from their rabbinic salaries, which were "extremely meager."[10] Under the circumstances, no one objected when the rabbi's wife supported the family by running a general store or when her parents provided living expenses for years after the marriage.[11] To build up their assets, some rabbis returned to business pursuits between rabbinic posts.[12]

Some trades happened to be particularly suitable for scholars seeking to supplement their rabbinic salaries. A rabbi might be employed as the community's scribe, notary, and archivist, copying books and deeds, issuing official documents, taking minutes at meetings, and keeping the community's records.[13] He might be engaged by various associations to lecture their members on religious topics on a weekly or monthly basis.[14] Rabbis instructed young children in the elementary classroom and were hired by the wealthy as private tutors for their sons.[15] The rabbi who headed a prominent yeshivah would receive the majority of his salary from the school and only a small stipend from his rabbinic post, which came to be regarded as an adjunct to his academic tenure.[16] A rabbi engaged as a moneylender or pawnbroker would be occupied in business affairs for only a brief period each day, freeing the remainder of his time for rabbinic pursuits, just as Maimonides had recommended.[17] Rabbis became printers, both to earn extra income and to disseminate their views and the views of other scholars.¹⁸ The rabbi who served as a matchmaker enjoyed a natural advantage over his competitors, for as principal of an academy he was acquainted personally with many eligible bachelors.¹⁹

Nor did the availability of salaries put an end to the scholar's traditional preferences and exemptions. The impact was cumulative. The salaried rabbi was still entitled to priority in the marketplace if he engaged in trade, enabling him to sell out his wares before anyone else.²⁰ In some communities, the rabbi was granted a monopoly for the sale of certain commodities in order to supplement his income.²¹ In many towns the Jewish community owned a house situated near the study hall and made it available rent free as the rabbi's residence.²² In addition, the tax exemption for scholars was retained as an important benefit of the profession.²³ The rabbi's share of government levies would be apportioned among the town's other residents and paid by them.²⁴

In most communities, in addition to his regular salary, the rabbi collected a fee for his services. Like the cantor who sang at a wedding and the sexton who arranged the hall, the rabbi received a fee for presiding. In Poland, the rabbi who performed a marriage received 1.6 percent of the value of the bride's dowry and remitted half to the chief rabbi of Poland.²⁵ The fees were not freewill donations but were assessed according to a graduated rate schedule adopted by ordinance in each community and stipulated in the rabbi's contract (*k'tav rabbanut*), also known as the *tena'im* or "conditions" of employment. The contract of Rabbi Menahem Spira of Friedberg, dating from 1575, guaranteed him a salary of twelve gulden a year, exemption from taxes, and a variety of fixed fees for his services: for arranging a marriage—one gulden; for administering the oath of a widow—one gulden per hundred gulden of the value of her marriage contract; for drawing a bill of divorce—six shillings; and for examining the competence of a ritual slaughterer—two chickens.²⁶ The contract of Rabbi Asher Loeb, the *Sha'agat Aryeh,* of Metz, France, dated 1765, stipulated a salary of one thousand pounds annually "with no possibility of increase," exemption from all taxes, and various fees for his services, including a stipend of eighteen pounds for conferring the preliminary rabbinic title of *haver.*²⁷ The town council retained the right to reduce the stipend in the case of a well-known scholar.

Fees for services were controversial at the start. The fifteenth-century scholar Rabbi Obadiah of Bertinoro criticized such fees severely in his Mishnah commentary: "Among the rabbis of Ashkenaz I observed something scandalous. The rabbi is not embarrassed to take ten zehuvim for spending half an hour in writing and delivering a divorce (*get*) and the witnesses take one or two zehuvim each. In my eyes the rabbi is a thief and an oppressor. He knows that in his town no one may obtain a divorce except under his authority so they are forced to give him what he wants. I am afraid such a divorce may be invalid."²⁸ Divorce fees may have been set high deliberately to discourage divorce.²⁹

Civil suits tried according to Jewish law also generated substantial revenue for the rabbi who presided.³⁰ This fee base was buttressed and enhanced by a prohibition under Jewish law against litigating a lawsuit between Jews in the Gentile courts.[31] In many cases, these fees were the main source of the rabbi's income, exceeding the amount he received as his salary.[32] At the same time, some halakhic authorities criticized communal ordinances that required litigants to pay the rabbi's fees. If the fee was based on the amount of the award, they feared rabbis might be tempted to inflate awards. When an ordinance required the litigants to tender a set fee, they feared the litigants might be tempted to offer more as a bribe. These authorities recommended that rabbis be paid their fees for presiding in court from the communal treasury. Unfortunately, the guardians of the communal treasury, the town's notables, preferred placing the burden of the rabbi's fees on the litigants' shoulders.[33]

Nothing prevented a scholar from being born into a wealthy family. Rabbi Abraham ben David of Posquières (*Rabad,* ca. 1125–1198) inherited a large estate from his father. The charitable purposes to which he dedicated his personal assets, including stipends for students studying in his yeshivah, made his generosity legendary among his contemporaries.[34] It was common for rabbis in Poland in the sixteenth and seventeenth centuries to come from wealthy families or to marry into them.[35] A fortunate match permitted Rabbi Joshua Falk (1555–1614), author of *Sefer Me'irat Eina'im,* to spend all his time engaged in study, teaching, and writing. His father-in-law, Israel Edels, supported the rabbi's family. Falk never accepted a salaried rabbinic post.

A rabbi might also accept the voluntary donations and gifts of his congregants. Residents of rural hamlets sent farm produce, while city dwellers tendered cash.[36] Some scholars became wealthy from this generosity, and it became an issue in the ethical literature of the day to determine the point at which a scholar should stop accepting gifts because his endowment had grown sufficiently large.[37]

At the other extreme some rabbis, particularly those serving Jewish communities in rural villages and small towns, were so indigent that volunteers had to forage for firewood to supply them with fuel for winter so that they and their families would not freeze.[38] Leon Modena, a rabbi in Venice during the first half of the seventeenth century, left the ghetto repeatedly to try his luck at the gambling tables in order to make up deficiencies in his income. When his rabbinical colleagues issued a ban against gambling, he wrote a legal tract to refute them, having failed to find gambling listed among the 365 prohibitions in the Torah.[39] In his autobiography, Modena writes of pawning his books in a lean year, practicing alchemy when he had no students, and in general earning his living "by using my pen, my tongue and my wits."[40]

Leon Modena's case illustrates the variety of rabbinic emoluments in an exemplary fashion. The rabbis of Venice were not communal appointees and did not receive salaries from the community. Instead, acting as free agents, they were hired by individuals and congregations to perform services for which they were compensated.[41] In a late passage in his autobiography, written not long before his death, Modena lists twenty-six endeavors in which he had engaged to earn a living, trying them, he says, "without success."⁴² Gambling is not mentioned. Among core rabbinic functions he lists six activities: the rabbinate itself, judging, preaching, rendering decisions of Jewish law, teaching in a yeshivah, and conferring rabbinic diplomas and titles. Cantorial work comprises a seventh endeavor. In the realm of instruction outside the yeshivah, there are entries for teaching arcane remedies, amulets, and writing to Jewish and Gentile pupils. Acting in a scribal capacity, Modena served as secretary for societies, transcribed letters for sending abroad, drew up contracts, and translated Hebrew documents for the Venetian government. On the creative side, he composed music, wrote poems for weddings and gravestones, wrote sermons for others, penned Italian sonnets, and authored comedies that he also directed. Among his commercial endeavors were commercial brokerage, matchmaking, printing, proofreading, and bookselling. These activities netted him a lower-middle-class existence and an income in the range of a master mason, 175–260 ducats a year.⁴³ He had difficulty providing his two daughters with dowries of 650 and 1,000 ducats, respectively. He died with an estate inventoried at 158 ducats, less than one year's average income.⁴⁴ It should be noted that a large number of the endeavors in which Modena engaged would be foreclosed to the majority of rabbis living in later eras and other cultures that were not heirs to the Italian Renaissance. For them, composing music, writing poems, and directing comedies for hire would not be options.

The sagas of prominent rabbis like Modena who died with small or insolvent estates were well known to the general public. There were rabbis whose estates could not afford to purchase burial garments or pay the sum stipulated in the widow's marriage contract.⁴⁵ This was considered praiseworthy, for it seemed to indicate a life spent pursuing Torah for its own sake and not for material gain, although in Modena's case unsuccessful gambling certainly played a role in his reduced circumstances.

On the whole, the availability of salaries—at least the adequate salaries paid by large communities, where most rabbis aspired to serve—increased public respect for the rabbinate and raised the social status of rabbis,⁴⁶ confirming the view of Maimonides' critics in this regard.⁴⁷ It could not be otherwise, for in virtually all societies, public prestige and social status are linked in some measure to a degree of success in the economic sphere. It would be surprising indeed if Jewish society were different. Ironically, however, in certain circles rabbinic salaries had the opposite effect. Some townsfolk, whether from traditional religious scruples or envy, questioned the propriety of their rabbi's material success. In addition, earnest students at some Talmudical academies frowned on the salaried rabbinate.⁴⁸ Believing that it detracted from the classic ideal of uncompensated devotion to Torah for its own sake, they accepted paid positions only when economic necessity forced them to do so. Teachers had to steer students gently away from their Talmud studies and encourage them to devote a modicum of time to studying codes and responsa so that they would be prepared and competent as rabbis to issue legal rulings for their communities. Parents had to prod their sons to end their studies and leave the yeshivah to take paid rabbinic posts.⁴⁹

Late in the nineteenth century, the innovative Rabbi Israel Salanter (1810–1883) of Kovno found a way to allow students to extend their yeshivah years despite difficult economic circumstances. With the assistance of a well-to-do donor, he created a postgraduate institution, the *kolel perushim,* that paid a small stipend covering basic subsistence needs to its mature student body of married men, permitting them to have families while they continued their full-time studies into adulthood.[50] Surely the challenges of modern times required intense and prolonged Torah preparation to equip the young men for committed Jewish life in general and the rabbinate in particular. Whether the early students were able successfully to reconcile the classic ideal of uncompensated Torah learning with their receipt of stipends is an interesting question. With the kolel supporting them while they deferred entering the rabbinate to continue their studies, they were receiving a *sekhar battalah* (suspension fee) for forgoing temporarily the sekhar battalah they would earn as practicing rabbis. The kolel, transplanted to the United States during and after World War II, remains to this day an established and highly regarded feature of the yeshivah landscape.[51]

It was perhaps inevitable that the availability of compensation for rabbis would create problems alongside the benefits it conferred. Indeed a host of problems arose that were much more serious than the bruised idealism of youth. Rabbis competed with each other for appointment in lucrative divorce matters and litigation.[52] Towns were forced to compete to extend their jurisdictions to surrounding rural villages as a way of expanding the material base available to support their rabbinates.[53] Ordination was given as a wedding present in an effort to guarantee a living to the as-yet-unqualified bridegroom.[54] Some individuals acquired rabbinic titles not to practice but only to take advantage of the tax exemption.[55] With future salary payments as the incentive, unqualified individuals sought rabbinic posts from government officials who welcomed the occasion both to exert authority over the Jews' religious leadership and to increase their revenues by the sale of rabbinic posts.[56] Imposters traveled the countryside posing as prominent rabbis and preachers, hoping no one in the town they were visiting would recognize them. This allowed them to secure a speaking engagement and pocket its attendant fee before anyone discovered the deception.[57] When selecting a new rabbi, communities sometimes passed over more learned scholars who were indigent and hired instead well-to-do rabbis who were less learned but would make fewer salary demands.[58] Some hard-pressed communities demanded that a rabbinic candidate contribute to its general fund or provide a loan from his personal assets in order to secure his post. Other communities sold rabbinic appointments to unqualified individuals. The purchaser then treated the post purely as an investment and looked to his rabbinic fees for an adequate return.[59] Regional rabbinic synods enacted ordinances repeatedly to try to stamp out these hardy and unsavory practices.[60]

There was turnover when incumbents vacated one post to secure another in a larger city with a higher salary. It was not uncommon for a rabbi to change posts five or six times in the course of his career.[61] Rabbis also left their posts because of age, illness, and emigration to the Holy Land, and they resigned in protest when their religious rulings were disobeyed. Communities suffered from the frequent loss of their accustomed spiritual leaders and the need to search for new ones. In an attempt to reduce turnover, community leaders insisted on writing disincentives into the rabbi's contract. When the Sha'agat Aryeh was engaged by the Jews of Metz to be their rabbi for a term of six years, the community retained an option to extend the rabbi's service for an additional six years. The first clause in his contract obligated him to take an oath not to accept a new position for twelve years. If he violated his oath, he was subject to excommunication. The contract also required him to deposit a letter of credit in the amount of six thousand pounds—six times his annual salary—to guarantee his undertaking not to leave.[62]

Enforcing such draconian provisions against a prominent rabbinic scholar who, it must be said, wanted to be free to leave so that he could satisfy the religious and spiritual needs of a larger Jewish population in another location, would naturally present community leaders with insurmountable problems. As an alternative, they might try to combat turnover in a more benign way by offering to increase the rabbi's salary to keep him in his post. As we have seen, this happened twice in the career of Rabbi Judah ben Asher.[63] He accepted the increases on both occasions and remained in Toledo until his death. A rabbi might seek an offer from a new town in order to elicit a salary increase from his current employers and then decline to accept the new post. Some communities actively opposed their rabbi's departure. The Jewish community of Saragossa sent a delegation to Calatayud to have their rabbi, Isaac ben Sheshet Perfet (*Rivash*, 1326–1408), released from his promise to relocate there and become its rabbi.[64] The prominent Lithuanian scholar Rabbi Isaac Elhanan Spector (1817–1897) had to be smuggled out of town twice to accept new posts, first in Novaredok and then in Kovno, so violent was the opposition of the townsfolk to his leaving them.[65] More typically, communities were forced to accept rabbinic turnover as a fact of life. A rabbi's leaving was marked by a respectful procession away from his old town and a celebratory procession of town notables accompanying him to his new home.[66] The rabbi's moving expenses would be defrayed by his new employers.[67]

The availability of a salary required new skills of rabbis, in particular a measure of business sense and bargaining ability, talents that were not likely to have been honed in the cloistered world of the yeshivah. In negotiating his contract with a town's notables, the rabbi would be facing across the table the community's most successful businessmen, merchants, and financiers, who, not incidentally, would have to contribute to the cost of employing him. The young, freshly minted rabbinic candidate was at a distinct disadvantage. Even seasoned rabbis who had weathered the process on previous occasions might feel constrained by their Torah-oriented values from pressing their demands too aggressively. In one instance of this type, when the citizens of Ponivezh sought to persuade their rabbi not to leave for another town, they offered to increase his salary from nine rubles a week to fifteen and he accepted. Only later did he learn that, if he had insisted, the town had been prepared to double his salary.[68]

The most serious problems arose when two rabbis competed for the same appointment. Entire Jewish communities could be riven into factions supporting the rival candidates.[69] These controversies, which could last for years, sometimes required the intervention of eminent outside halakhic authorities to resolve them and always left a legacy of bitterness, no matter which candidate ultimately prevailed. A dispute over the rabbinate in Riga was resolved by the eminent Rabbi Isaac Elhanan Spector in 1882, much to the chagrin and disappointment of the losing candidate, who wrote, "The shame I suffered because of this cannot be described in words."[70]

Rabbis now competed for the scarce material resources of the Jewish communities. They competed with other religious functionaries who also required compensation for their services. The *Shulhan Arukh* laid down the following rule: If a community needs to hire both a rabbi and a cantor but does not have the resources to pay salaries to both, then if the candidate for rabbi is a prominent scholar, great in wisdom of the Torah and an expert in deciding matters, it should hire the rabbi; but if the candidate for rabbi is ordinary, then it should hire the cantor.[71] Rabbis also competed with each other. We shall consider this competition and the rabbis' attempts to regulate it in part 2 of this study.

PART 2

Competition

Chapter 6

"THESE FEES EMBARRASS US"

Having won the right to support themselves as rabbis and scholars, incumbent rabbis tended to regard newcomers as interlopers who imperiled their livelihoods. Rabbis acquired their positions with varying degrees of deliberate formal involvement by the community or its representatives. At one extreme, a rabbinic scholar, young or old, might arrive uninvited and unannounced in a new place of residence. In the course of time, as his qualifications became known to the residents and they increasingly consulted him on matters of Jewish law, he might come to occupy a de facto position as their religious authority by common consent without any formal communal appointment. At the other extreme, an individual's appointment might have been the result of a community's formal search for a new religious leader. The community at large, or its board of electors, would interview a number of candidates, assess their respective merits, invite some to visit and deliver a Sabbath sermon, and then vote on the candidates to fill the vacant rabbinic chair. The winning applicant received a formal invitation to serve as the town's spiritual leader. Often, the electors would hold a second choice in reserve in case their first choice declined their offer.[1]

Over time, as the rabbinate became salaried, the formal electoral process replaced informal appointment by common consent as the usual method for selecting communal rabbis. This did not occur all at once but gradually over time. In most communities, this happened during the course of the sixteenth and seventeenth centuries.[2] Yet uncertainty over the correct method for selecting rabbis persisted. When Napoleon asked the assembly of Jewish notables he convened in Paris in 1806 the straightforward question, "Who appoints rabbis?" the assembly answered as follows: "Since the revolution, the majority of the chiefs of families names the Rabbi, wherever there is a sufficient number of Jews to maintain one, after previous inquiries as to the morality and learning of the candidate. This mode of election is not, however, uniform; it varies according to place, and, to this day, whatever concerns the elections of Rabbis is still in a state of uncertainty."[3]

A third route to a rabbinic post was sometimes available. In regions where civil authorities sought control over religious appointments or revenues from the sale of religious offices, there was the possibility of securing a government appointment.[4] Under Jewish law, the validity of these appointments was questionable. Although some halakhic authorities condoned them under the general rule that "the law of the land is law," most found them acceptable only as after-the-fact government confirmation of candidates whom the communities had themselves selected.[5] Absent their approval, Jewish communities were reluctant to accept the official appointees and resisted them when possible.

Once a rabbi became established in a town or region by any method, whether by common consent, formal election, or government appointment, then whether a newcomer was at liberty to repeat the process required answers to two separate questions under Jewish law. First, could a new scholar establish his residence in a town already served by a rabbi? Second, could he practice as a rabbi in the town, accepting fees for his services? The halakhah prohibited this conduct in the case of a former student who had matured and achieved rabbinic stature. He could not establish himself as an independent rabbinic authority in his teacher's community without first obtaining his teacher's permission.[6] This rule, observed before the rabbinate became salaried, was based on principles governing the student-teacher relationship, such as deference to the teacher, avoiding the potential for conflict with his rulings, and respect for his authority.[7]

As to competitors from the outside who were not former students of the local scholar, different principles governed, and initially the conduct was permitted. Thus both questions were answered in the affirmative in the middle of the fifteenth century by two prominent authorities, Rabbi Jacob Weil of Erfurt (*Maharyu*) and Rabbi Israel Isserlein, head of the Talmudical academy in Neustadt. They were consulted by the elders of the Jewish community of Regensburg (Ratisbon) about a troubling situation that had arisen in their town. In 1454, Rabbi Israel Bruna immigrated to Regensburg upon leaving his rabbinic post in Brünn (Brno) when the Jews were expelled from the city. Upon arrival, Rabbi Israel intended to continue his rabbinic practice, but a venerable sage who lived in Regensburg, Rabbi Anshel, attempted to prevent him from doing so, seeking to preserve the prerogatives and emoluments of Regensburg's established scholars, including himself.

Rabbi Isserlein issued a strong ruling in favor of the newcomer's right to practice in Regensburg.[8] Isserlein was personally acquainted with Rabbi Israel Bruna and knew him to be a well-qualified scholar. The only possible legal objection to his activities in Regensburg would be the argument that he was impermissibly reducing the livelihood of the town's other rabbis by infringing on the economic boundaries they had staked out for themselves. But if this was the argument against him, it was misapplied in his case. According to Isserlein, infringing on economic boundaries (*hasagat gevul*) might be raised as an objection to a foreign tradesman seeking to establish his business in a town already served by existing tradesmen in the same line of work, but it may never be asserted against a Torah scholar to prevent him from settling in a town and practicing as a rabbi. The crown of Torah is resting like "abandoned property" for all who wish to take it and exercise authority in its name.

Rabbi Isserlein acknowledged that a new arrival might deflect some fees from the town's established rabbis. But for Isserlein, "these fees are an embarrassment to us and we have to strain to find legal grounds to accept most of them."[9] Isserlein makes this admission in the context of the traditional strictures against receiving compensation for one's Torah knowledge.[10] In his view, compensation with such uncertain legal justification could never rise to the level of a protected livelihood with economic boundaries that had to be respected by other scholars.

Rabbi Jacob Weil, the second authority to issue a ruling in favor of Rabbi Israel's right to practice in Regensburg, based his decision on a factor that Isserlein did not mention at all. Neither of the disputants in Regensburg had been formally appointed as the town's rabbi. Rather, both had achieved their rank by common consent, demonstrating over time their abilities as religious authorities and scholars and obtaining the recognition of the townsfolk as such. Weil held that Rabbi Anshel's mere priority in time did not confer upon him any superiority of rights.[11] Hence neither had the greater right to practice in Regensburg and neither could exclude the other. In support of his conclusion, Weil cited a passage from the authoritative halakhic treatise *Or Zaru'a* that affirmed the right of a new scholar to emigrate to a city already served by a rabbi, engage there full time in the study and teaching of Torah, and benefit from the same public support and tax exemption granted to the first scholar. Weil noted that the passage did not distinguish between incumbent rabbis who had been formally appointed to their posts and those who had received only informal recognition by common consent; in both cases, the new arrival may settle in town and compete.[12]

Both rulings settled the Regensburg controversy in favor of the newcomer's right to practice, yet in the course of time each ruling proved to be a two-edged sword. Later authorities cited Weil's ruling *against* new arrivals after formal appointment had, over time, largely replaced informal appointment by common consent in the selection of rabbis.[13] They inferred, despite Rabbi Weil's citation of the *Or Zaru'a*, that he would have ruled against the newcomer in Regensburg if in fact his predecessor had been formally appointed to the post.

Isserlein's ruling also proved to cut two ways. In disputes between established rabbis and recent arrivals, the ruling clearly favored the newcomer, guaranteeing him the right to earn a living as a rabbi alongside the established scholar in his new town. But in disputes between rabbis, old or new, and the Jewish communities from which they sought their livelihoods, the ruling favored the communities. As long as rabbinic compensation officially remained a legal embarrassment, rabbis were at a disadvantage in pressing their economic claims too vigorously against the straitened Jewish communities they served.

This impact of Isserlein's ruling was perfectly illustrated by the case of David ibn Yahya, rabbi of the kingdom of Naples from 1525 to 1540. Before accepting the post, community leaders had assured him there would be compensation, but he went unpaid for his first five years in office.[14] He refrained from pursuing the matter because the Jews of Naples were sorely pressed for cash. They had to raise huge sums for two purposes that were all too common at the time—redeeming Jews who had been sold into slavery by pirates and staving off an edict of expulsion that would have forced the Jews out of Naples in 1533. In addition, Ibn Yahya declined to accept compensation for acting as a scribe. He considered his scribal duties to be beneath his dignity and transcribed his congregants' letters only because he did not want any unworthy Hebrew prose issuing from his community. Neither would he accept fees for teaching young children. This service he believed should be rendered to the community gratis. He finally decided to leave Naples, but at that point the elders promised their rabbi an annual salary of one hundred scudi in gold.[15] Ibn Yahya thought the agreement would apply retroactively and cover the arrearages as well. The community disagreed, however, because the question of payments for years past was never raised during the negotiations.

Ibn Yahya sought a resolution of the dispute from the prominent authority Rabbi Meir of Padua (*Maharam Padua*). Rabbi Meir sided with the community against his colleague. He ruled that the community's silence on the question of the arrearages during the negotiations did not indicate their acquiescence to Ibn Yahya's position, since he had never expressly raised the matter with them.[16] He quoted verbatim the passage from Rabbi Isserlein's work that expressed embarrassment over rabbinic fees in view of their uncertain legal basis. In light of this, he advised Ibn Yahya, there could never be a valid claim for compensation that was at best implicit, such as fees for past services that the community had never explicitly fixed and agreed to pay.

It took many generations for halakhic authorities to gradually overcome the embarrassment over fees that Isserlein so candidly expressed. As we shall see, when they did overcome it, they tended to defend the incumbent rabbi's livelihood from encroachment by newcomers, something Isserlein and Weil were unwilling to countenance.

Chapter 7

THE RESIDENCE RIGHT AND THE RESIDENCE BAN

A scholar's right to take up residence in the community of his choice, affirmed by both Rabbis Isserlein and Weil in the Regensburg case, was one facet of the broader question of freedom of movement for Jews in pre-Emancipation times. In general, the Jews were precarious inhabitants of their nations and localities, excluded from some territories and welcomed in others but always subject to expulsion en masse by princes and local authorities. Our concern, however, is the narrower question of freedom of movement between Jewish communities. We will focus on the internal regulations the Jews adopted for themselves to control the flow of newcomers and how these regulations applied to rabbis, scholars, and teachers.

Under Jewish law, the Jewish inhabitants of a town acquired a right to reside there known as a "residence right" (*hezkat hayishuv*). The right to reside encompassed the right to earn a living in the town. The residence right was based on the charter the original Jewish inhabitants had purchased from local authorities, granting them the right to settle and to trade and limiting the number of Jews permitted to reside in the locality.[1] To support the residence right, Jewish law enforced a "residence ban" (*herem hayishuv*).[2] The ban prohibited a new arrival from settling in a town without receiving the consent of the Jewish residents. In most communities, unanimous consent was required.[3] A Jewish immigrant who took up residence in violation of the ban was subject to severe social and religious ostracism by his coreligionists. Thus an ordinance enacted in 1583 by the Jewish council of Padua, Italy, provided that a Jew who settled in Padua without the community's consent would be ostracized from the community, not allowed to participate in the slaughtering of kosher meat, refused the circumcision of his sons, shunned on festive occasions, and denounced as a renegade in the synagogue every Monday and Thursday until he left.[4]

Jews who were fleeing from religious persecution were exempt from the residence ban, but upon arrival, their right to engage in trade was restricted.[5] Refugees could engage in trade only to the extent necessary to earn a living at a subsistence level.[6] This minimized the impact of their arrival on the town's existing businesses, while at the same time ensuring that they did not become public charges.

The residence ban served many important purposes, such as avoiding overcrowding in the Jewish Quarter, excluding the morally objectionable from the community, and reducing anti-Jewish sentiment among the Gentile population.[7] These purposes, however, were incidental to the ban's primary goal: protecting the livelihoods of established residents from the competition of newcomers. What was in form a regulation of residence was in substance a system of trade protection,[8] as the treatment of refugees illustrates.

Whether the residence ban was the original creation of medieval Jewry or whether it had its origins in Talmudic jurisprudence was uncertain. Some attributed the ban to the tenth-century Franco-German authority Rabbenu Gershom of Mainz, a seminal figure in the organization of the Jewish communities of Europe to whom many regulations of a constitutional nature are attributed.[9] Others held the ban was ancient and had a basis in the Talmud's discussion of economic competition among the residents of a lane. The passage relates a difference of opinion between two scholars named Huna. The first Rav Huna ("Huna I") held the opinion that a resident of a lane who operated a mill could prevent a second resident from opening a similar establishment in the lane by claiming, "You are interfering with my livelihood." The second, Rav Huna ben Rav Joshua ("Huna II"), disagreed. In his view, the second resident could open his mill despite the prior miller's objection, and the same rule applies even when the potential competitor is a nonresident, someone who comes from another town, provided the newcomer is willing to pay his share of taxes in his new town.[10]

Huna I's position on the nonresident competitor is not stated but can be inferred from the passage. Since he denies a current resident, someone already obligated to pay taxes in the town, a right to open a competing establishment, then he would surely deny the right to a nonresident despite that person's undertaking to pay taxes. The Talmud does not explicitly resolve the dispute, but most students of the passage concluded that the view of Huna II should prevail.[11] Maimonides and Joseph Karo ruled in their codes in accordance with Huna II's position, permitting a nonresident to settle in a new town and open a competing business upon his undertaking to pay local taxes.[12]

Adhering closely to the tenor of the Talmudic passage and its treatment by the codifiers, Jewish communities in Spain, North Africa, and the Middle East permitted free entry to foreign Jews who agreed to participate in communal tax levies. By contrast, in France, Germany, England, Italy, and Eastern Europe, while agreeing to pay taxes was of course necessary to gain admission to a Jewish community, it was not sufficient.[13] A newcomer would still have to obtain the unanimous consent of the residents, any one of whom could object if he feared economic competition from the new arrival.

The difference in approaches between Sephardic and Ashkenazic Jewries has been explained by reference to the difference in their economic circumstances.[14] Although Jews in the Muslim world were second-class citizens, they were largely unrestrained in their economic pursuits. By contrast, Jews in Christian Europe before Emancipation faced many barriers to earning a livelihood. In most places they were not permitted to own land, till the soil, bear arms, or join Christian craft guilds. Jews were employed largely as merchants, peddlers, moneylenders, and bankers. Those who were trained as artisans by Jewish guilds had to ply their trade exclusively among fellow Jews. But a small Jewish community could support only so many local merchants, carpenters, tailors, butchers, and bakers, hence the incentive among Ashkenazic Jews to utilize the residence ban as a way to insulate the livelihoods of established residents from competition by newcomers.

The practice of the Ashkenazic communities led to a dissonance between the law written in the legal codes and the law applied in their communities. The residence ban as they applied it conformed better with the anticompetitive position of Huna I, which the codifiers had rejected, than with the position of Huna II, which the codifiers had endorsed. As a result, some halakhic authorities tried to limit its application in their communities. For example Rabbenu Tam held the ban should be utilized selectively to exclude only tax resisters and informers.[15] But the economic incentive to apply the ban broadly was too strong. It remained a potent limitation on the free movement of Jews in Europe until Emancipation.[16]

How did rabbis, scholars, teachers, and their students fare during the heyday of the residence ban? They were exempt from its application.[17] There was a simple explanation for this—scholars did not pose a direct economic threat to the livelihoods of the local residents, apart from the local rabbi, a matter we shall consider shortly.[18] Students at the Talmudical academy did not work at all, and the rabbi did not ordinarily compete with the local residents in any of their lines of work. Now it is true that if the rabbi engaged in trade, he was entitled to priority in the marketplace, but his trade would be incidental to his rabbinic practice, undertaken to supplement his rabbinic salary.[19] It posed competition of a lower degree of magnitude than that of the nonrabbinic newcomer who engaged in commerce full time as his sole means of support. Thus the competition to the town's regular merchants arising from a new scholar's incidental trading activities would be slight, and the townsfolk even gained a small economic benefit from his trading. If the town allowed the new scholar to support himself and his family, it prevented them from becoming wards of charity whom the townsfolk themselves would have to support with contributions from their pockets. It is also true that new scholars would increase the tax burden of local residents, since the scholars' taxes would be apportioned among the community at large.[20] This did occasion some complaining, but on the whole the impact of such apportionment on any given household was hardly noticeable, and in the community at large the impact was diffuse and indirect.[21] In any case, any untoward economic effects resulting from the arrival of a new scholar would naturally be offset against the recognized intellectual and spiritual benefits and the increase in prestige that accrued to a community from having a new rabbinic scholar settle in its midst.

The rulings of Rabbis Isserlein and Weil in the Regensburg matter were consistent with the scholar's exemption from the residence ban. They upheld the right of the newcomer, Rabbi Israel, to emigrate from Brunn, settle in Regensburg, and practice as a rabbi. Neither based his decision on Rabbi Israel's status as a refugee nor did either restrict the newcomer's right to earn a living to his bare subsistence needs as required in the case of a refugee. But Rabbis Isserlein and Weil did not have the last word on the question of rabbinic competition. The question continued to be debated, and in time the scope of the newcomer's permissible activities was circumscribed. As we shall see, in the end the positions of Rabbis Isserlein and Weil were superseded by other more restrictive rulings, far less favorable to the free movement of scholars.

Chapter 8

"THE ENVY OF SCHOLARS INCREASES WISDOM"

While ordinary townsfolk, who were not threatened economically by the arrival of a new scholar, were not likely to object to his settling in their midst, the local rabbi might view the situation from quite a different perspective. He faced a host of delicate issues occasioned by the newcomer's arrival, involving their religious and legal authority vis-à-vis each other. These issues included entitlement to priority and honors in the synagogue, the community's assessment of their respective ranking as scholars, and the adjustment of their differences of opinion should they issue rulings that conflicted. In addition, the local rabbi faced direct economic competition from the new scholar. The question arose whether an incumbent rabbi, like the town's merchants and craftsmen, should have the legal right to protect the boundaries of his livelihood by raising an objection to a newcomer's rabbinic practice.

The starting point for resolving questions of this type was again the passage in the Talmud where two sages named Huna debate competition among the residents of a lane.[1] In a coda to the passage, Rabbi Joseph states a rule concerning competition among schoolteachers. A teacher who runs a schoolroom in a lane cannot object to a second resident opening a competing schoolroom in the same lane. Since teachers of young children receive fees for watching over their charges during school hours,[2] the second teacher poses a direct economic threat to the first. Still, according to Rabbi Joseph, unlike the first miller in a lane, the first teacher cannot compel the second to close the rival schoolroom and cease operation in the lane.

Rabbi Joseph's rule for schoolteachers is perfectly consistent with the position of Huna II, who favors competition among residents of a lane. But according to Rabbi Joseph, even Huna I, who was inclined to protect the livelihood of the first entrant into a market, would agree with Huna II in the case of schoolteachers because "the envy of scholars increases wisdom."[3] The religious well-being of the community at large requires "the maximum availability of Torah teachers."[4] The economic interests of the first teacher must give way to this religious and spiritual interest of overriding importance.

Rabbi Joseph's statement is limited to schoolteachers and does not mention rabbis or scholars who instruct mature students. This is understandable since rabbis and scholars did not receive fees for teaching Torah in the Talmudic era.[5] Hence the issue of economic competition between them was a moot point. It is plain, however, that Rabbi Joseph's rationale for allowing competition among schoolteachers—"the envy of scholars increases wisdom"—must apply with equal force to all expositors of the Torah, including rabbis and scholars. Community welfare demands the maximum availability of Torah teachers at every level of instruction, from the elementary to the most advanced.

The rule for schoolteachers is cited in the codes of both Maimonides[6] and Karo[7] as settled law. Neither of their rulings carries the discussion of competition beyond schoolteachers even though, in the centuries after the close of the Talmud, the emoluments of the rabbinate had developed into a significant source of income for rabbis and scholars who teach mature students. It is Rabbi Moses Isserles (Rema), in a gloss he appends to Karo's ruling, who draws out its implications for the salaried rabbinate, writing as follows:

> Where a rabbi resides in a town and instructs the public, another sage may come and teach also in the same place, even if he deprives the first to a certain extent of his livelihood. For example, where the congregation accepted the first as their rabbi and he receives compensation from them for this, the second may still settle there and establish himself in all aspects of the rabbinate like the first, provided he is great [in learning] and qualified for this.[8]

Like the first schoolteacher in a lane, the town's established rabbi cannot object to the newcomer's arrival and rabbinic practice. As we shall see, however, there is an opening for an exception to this general rule where the new arrival deprives the incumbent of his livelihood more than "to a certain extent."[9]

Some cite Rabbis Jacob Weil and Israel Isserlein as authority for the Rema's ruling.[10] Indeed the situation the Rema describes in generic terms is very similar to the facts of the Regensburg case a century earlier, where Weil and Isserlein overturned the resident scholar's objection and ruled that a new arrival could not be excluded from rabbinic practice in the town.[11] In his ruling, the Rema affirms the free movement of qualified scholars that both of his predecessors had endorsed. At the same time, he parts company with them over the question of the newcomer's fees. The Rema would permit a recent arrival to deprive the resident rabbi of his livelihood "to a certain extent" only. The rulings of Weil and Isserlein contain no such express limitation.

This is not a small difference of opinion. It signifies a fundamental difference in their basic approach to rabbinic compensation. Isserlein had written that most rabbinic fees were an embarrassment because they had an uncertain basis in the law.[12] As a result, he held rabbinic compensation could never rise to the level of a livelihood that warranted legal protection against newcomers. By contrast, the Rema's ruling elevates the status of rabbinic fees to the rank of a livelihood entitled to a degree of legal protection against encroachers. In his view, the new scholar is legally entitled to deprive the incumbent rabbi of his fees to a certain extent but no further.

The Rema's position is reiterated in his ruling regarding a visiting rabbi: "But if a sage has come to the town for a temporary sojourn, he may not infringe upon the livelihood of the resident rabbi by performing weddings and taking fees, for this is the livelihood of the resident rabbi; however he is permitted to perform the wedding and remit the fee to the resident rabbi."[13]

A visiting rabbi may not infringe upon the livelihood of the town's rabbi to any extent. He may perform religious functions such as weddings, but only if he remits the customary fee to the resident rabbi. In a sense, the fee belongs to the resident rabbi even if he does not perform the service that earns it. As the Rema puts it, "This is *the livelihood* of the resident rabbi" (emphasis added).[14]

The key to understanding the Rema's position is Rabbi Joseph's epigram "The envy of scholars increases wisdom." This maxim has two connotations. Anyone who has spent time in academia understands the first. Scholars are jealous of each other's accomplishments. Although they are engaged in the world of ideas and learning for its own sake, they nonetheless seek recognition and tend to envy those who advance beyond them in stature, rank, and title. This phenomenon was not entirely unknown among the rabbinic sages, as demonstrated by Rabbi Zadok's admonition against using the Torah as a crown for self-glorification.[15] If at least some of his colleagues were not doing just that, then whom was he addressing? Still, when the phenomenon manifested itself, the sages did not condemn it completely. The striving for recognition acted as a spur to intellectual achievement. It generated fresh ideas, new interpretations of texts, and innovative solutions to problems, the net result of which was an increase in the quantum of Torah knowledge in the world. In this sense, the maxim expresses an insight into the psyche of the scholar that explains what makes him strive for excellence and toil long and hard at his intellectual pursuits.

The maxim has a second, purely economic connotation. For this purpose, it is better to render the Hebrew word for envy as "competition" and to restate the phrase as "competition among scholars increases wisdom." Competition among scholars is not like competition among merchants or craftsmen. A small local economy can support only so many tradesmen engaged in a given line of work. If, for example, a second cobbler enters a town already served by one, there may be more shoes available to the public for a short time, but eventually the situation will change. The local market for shoes being only so large, one of the competitors will be driven out of business, and the town will revert to being served by a single cobbler. In the end, there will be no net gain in the number of shoes available to the public. Enforcing the residence ban as a system of trade protection tended to prevent this vicious cycle from occurring.

The same is not true in the case of rabbinic scholars. Their stock-in-trade is knowledge of the Torah. Wisdom is not like shoes—there is no limit on the market for wisdom. Hence competition among scholars is not like competition among cobblers, for the Jews can absorb the insights, interpretations, and teachings of an unlimited number of Torah scholars. The arrival of a new one in a town will in no wise drive an established scholar out of the marketplace for ideas. For this reason, those who held that Rabbenu Gershom instituted the residence ban[16] also held that he exempted scholars, recognizing that competition among scholars increases wisdom.[17]

But the application of the maxim in this second sense is apt only so long as Torah sages perform their functions gratis. Its application to scholars who accept fees for their services is questionable. When scholars take fees, an analogy can be drawn between them and ordinary tradesmen like cobblers. There are only so many weddings and divorces for the rabbi to perform, yeshivah students to teach, witnesses to depose, and lawsuits to try in a single community. If a newcomer attracts fees that would otherwise flow to the established rabbi, it is quite possible that in the course of time one of them will not be able to support himself and his family from his rabbinic practice. He will have to leave the town or change his profession. The town will revert to being served by a single rabbi, and there will be no net gain of either scholars or wisdom in the town.

More than a century separated Rabbi Isserlein's decision in the Regensburg case, dating from 1454, and the Rema's ruling in the *Shulhan Arukh*.[18] Trends that were just noticeable in Isserlein's day had become entrenched by the time of the Rema. We have seen how, once accepting compensation became the norm, there were frequent instances of intense competition among rabbis for positions and fees.[19] As a concomitant development, rabbis began to level the charge of trespass against colleagues who encroached upon their economic territory.[20] The Rema's ruling takes these developments into account, seeking to regulate and moderate the impact of the new economic competition on the newly salaried rabbinate. He rules that scholars, while exempt from the residence ban so that they may settle anywhere, even in a town already served by a rabbi, may encroach on an incumbent's livelihood "to a certain extent" only. He fully appreciates that if a newcomer reduces an established rabbi's income to a greater extent, and certainly if he deprives him of his livelihood entirely, the incumbent may be driven from the rabbinate. Instead of an increase in the number of scholars in the town, a new scholar's arrival may herald only the replacement of the old rabbi by a new one. Given such an outcome, it would be hard to argue that competition among scholars had resulted in an increase in wisdom.

The Rema perceived that in his day, when rabbis were earning their living from their rabbinic practices, Isserlein's view of rabbinic compensation was already outmoded. The Rema was willing to protect an established rabbi's livelihood to the extent necessary to prevent a new arrival from replacing him, even if it meant departing from Isserlein's view that rabbinic compensation was not to be deemed a "livelihood" entitled to legal protection.[21] As we shall see, halakhic authorities that came after the Rema were prepared to go further to protect the incumbent's fees.

Chapter 9

"NO BETTER THAN AN OUTRIGHT THIEF"

The Rema's ruling limiting a newcomer's competition marked a watershed because of the authoritativeness of the author and the thrust of his position extending legal protection to the established rabbi's livelihood. In the end, it offered little practical guidance for regulating competition among rabbis. Just what marked the "certain extent" to which a new arrival might lawfully reduce the resident rabbi's income? The incumbent might draw the line at any amount that exceeded a de minimus reduction of his income. A careful newcomer who wished to remain within the bounds of propriety might not necessarily disagree. This restraint, however, would make it next to impossible for him to earn his own livelihood in the rabbinate, rendering his right to settle in the new town and practice as a rabbi largely useless. On the other hand, if the new scholar interpreted the Rema's ruling as a license to earn from his rabbinic practice at least enough to support himself and his family, he was almost certain to violate the ruling by depriving the established rabbi of more than "a little" of his customary income.

To resolve controversies of this type, the Rema's successors needed to explore the implications of his ruling and apply it in concrete cases. In the process, they enlarged the scope of protection afforded the incumbent's fees. In their rulings one can discern the embarrassment over rabbinic salaries and fees, so candidly expressed by Rabbi Israel Isserlein in the Regensburg case, dissipating generation by generation as the emoluments of the office become more and more entrenched. In the end, they ruled competition among rabbis completely out of bounds.

One approach involved giving the Rema's ruling and the passage in Rabbi Isserlein's work on which it was based a very close reading. This was the approach of the *Shakh,* Rabbi Shabbetai Hakohen, in his authoritative commentary on the *Shulhan Arukh*.[1] There are indeed fees paid to rabbis that have an uncertain basis in Jewish law and cause embarrassment, just as Rabbi Isserlein had written. These are the fees paid for core rabbinic functions such as officiating at weddings and divorces. But there are also fees that have a solid foundation in the law and do not cause any embarrassment. Isserlein wrote that we have to strain to find legal reasons to accept *most* rabbinic fees, not all of them. Examples of acceptable payments are the fees rabbis receive for their scribal activities and for their service as arbitrators. These fees did not cause Rabbi Isserlein any embarrassment, and rabbis may accept them without qualms. The Rema's ruling, which allows a newcomer to compete while limiting him to reducing the incumbent's livelihood just a little, applies to the first category of fees only—those that cause embarrassment. As to the second category of fees, which do not cause any embarrassment and are perfectly proper to accept, the newcomer may not encroach at all.

Rabbi Shalom Schwadron, the *Maharsham,* applying the distinction between the two categories of fees in a dispute between an established rabbi and a newcomer, demonstrates the potential economic threat of a new scholar's arrival.[2] The local rabbi in a town had established a court in his home where he issued rulings, arranged marriages and divorces, and accepted the customary fees for his services. When a new scholar settled in the town, at first he satisfied himself with the honor the townsfolk bestowed upon him and did not accept fees for services. Up to this point no one raised any objections to his presence. When in due course the newcomer wished to open a court at home and accept fees, the established rabbi objected. He charged the newcomer with invading his economic territory. The Maharsham ruled that "for the sake of peace," the site of a court should never be changed—a principle that will resolve every such dispute in favor of the established rabbi. Further he ruled that the newcomer may not compete at all over the second category of payments, the type rabbis are permitted to accept without embarrassment, such as scribal fees and arbitration fees. If he reduces to any extent the income the complaining rabbi derives from these sources, the newcomer will be guilty of trespassing on the incumbent's livelihood. This case, which must be emblematic of many similar instances, shows how the economic threat posed by a newcomer could be both insidious and real, and how halakhic principles were marshaled to check the newcomer's ability to compete.

A second approach to the Rema's ruling afforded even greater protection to the established rabbi's livelihood. It acknowledged the distinction between the two categories of fees, those that cause embarrassment and those that do not, but held the distinction exists purely as a matter of law. The Rema's ruling was accurate in restating the law, but the ruling should not govern the newcomer's conduct. Today it is the custom not to differentiate between the two types of fees. This custom dictates that the new scholar should refrain from depriving the established rabbi of any part of his income, whether derived from one class of fees or the other.[3] Thus, binding custom rules out competition where the law would permit it.

A third approach challenged the view that the Rema's ruling correctly stated the law for his or subsequent generations. This was the approach of the *Hatam Sofer,* Rabbi Moses Sofer of Pressburg.[4] In his opinion, when the Rema adopted Rabbi Isserlein's division of rabbinic fees into two classes, one embarrassing and one not, he had affirmed an outmoded rule of law, one that had been superseded. According to Rabbi Sofer, a discerning eye that looks closely into the responsa of Rabbis Weil and Isserlein upon which the Rema's ruling was based would see that their decisions were limited to their day, when appointment as rabbi was informal.[5] In those days, when a community turned to a scholar who happened to live in their midst to serve as their rabbi, their fees flowed to him as a natural consequence of his service. But since he had never been appointed to his post officially, no one was prevented from turning to a new scholar to serve those same needs. The newcomer would naturally be rewarded for his services just as the first rabbi had been.

In our day, according to Rabbi Sofer, the situation is quite different. Today a community deliberately invites a candidate to come and serve as their rabbi, often requesting him to relocate from a distant place. They hire him as an employee, and as a community they are obligated to provide him with a livelihood. The best way for the community to discharge its obligation would be to pay the rabbi from its general fund. Instead, many communities delegate their obligation to support the rabbi to those individuals who utilize his services. The clients' payments discharge the community's obligation to provide its rabbi with a livelihood. This practice is widespread, Rabbi Sofer wrote, and we have completely overcome our embarrassment over these fees. In fact, if the rabbi has any qualms about taking them, we force him to accept them. Anyone who encroaches on his fees to any extent is an evildoer.[6]

In an earlier discussion of the Regensburg case,[7] it was noted that only Rabbi Weil had based his holding on the fact that the incumbent had never been formally appointed to his post, while Rabbi Isserlein did not mention this factor at all. Further it was unclear how Weil would have ruled if Rabbi Anshel, the target of the competition, had been the recipient of a formal rabbinic appointment from the town. Nevertheless, Rabbi Sofer's reinterpretation of their holdings in the case was itself considered so authoritative that it provided the basis for subsequent restatements of the Rema's ruling. Thus, Rabbi Yehiel Epstein in his late code of law, *Arukh Hashulhan,* which appeared in the nineteenth century, after quoting the Rema's formulation in full, adopts Rabbi Sofer's view of the matter, ruling that it is forbidden in our day for a rabbi to settle in a town already served by a rabbi and to encroach on his fees.[8] A newcomer who deflects fees away from the appointed rabbi to any extent is no better than an outright thief.[9]

The reassessment of the Rema's position by his successors achieved two results. First, it strengthened one part of his ruling, the part that protected an established rabbi's livelihood, at the expense of the other part of the ruling, the part that exposed his fees to some competition from a recent arrival. Second, it formally ended the traditional embarrassment over rabbinic fees that Rabbi Isserlein had expressed. The pendulum had swung decisively against the newcomer. Labeled an evildoer by the Hatam Sofer and an outright thief by Rabbi Yehiel Epstein, he was liable to feel more embarrassment over deflecting fees from the established rabbi than the incumbent felt upon accepting them. Without the ability to compete for fees, the new scholar's right to settle in a new town, which Isserlein, Weil, and the Rema had all endorsed, was rendered more theoretical than real.

Chapter 10

RABBIS AND SCHOOLTEACHERS
Two Competitive Regimes

The Rema and later halakhic authorities made it clear in their rulings that competition among rabbis was subject to legal limitation. The halakhah would protect the economic well-being of the newly salaried rabbinate. Particularly objectionable was conduct that might ruin a colleague's rabbinic practice and drive him from the profession. In this respect, there was a marked difference between the rules for rabbis and those that governed schoolteachers. The rules for teachers permitted them to engage in vigorous, even predatory, competition. In his code, Maimonides states the rule for schoolteachers in the following terms:

> And so in the case of a schoolmaster, where another has come and opened a schoolroom next door in order to attract new pupils or to attract pupils of the first, he cannot object, for it is written (Isaiah 42:21), "The Lord was pleased, for His righteousness' sake, to make the teaching great and glorious."[1]

Thus, a new teacher may open a school and enroll new students; this will increase the total number of students in the town. But he may also open his school with the deliberate intention of attracting currently enrolled students away from an existing school. In either case, the old schoolmaster may not object.

In his code, Joseph Karo repeats Maimonides' formulation virtually word for word—but not quite. Where Maimonides had written that it is permissible for the new schoolteacher to recruit pupils of the first teacher, he used a phrase that signifies "*some* pupils of the first" (*mi-tinokot shel zeh*) but not all of them. Karo, replacing a single letter, formulates a rule that allows the new teacher to recruit "*the* pupils of the first" (*ha-tinokot shel zeh*),[2] suggesting that the newcomer may take all of them. Quite obviously this poaching will put the existing schoolroom out of business.

The prooftext, Isaiah 42:21, supplies the reason why schoolmasters are permitted to recruit students away from each other: "The Lord was pleased, for His righteousness' sake, to make the teaching [*torah*] great and glorious." Both Maimonides and Karo cite this verse in place of the Talmudic maxim "The envy of scholars increases wisdom." Perhaps they preferred to use a biblical verse as a prooftext rather than to cite a Talmudic maxim. Perhaps they felt it would be inappropriate to apply a Talmudic term for scholars or scribes (*soferim*) to the lowest member of the educational hierarchy, the schoolteacher (*melamed tinnokot*). In any case, the verse states clearly the aim of competition among schoolteachers—to improve teaching, to make it "great and glorious."

Rabbis and schoolteachers were members of two separate professions, with distinct training, licensing, employment arrangements, functions, and prestige. They shared a common professional interest in the education of the young, but the Jewish community typically assigned this task to schoolteachers, not rabbis. Rabbis performed other tasks. They served as judges on rabbinic tribunals, tried lawsuits and arbitrated disputes, and administered the Jewish community alongside the lay leadership. They answered their congregants' halakhic questions, arranged marriages and divorces, lectured in the yeshivah, the synagogue, and the study hall, and supervised the community's charities and its ritual institutions—the kosher slaughterhouse, the Sabbath boundaries, and the ritual bath. In addition, prominent rabbis —those of regional and international stature—responded to halakhic inquiries from rabbinic colleagues, founded important yeshivahs and lectured in them, wrote learned treatises, commentaries, and novellae, and convened periodically in regional synods to enact broad-ranging communal ordinances. Schoolteachers performed none of these important tasks. Rabbis, who had been ordained since medieval times, received honors in the synagogue and enjoyed large measures of communal authority, deference, and prestige. They had a degree of professional mobility and were favored on occasion with tax exemption, lifetime tenure in office, and inheritance rights for their heirs. Schoolteachers, who were not ordained, lacked all authority and prestige and enjoyed few benefits.[3] When a rabbi who had fallen on hard times turned to school teaching to make a living, he left one profession and joined another.

In a given locale, prominent rabbis might be engaged in elementary instruction. On these occasions, there was some overlap in personnel between the rabbinate and school teaching. The occupants of rabbinic chairs sometimes taught young children, either to supplement their incomes or because the community required it, but this task they considered incidental to their core rabbinic functions. This was true, for example, in the case of David ibn Yahya, the chief rabbi of Naples, who refused compensation for teaching youngsters as an incidental part of his duties as rabbi until his later years when reduced circumstances forced him to accept gifts from their parents.[4] For performing his core rabbinic duties, however, he expected to be compensated by the community and threatened to vacate his office when he was not.[5]

Rabbis, of course, were qualified to instruct young children at the elementary level. Perhaps, in their own eyes, they were overqualified. No doubt some rabbis were conscientious instructors of the young, but others regarded school teaching and tutoring youngsters as less than pleasant tasks that were beneath their status. In his autobiography, Rabbi Leon Modena relates, "In order not to remain idle, I began to give lessons in Torah [to the sons of prominent individuals]. . . . I continued in this profession . . . in spite of myself, because it did not seem fitting to me."[6] In a letter describing a typical day, Modena wrote, "I go to the elementary school to serve my sentence, as the wicked do in hell."[7]

The rabbinate's intermittent and supervisory involvement in the instruction of young children was not enough to ensure its overall quality.[8] The need for better elementary education is a persistent theme in the history of Jewish education.[9] The general quality of instruction was low in the traditional elementary classroom, the *heder*.[10] All grade levels met in the same room at the same time and carried out different lessons simultaneously. The curriculum typically consisted of the Hebrew alphabet, prayers, the weekly Torah portion, and Rashi's commentary. Hebrew grammar was an infrequent addition to the curriculum, as was secular knowledge, where permitted. Typically there were no texts formulated specifically for the education of young students. The texts were volumes readily at hand—the prayer book, Bible, commentaries, and the Mishnah. The academic attainments and intellectual caliber of the ordinary teachers were low. Anyone who could read and write could open a school or hire himself out as a private tutor, with two exceptions. Bachelors were not allowed to be teachers, to prevent them from meeting the pupils' mothers. Women were excluded from the profession to avoid contact with the pupils' fathers.[11] Teachers typically had no training in pedagogy or child development. School teaching often was a calling of last resort. Men became teachers after failing in other lines of work, and down-at-the-heels refugees turned to teaching when they discovered other trades were closed to them.[12] This flawed institution achieved one notable success in premodern society—near universal Hebrew literacy among Jewish males. In every other respect, there was a profound and continuing need for improvement.

One who wished to open a new school would have to compete with existing schools on some basis. It was impossible to compete by charging lower fees because *melamdim* (elementary schoolteachers) were never paid more than a pittance and often had difficulty collecting even these small sums from parents.[13] Accepting even less to attract students was not economically feasible. Sometimes it was not permitted, for often school fees were fixed by communal ordinance and the individual teacher was not permitted to deviate from the established rates. But a new teacher could compete by offering superior instruction. Since the halakhah permitted parents to remove their children from one school and place them with a better teacher in another,[14] schoolmasters' competing to provide better education could have an impact on enrollments. If one teacher's methods did indeed achieve superior results, this would become known in the community. Parents would notice the improvement as it was customary to engage young children in conversations about their studies on the Sabbath.[15] Many towns employed an official examiner who tested local schoolchildren periodically.[16] Sometimes the town's rabbi served in this capacity. Perhaps, in order to survive, the old schoolmaster would improve the quality of instruction at his school in response to the new competition. If, however, the old school was forced to close for lack of students, it was not likely to have been much of a credit to the community in the first place. In sum, the impact of robust, even predatory competition between schoolteachers was "to make the teaching great and glorious," that is, by permitting the entry of new and better teachers, to improve the overall quality of elementary education through the gradual improvement or elimination of the weaker institutions.

The case of rabbis was entirely different. Many factors argued for a competitive regime that was restricted and more subdued. First there was the patent unseemliness of respected rabbinic figures competing aggressively for business and fees. Second, rivalries among eminent rabbis would resonate on a community-wide and even regional basis in a way that competition among anonymous local schoolteachers did not. As vocal public factions coalesced around rabbinic contenders, their competition had the potential to divide communities, upset social cohesion, and shatter communal peace. In addition, competition that forced a rabbi from his practice implicated important religious tenets that were not present in the case of schoolteachers. As we shall see, the Talmudic principle that "we ascend in matters of holiness but we do not descend" applied to rabbis.[17] It buttressed their contention that once appointed to a post, they were entitled to hold it for life. Competition that might force a rabbi out of his post jeopardized his expectation of secure tenure and, if permitted, might lead to a violation of the religious stricture against removal.

Most important, in contrast to schoolteachers, the rabbinate as a whole comprised a true intellectual elite. This remained true despite the shortcomings of individuals, the abuses of some unscrupulous types, brief periods of low standards, and occasional pockets of poor performance. Nor did calls by prominent religious leaders for even higher standards contradict this fact. Unlike schoolteachers, rabbis' academic preparation entailed many years of intense, full-time study under the tutelage of seasoned scholars of recognized rank. Rabbinic training consumed all of a young man's adolescent years and perhaps a decade after his marriage.[18] Ordination was awarded only after earning the approbation of a mature scholar with personal knowledge of the candidate's abilities. Rabbinic title did not itself confer any position of communal authority. To secure an appointment, a rabbi would have to convince the townsfolk (or their designated electors) of his qualifications for the post. As products of their training and as a result of the selection process, rabbis were not ordinarily unqualified for their tasks in the way many schoolteachers were. Nor was it likely that a newcomer would be more qualified than an experienced rabbi with many prior years of service in his post. Hence, to permit a new arrival to compete with an incumbent rabbi and, by siphoning away his fees, drive him from office was not likely to result in a new rabbi who was superior to the incumbent, and it might even have the opposite effect.

In the end, it was the rabbis themselves who formulated the rules of competition in their codes and responsa. They established two competitive regimes.[19] For the humblest of Jewish educators, elementary schoolteachers, they sanctioned a regime of unrestricted, even cut-throat competition. They allowed the opening and operating of rival institutions side-by-side, poaching one another's students, and driving one's fellow from the school-teaching business, all with the stated aim of increasing the quality of instruction. The practices the halakhah sanctioned were so disruptive that town elders recognized the need to temper the competition, for example, by passing ordinances that prohibited parents from removing children from a school at least until the current term had ended. But for themselves and their rabbinic practices, once the rabbinate became a salaried profession and their own livelihoods were threatened, the rabbis reined in competition by colleagues. They prohibited newcomers from siphoning fees away from established rabbis and engaging in other competitive practices that might drive incumbents from their posts, like changing the location of a court.[20] Compared to schoolteachers, the competitive regime rabbis established for themselves was less robust and more subdued, designed to reduce the negative communal consequences that might flow from unrestricted competition while, not incidentally, providing a large measure of protection for the established rabbi's livelihood.

PART 3

Tenure

Chapter 11

"ALL THE SAME, GO AND CONSULT THEM"

Rabbinic tenure denotes a rabbi's entitlement to retain his position for life subject only to removal for cause.[1] It both complements and supplements the principles discussed in parts 1 and 2, for once the rabbi's salary was legally sanctioned and his livelihood insulated from competition, tenure would guarantee his ability to enjoy the benefits of office for the longest possible time—the remainder of his life. Still, like all legal assurances, a rabbi's ability to realize lifetime tenure varied from time to time and from place to place, and not every rabbi desired to retain his post for life. Thus, alongside lifetime tenure, rabbis also wanted freedom to leave when offered a new position in a larger, more prominent community with greater prestige and a more generous stipend.[2]

The concept of tenure was a broad one that protected native rabbis as well as those imported from afar, but rabbis who had been invited by a Jewish community to relocate from a distant place and take up residence as spiritual leader in a new town made an especially compelling argument for tenure. Some argued it would be unduly harsh for the appointee to have uprooted himself and his family and traveled to his new post at the town's invitation only to be told after the passage of a number of years that his services were no longer required.[3]

Removal by the community at will could have profoundly negative consequences. Disputes over rabbinic appointments could engender bitter divisiveness within a community.[4] To keep an incumbent rabbi in jeopardy of removal would mean that a new controversy might erupt at any moment and shatter communal calm. Perhaps it was better, once an appointment was made, to regard the matter as closed "for the sake of peace."[5] By the same token, granting the incumbent tenure for life delayed the onset of the next appointment controversy for the longest possible time. Tenure had additional benefits for the community. The rabbi's long service would permit him to become intimately acquainted with the community and its affairs. His job security would give him the freedom to render unpopular decisions and, when necessary, chastise his congregation in his sermons.[6]

Designating the topic as "tenure" naturally invites comparisons with academic tenure, a concept it resembles in some respects. Rabbinic tenure could serve one of the functions that academic tenure serves in modern universities, affording the tenured rabbi the equivalent of academic freedom, enabling him to teach and to preach as his conscience dictated. There is an important distinction between the two, however. While a university professor must earn academic tenure over time, rabbinic tenure is an entitlement conferred automatically upon appointment to a post. For the rabbi there is no probationary period during which his performance is judged by peers applying objective and subjective criteria.[7] Of course the rabbi's qualifications for office would have been evaluated by the community when initially considering him for appointment, but it is upon assuming the post,[8] at a time when his actual performance in office is unknown, that his lifetime tenure commences. Thus alongside the benefits there is some risk to the community in acceding to the rabbi's demand for tenure at the time of his initial appointment.

On a practical level, the community was always in control of the rabbi's employment because it possessed the power of the purse. There were instances, referred to earlier, in which community leaders, claiming funds were needed for other purposes, neglected to pay a rabbi's salary, in one case for forty weeks, in another for five years.[9] In the first case, the rabbi went on strike, refusing to issue halakhic rulings until payments resumed; in the second, the rabbi threatened to leave his post. But for every rabbi who merely threatened to leave his post, there may have been another who actually did when his salary went unpaid. We lack realistic accounts of disputes of this type because few rabbis wrote autobiographies, and incidents of this sort were not likely to be included in the admiring biographies written by their students and descendants.[10] If some rabbis were resigned to an income stream that was sporadic, other rabbis who were less patient or more impoverished, or who had viable employment alternatives elsewhere, might view the salary interruption as an occasion to leave their posts or as the community's not-so-subtle suggestion that they ought to do so.

Apart from his salary from the town, the rabbi received fees for services. He could be deprived of these as well if people shifted their patronage away from one scholar to another whom they preferred. When students left the yeshivah of Rabbi David ben Isaac of Fulda, he lost the economic base of his rabbinate. He was forced to leave town and seek a position elsewhere.[11] In the responsa of Rabbi Malkhiel Tenenbaum, we learn of a town that was served by two rabbis, one Ashkenazic and the other Sephardic. Most of the townsfolk, including the Sephardim, preferred the Ashkenazic rabbi and took their matters to him when they required a rabbi's services. When the Sephardic rabbi died, the Sephardic community accepted the Ashkenazic rabbi as their own rather than appoint the Sephardic rabbi's heir. Here the townsfolk voted with their feet, so to speak, effectively removing the Sephardic rabbi and his heir by transferring their patronage to his colleague.[12]

In addition to these practical considerations, there is a more fundamental objection to lifetime tenure for rabbis. This arises from the community's acknowledged authority to consent to the appointment of its leaders. That community consent is required for their appointment is a fundamental principle of Jewish law, embodied in a Talmudic dictum that states, "We must not appoint a leader over a community without first consulting it."[13] Communal consent to the appointment is implicit in the dictum, for otherwise the consultation would be an empty gesture.[14] Rabbinic commentators found support in the Mishnah for the proposition that even a king who inherited his office from his father required the consent of the people's representatives before ascending to the throne.[15] In the archetypal case, the Talmud relates how God commanded Moses to present to the Israelites for their approval Bezalel, the man whom God called to serve as chief artisan of the Tabernacle. When Moses hesitated in deference to God's selection of Bezalel, God commanded him, "All the same, go and consult them."[16]

That rabbis required communal consent for their appointment was never doubted.[17] According to the dire warning of the Rema, the rabbi who serves without the community's consent "in the end will be destined to answer in Judgment."[18] The principle was affirmed by Rabbi David ibn Abi Zimra, the *Radbaz* (ca. 1479–1573), in the middle of the sixteenth century.[19] In 1541, a dispute erupted in Salonika over who should be the rabbi of the congregation of Aragon after the death of its leader, Rabbi Jacob Sarfati. The rival candidates were his son, Judah, and another prominent scholar, Rabbi Isaac Arama. The congregation split into quarrelsome factions. It was agreed to submit the matter to the binding arbitration of two rabbinic authorities. The arbitrators decreed that the matter should be decided by the unanimous decision of the congregation's five lay leaders, the *parnassim*. After several months of deliberation, the parnassim announced their unanimous decision. They decided that neither candidate was suitable to lead and stripped both of all rabbinic functions vis-à-vis the congregation. Rabbi Judah complained about the outcome to the Radbaz, arguing that various conditions of the arbitration had been violated. The Radbaz was unstinting in his condemnation of Judah's conduct, for "no one may become an official of the congregation without the congregation's consent, and the lay leaders stand in the congregation's place" for this purpose.[20] He ordered Judah to repent and to accept the lay leaders' decision under threat of excommunication. That Judah was the departed rabbi's son and had preached in the synagogue on several occasions since his father's death did not alter his conclusion.

Given the requirement of consent for a rabbi's appointment, the question arises whether it is not inconsistent to withhold from the community discretion over removal, for it is the community's withdrawal of its consent to his continued service that will act as the catalyst for seeking a rabbi's removal. Put another way, why does the need for the community's consent dissipate once an individual takes office? Rather, should not an incumbent, when he loses the public's mandate to serve, be subject to removal by them at will?

That the community's power to remove at will follows logically from its necessary consent to appointments is suggested by the *Tosafot,* who wrote: "And one may say that the high priest is appointed orally and removed orally. In the Jerusalem Talmud they derive this from Scripture, and it is logical that the matter should depend on the king and his fellow priests."[21] That the high priest's *appointment* depends on his fellow priests follows from the general rule, "We do not appoint a leader over a community without first consulting it," for the priests are the community that the high priest leads, and they must consent to his leadership.[22] The question is whether the same principle applies to *removal,* and the clear import of the passage is that logically it does. Read this way, the implication of the passage is problematic for those who argue that Jewish law grants communal appointees lifetime tenure, denying the community a right to remove officeholders at will.[23]

The following chapters of part 3 examine first the justifications that halakhic authorities offered for rabbinic tenure, next the relationship between tenure and merit in the selection and retention of rabbis, and finally the way custom and case-by-case challenges to incumbents preserved for Jewish communities a measure of control over their spiritual leadership notwithstanding the principle of lifetime tenure for rabbis.

Chapter 12

JUSTIFICATIONS FOR TENURE

In making their case for rabbinic tenure, the authorities of Jewish law developed a variety of arguments. They equated the rabbinate with two tenured positions, those of king and high priest. They weighed the harm that might be caused to a rabbi's reputation if he were removed from office without just cause. They applied to rabbinic posts the Talmudic maxim, "We elevate in matters of sanctity but we do not decrease." In this chapter we survey these three justifications for rabbinic tenure.

THE ANALOGY TO MONARCHY AND PRIESTHOOD

Halakhic authorities drew an analogy between the rabbinate and two institutions of communal leadership mentioned in the Bible, monarchy and priesthood. It was clear from scriptural verses that monarchy and priesthood were lifetime callings that passed by inheritance to heirs.[1] It was also plain from biblical narratives that many kings and high priests served in Israel while more worthy individuals were available to replace them, yet the incumbents were never removed from office on this account.[2] By analogy, halakhic authorities invested rabbis with lifetime tenure and ruled they were not subject to removal solely because better qualified candidates became available to replace them.[3]

The analogy yielded an additional argument in favor of rabbinic tenure. Most halakhic authorities held that rabbinic posts, like monarchy and priesthood, descended by inheritance to an incumbent's qualified heir.[4] From this they constructed an a fortiori argument in favor of lifetime tenure. If the rabbi's appointment guarantees the post to his heir at his death, then it must surely guarantee the post to the incumbent himself for his life.[5]

These arguments have merit to the extent the analogy is apt. Is a rabbinic post rightly to be regarded as sufficiently akin to the position of monarch or high priest to warrant similar treatment for purposes of tenure and inheritance? Jewish tradition recognizes three separate and distinct spheres of authority—the royal crown of monarchy (*keter malkhut*), the priestly crown of the priesthood (*keter kahunah*), and the Torah crown of the sages (*keter Torah*).[6] But the rabbis, who regarded themselves as custodians of the third crown, also, after the destruction of the Temple, regarded themselves as successors to the first two.[7] The analogy was persuasive for them, and they deliberately employed it to afford a scriptural basis for the rabbinate, essentially a postbiblical institution.[8]

To Avoid Creating Suspicion

Under Jewish law, the occupant of any communal office can be removed for cause, whether for misappropriating funds, leading an immoral life, violating precepts, or straying into foreign cultures.[9] Like the high priest who sinned and was flogged and then returned to office, the official who repented and accepted punishment could resume his post.[10]

Allegations against communal rabbis in which the community sought their removal for cause were infrequent but serious. Typically a community resident would bring the charges to the attention of the town's lay leaders and they would act on their own accord or refer the matter to a prominent halakhic authority in a neighboring town or region. In some cases the charges were brought to a rabbinical synod or to government authorities. The allegations ranged from the serious, such as holding heretical views,[11] to the more prosaic, such as not studying Torah sufficiently.[12] Sometimes the controversy was but one aspect of a more far-reaching religious and social upheaval affecting the Jewish people at the time. This was true when the rabbi of Altona, Jonathan Eybeschutz (1690–1764), was temporarily suspended under suspicion of adhering to belief in the false messiah Sabbatai Zevi,[13] and when Levi Isaac of Berdichev (ca. 1740–1810) was dismissed from his position as rabbi, first in Zholikhov (Zelechow, Poland) and then in Pinsk, for promoting the tenets of the Hasidic movement.[14] Similarly, early in the twentieth century, Emil Cohn was removed from his position as rabbi in Berlin when he expressed support for the Zionist movement.[15] Rabbis were particularly vulnerable to the charge of leading their congregations astray by issuing erroneous halakhic rulings,[16] especially in intimate matters of Jewish family law, given the complexity of the rules and the rabbis' varying abilities.

There was no fixed procedure nor any central tribunal for adjudicating complaints against rabbis. Fact finding was often limited to the written record. If the halakhic authority to whom a matter of this type was addressed had confidence in the trustworthiness of the complainants, he would publicize the allegations in a responsum, chastise the offending rabbi, pronounce a ban against him, deprive him of the use of his rabbinical titles, demand remedial action, and pending such action forbid him from issuing halakhic rulings. In response, the rabbi's supporters and the accused himself would pen tracts disputing the charges. If in due course the allegations failed to be established by two credible witnesses or if it became clear that the charges were raised falsely by opponents, the rabbi was reinstated and the authorities who had removed him would attempt to make amends. In a noteworthy instance of this type, the prominent fifteenth-century Italian scholar Rabbi Joseph Colon sent his son Perez to Istanbul to seek forgiveness from Rabbi Moses Capsali, whom Colon had banned upon receiving a false charge, leveled by Capsali's enemies, that he was lax in matters of family law.[17] Whatever the eventual outcome, allegations of wrongdoing against a sitting rabbi shattered communal tranquility, divided communities into factions, and created bitterness and resentment among the participants.

The dire scenario occasioned by a removal for cause provided an argument for lifetime tenure for rabbis who were innocent of any wrongdoing. Removing someone who was blameless simply because the community changed its allegiance and now preferred another would arouse the suspicion, among those unfamiliar with the facts, that the incumbent had been removed for cause. This blemish to his honor was a stain that a rabbi who properly discharged his duties did not deserve. Lifetime tenure thus secured not just the innocent rabbi's post but also his good name and reputation.[18]

Chief Rabbi Abraham Isaac Kook (1865–1935) wrote movingly of the terrible distress an individual experiences upon removal from office, when he is stripped of his honors and sees his position pass to another.[19] The psychological trauma of removal is compounded when there is no just cause.[20] Rabbinic tenure ensures that the rabbi who is blameless will not suffer this distress gratuitously.

The Holiness Principle

Perhaps the most important justification for rabbinic tenure was rooted in a fundamental tenet of Judaism. The Jewish tradition seeks to attain holiness in the world. When, in the wilderness of Sinai, God revealed His intention to transform the Israelites into "a kingdom of priests and a holy nation" (Exod. 19:6), He commanded them to be holy "for I the Lord your God am holy" (Lev. 19:2).[21] The course of Jewish history as well as the trajectory of each individual's life must be away from that which defiles and toward that which sanctifies.

In the Talmud, this principle is embodied in a legal maxim that states, "We elevate in matters of sanctity but we do not decrease."[22] Sacred status, once achieved, is permanent, and while one may ascend to a higher level of sanctity, one may not revert to a lower level.[23] We shall refer to this principle as "the holiness principle."

The principle found many applications in Talmudic jurisprudence,[24] among them two that have a bearing on tenure in office. In the first, the Mishnah relates how, seven days prior to Yom Kippur, an ordinary priest was designated as substitute high priest.[25] Then, if the high priest became unable to perform the Temple rites on the holy day by reason of illness or ritual disqualification, the substitute officiated in his place. Once such an event did occur, and Joseph ben Ulam was called upon to substitute. When the high priest recovered, he resumed his position. As to the future status of Joseph ben Ulam, the substitute, the sages ruled as follows: He cannot continue to serve as high priest, to prevent the rivalry that was sure to arise if two individuals held the same post. Nor, having attained the status of high priest, even temporarily, could he revert to his former rank as an ordinary priest because "We elevate in matters of sanctity but we do not decrease."[26] The substitute retired from priestly service with the rank of "former high priest."

That the holiness principle should apply with full vigor to the sacred personnel who ministered in the Temple seems plain. That it applies as well to rank and status outside the Temple precincts was demonstrated by a second matter related in the Talmud. After the destruction of Jerusalem in 70 C.E., a group of scholars assembled in the village of Yavneh (Jamnia) to preserve the oral traditions of the Jewish legal heritage. For decades starting after 80 C.E., a scholar named Rabban Gamaliel served as president of the assembly. The Talmud relates an occasion on which he behaved in an insulting manner toward Rabbi Joshua, a member of the assembly who disagreed with him on a legal point. This was the third occasion on which Rabban Gamaliel had behaved in this fashion, and as a result the assembly removed him from the presidency. They appointed Rabbi Elazar ben Azariah to replace him. A short time later Rabban Gamaliel and Rabbi Joshua were reconciled, and the latter persuaded his colleagues to restore Rabban Gamaliel to his post. This presented the scholars with a dilemma, for restoring Rabban Gamaliel would mean removing Rabbi Elazar, and this would violate the holiness principle. They solved the problem by establishing a copresidency. Thereafter Rabban Gamaliel delivered the president's address on three Sabbaths each month and Rabbi Elazar preached on one.[27]

Rabban Gamaliel's removal did not violate the holiness principle, for he had committed an impeachable offense—insulting a scholar—and was removed for cause. But the copresidency presented difficult problems under the holiness principle. It seemed that both Rabban Gamaliel and Rabbi Elazar were experiencing some reduction in status by having to share the honors of office with each other. Rabbinic commentators offered a number of semantic arguments to explain the result.[28] Conceding Rabban Gamaliel was demoted "somewhat," they argued that he retained the essence of his office and that a partial reduction in status did not constitute the degree of demotion that would violate the holiness principle. As for Rabbi Elazar, he, unlike Rabban Gamaliel, was not a descendant of the great sage Hillel, who himself had served as president of the scholars' assembly some seventy years earlier. Having been appointed president without the benefit of inherited right to the office, Rabbi Elazar's ascent did not constitute a full-fledged ascent, so that his reduction in status did not constitute a full-scale reduction.[29] Again, with this explanation no violation of the holiness principle was deemed to have occurred. It was also possible that Rabbi Elazar had experienced no reduction at all, for the reappointment of Rabban Gamaliel may have come within a week of his removal, by which time Rabbi Elazar had delivered the president's address only once.[30]

In truth, the efforts to reconcile the copresidency arrangement with the holiness principle were not totally successful, and the propriety of joint appointments remained open to question.[31] It was clear from the narrative, however, that the holiness principle *did* apply to rank among the Talmudic sages. Since the sages were the precursors of the rabbis, it followed that the principle applied to rabbinic rank as well. The rabbis' close association with the study and dissemination of the holy Torah fortified the conclusion, for appointment to a rabbinic chair was considered a sacred calling.[32] As applied to rabbinic appointments, the notion that "We elevate in matters of sanctity but do not decrease" means that once appointed, a rabbi, absent cause, could not be removed from his post. In this fashion, the holiness principle served as an important underpinning for the concept of rabbinic tenure.

Chapter 13

TENURE AND MERIT

The ancients believed in miracles, among them the miracle of appointment. For them officeholders who overcame personal shortcomings to perform extraordinary service when circumstances required were not simply rising to the occasion. They believed that installation in high office miraculously transformed the appointee into something better than he was.[1] A midrash relates how David, who was shorter than King Saul, immediately upon trying on the King's armor grew in stature so that it fit,[2] teaching that the short become tall upon attaining royal rank. So too upon appointment the high priest became tall if he was short, light if he was dark, and cheerful if he was troubled.[3] Rabbi Joseph struggled for twenty-two years to solve a problem until he was appointed head of the academy, when he immediately solved it.[4]

With the transition from ancient to modern times, however, one can no longer rely on the miracle of appointment. Among candidates for office, who vary in ability, difficult assessments will have to be made to ensure an appointee's qualifications for office. Even an incumbent may fall short in comparison to another individual who arrives on the scene later and appears better qualified to hold his post.

In the case of rabbis, does such a comparison allow a community to remove its rabbi and replace him with someone else? In the view of most halakhic authorities, removal is not permitted in these circumstances, for rabbinic tenure entitles a rabbi to retain his post even after someone more learned becomes available to replace him. Rabbi Moses Isserles (Rema) formulated the rule as follows: "One who is established as rabbi in a town, even where he established himself in his post, should not be removed from his post even though there may come to the town another who is greater [in learning] than the first."[5]

This preference for incumbency over merit is a problematic feature of rabbinic tenure. It is true that many important values can be cited to support it, including communal peace and stability, the honor of the incumbent, and the value to the community of his accumulated experience. There is also the admitted difficulty of accurately comparing the scholarly attainments of two learned individuals and the ever-present danger of making a mistake, especially serious when the current livelihood of one of them depends on the outcome of the assessment. But it seems certain that under the doctrine of rabbinic tenure there will be instances in which the supreme value—the provision of the highest possible level of Torah scholarship to any given Jewish community—will be sacrificed. The mediocre incumbent will retain his post. The brilliant newcomer cannot claim it.[6]

Two expectations mitigate to some extent this consequence of rabbinic tenure. First, an incumbent rabbi, obligated like every Jew to study the Torah each day, is expected to continue his studies while in office. Thus, whatever the state of his knowledge upon taking office, he will increase it over time. Second, divine guidance will counteract any deficiency in his ability. He will be assisted from on High to issue rulings that are correct.[7] The minimum qualifications for the rabbinate, some learning and a fear of Heaven,[8] lend credence to both expectations. Possessing at the very least the rudiments of scholarship, a rabbi will be able to tutor himself. His fear of Heaven assures that he will not treat the obligation to do so lightly.

A legal opinion from the prominent Spanish authority Rabbi Joseph ibn Migas (1077–1141) sheds light on the intermediate category of scholar, neither completely learned nor completely ignorant.[9] He was asked for his view of the rulings of those who had never studied halakhah under the tutelage of a rabbi and did not understand its operation but were able to read the summaries of the law prepared by the geonim, the scholars in Babylonia in the four centuries after the close of the Talmud. Often these individuals issued contradictory rulings. They did not realize that the manuscripts on which they relied contained scribal errors nor were they aware that the geonim sometimes retracted their views in later opinions. The inquirer asked Ibn Migas whether one could rely on the rulings of people like these, who used secondary sources for the halakhah but lacked the ability to support their conclusions directly from the Talmud, the source of the laws.

For Ibn Migas, these admittedly marginal scholars were better qualified to issue rulings than many who had undertaken the task in his day. At least, in consulting the works of the geonim, they were relying on the opinions of experts. In their works the geonim presented the laws in a clear and concise manner, very much unlike the complex labyrinth of Talmudic argumentation, and one who relied on them was less likely to make an error than one who consulted the Talmud directly. By contrast, many who had arrogated to themselves the authority to decide the law in Ibn Migas's day lacked in his opinion the ability either to study the Talmud directly or to understand the works of the geonim. In our day, Ibn Migas writes, we do not have scholars with the ability to consult the Talmud directly and reach correct conclusions. Only presumptuous individuals believe that by consulting the Talmud directly they can ascertain the correct rules. They are wrong and should be prevented from even attempting to do so.[10]

Given this broad range of intellectual ability among rabbis, there is an important exception to the rule granting lifetime tenure. A rabbi may be removed from his post and replaced by a greater scholar when the incumbent is not learned at all—that is, when he is an ignoramus.[11] An ignorant person may never rely on his incumbency to preserve his office against a person with learning, for this would dishonor the Torah knowledge possessed by the learned individual in favor of an empty vessel who possesses none. Further, there is no hope that an ignoramus will be able to tutor himself adequately to discharge his duties as rabbi.

That an unlearned person might come to occupy a rabbinic chair seems startling at first blush, but it could occur quite innocently. Small, poor, distant Jewish communities would always have difficulty attracting and maintaining qualified scholars and might have to settle for someone with minimal qualifications.[12] Also, it must be conceded that there were unscrupulous persons who purchased or forged certificates of ordination and then purchased rabbinic offices.[13] Halakhic authorities considered such behavior an abuse,[14] but distinguishing these rabbinic pretenders from persons with the requisite training sometimes proved difficult for the lay leaders of Jewish communities, especially in periods of persecution and natural disaster when learning and scholarship naturally declined and qualified rabbis were few. A notable example of this occurred in the fourteenth century when first the Black Death and then popular uprisings against the Jews decimated Jewish communities and their scholars, disrupting religious and educational life, including the training of rabbis.[15] Yeshivahs were closed and rabbinical training was interrupted again after massacres in the Ukraine in 1648–49.[16]

Thus, for a variety of reasons, there was the possibility that a rabbinic chair would come to be occupied by someone whose qualifications were marginal or nil. Our concern is the way rabbinic tenure impacts on a community's ability to remove such an individual from his post and replace him when, in due course, a more qualified candidate becomes available. Rabbinic tenure, as most halakhic authorities understood it, protected the post of the marginal scholar, although no one argued that it protected the post of someone who was completely unfit to serve.

Not every halakhic authority was willing to concede the case of the marginal scholar. Rabbi David ben Hayyim of Corfu (the *Radakh*) held that a greater scholar can *always* displace a lesser light, and this is true even with respect to the appointed rabbi of a town.[17] He cited in support of his view the Talmudic dictum "In a place where there is no man, there be a man."[18] He held that the holiness principle, "We elevate in matters of sanctity but we do not decrease,"[19] applied only where two individuals are equal. In such cases, there are no grounds for removing the incumbent. But in all other cases, the greater scholar takes precedence.

The Radakh, like Ibn Migas four centuries earlier, was concerned about the quality of the rabbinate in his day, writing that "on account of our many sins, there are judges who are unfit, who ordain empty vessels and who profane the name of God in public and plant an idol next to the altar of the Lord."[20] But the situation may have improved, for he was willing to concede that the majority of rabbis were not in this category.[21]

With a view towards improving the quality of the rabbinate, the Radakh's position has a great deal to recommend it. Under his approach, greater scholars may always replace lesser ones. Over time this approach would weed out marginal scholars from their posts. The net result would be an incremental improvement in the quality of the rabbinate, achieved at the expense of the second-rate scholars' positions. His, however, was the minority view. The majority held that rabbinic tenure protected a lesser scholar who was otherwise blameless, so long as he was not an ignoramus. This preference for incumbency over merit remains a troubling aspect of rabbinic tenure, a striking departure in a tradition that claims excellence in Torah studies as its paramount value.

Chapter 14

ALTERNATIVES TO TENURE

The rabbis' striving for security in their posts was checked in many places by local customs that were inconsistent with granting them lifetime tenure. Since custom is a recognized source of Jewish law,¹ such customs are not necessarily invalid. It is the task of halakhic scholars to distinguish good customs from bad ones and to invalidate those that are erroneous or illogical or violate fundamental principles of equity.² In this chapter we examine how they performed this task in relation to customs that provided alternatives to rabbinic tenure.

ROTATION IN OFFICE

In some towns, it was the custom to rotate public offices regularly among the adult male residents. This distributed the honors as well as the burdens of public service and prevented any individual or a single family from monopolizing power.³

Could rabbinic posts rotate in this fashion? The notion seems farfetched when applied to the later eras of the rabbinate's development and professionalization. But during the early ages of Jewish settlement in Europe, and especially in small communities, even the spiritual leadership of the community could rotate in this fashion, for at the head of many families there stood a learned patriarch able to perform this task.⁴ To illustrate Rabbi Israel Isserlein's famous lament that "the ordained are many but the knowledgeable are few," Simha Assaf cites a small village in sixteenth-century Poland consisting of fifty Jewish households, twenty of which were headed by individuals who held rabbinic titles.⁵ In a village like this, rotating the rabbinic chair among the twenty would have been possible.

With rotation in office came welcome social and communal benefits. A system of rotation in office, which gave every qualified individual a turn to serve, tended to decrease the natural social tensions between those in and out of power.⁶ The first Jewish rebel leader, Korah, who challenged Moses' leadership in the wilderness of Sinai, implanted the notion that all Israelites are worthy of holding high office when he claimed, "All the congregation are holy, every one of them" (Num. 16:3). In later generations, whenever the general public became dissatisfied with their leaders, they echoed Korah's claim. Rotation in office answered Korah's challenge by affording every qualified resident an opportunity to serve.

Although it was inconsistent with the principle of lifetime tenure, halakhic authorities regarded rotation in office as an acceptable alternative.⁷ The practice satisfied most of their concerns regarding removal from office. The greatest threat to rabbinic security was a fickle public, perhaps aroused by the passions of the moment, that could remove from office at will. So long as rotation was a regularized practice and applied to all officeholders in a community, turning them in and out of office according to a fixed schedule, then public animus against a particular individual would not be the motivating cause for anyone's dismissal. Further, no suspicions of wrongdoing were aroused when one resident passed from office and was replaced by the next in line according to a preset formula.

Appointments for a Limited Term

Similar arguments can be made in support of another custom inconsistent with lifetime tenure. In many communities officeholders served for fixed terms determined at the time of their appointment. Upon the expiration of the term, it could be renewed or extended or the contract could be terminated.

In the case of rabbis, it was the practice in many communities to insert a fixed term, often three or five years, in their contracts of appointment. The Rema ruled such provisions were proper: "In a place where it is the custom to accept a rabbi for a fixed term or to appoint whomever they wish, they have authority to do so."[8] In some cases, custom or regional ordinance required the community to notify the rabbi of nonrenewal six months before the expiration of his contract. Absent notification, the rabbi's contract was automatically renewed. In other communities, if the congregation was silent when the rabbi's contract ended, it was deemed to have been terminated.[9]

Early authorities tended to interpret fixed-term provisions in a straightforward way, giving both parties at the expiration of the term free rein to renew or not to renew.[10] This view was supported by simple logic and in addition satisfied many of the halakhic concerns regarding removal from office. Leaving at the expiration of a set term would not incite any suspicions that the incumbent was removed for cause. It would not violate his fair expectations regarding the duration of his employment, for he had agreed to the term before accepting the post. And it need not be deemed a violation of the holiness principle if we are permitted to say that appointment for a limited term is not a full elevation in sacred status nor is leaving when a term expires to be deemed a demotion, for the appointment merely expires of its own accord at the end of the term.

There are counterarguments, of course. If the community has the option to renew an appointment and does not, then one might ask why it has not done so, thus raising suspicions about the rabbi's performance in office. Nor was the inapplicability of the holiness principle so clear-cut. The substitute high priest was promoted for a limited time only—until the high priest recovered—yet the holiness principle applied and he never reverted to the status of an ordinary priest.[11] Rabbi Elazar ben Azariah was appointed president for a limited time only—until Rabban Gamaliel apologized to Rabbi Joshua—and he too was covered by the holiness principle.[12]

Later authorities revised the interpretation of fixed-term rabbinic contracts and read them in a way that departed from their plain meaning. In order to understand the contracts, they held, it was necessary to take into account the context within which they were drafted and signed. Jewish law disapproves of open-ended employment contracts or, according to some, contracts that exceed a term of three or six years,[13] because they are too reminiscent of the biblical institution of Hebrew bondage. The Hebrew slave served for six years and could go free earlier only upon receipt of a bill of manumission from his master. He could elect not to go free and serve for an open-ended term that would end upon the occurrence of a jubilee once in fifty years.[14] In the rabbinic view, Hebrew slavery was in conflict with the fundamental notion that each Jew is subservient only to God.[15] They held that an employment contract should embody at most a term that is appropriate for a hired worker, three to six years,[16] and not a term that characterizes a Hebrew slave, six years or longer.[17]

Interpreting rabbinic contracts in light of this background yielded a result that was not apparent on their face. The stated three- or five-year term was never intended to give a community the right to remove its rabbi and replace him at the end of the term. Rather it was a formal or stylistic device inserted to remove any appearance of Hebrew slavery from the agreement.[18] This reading was supported by Talmudic dicta that equated leadership positions with slavery to the public welfare.[19] As Rashi explained, "Leadership is slavery to the yoke of the many for the person on whom it is bestowed."[20] Under the revised reading, the three- or five-year term might have been inserted as the minimum number of years the rabbi was committed to serve, marking the point at which he could voluntarily relinquish his post.[21] The fixed term might have been inserted to negate the inference that upon the incumbent's death, his heir automatically would be entitled to inherit his post.[22] But if the provision had any practical effect, it was only to the advantage of the rabbi, permitting him to leave. It did not confer any benefits on the community, permitting them to remove him. Under this construction, unless the parties had expressly stipulated to the contrary at the time of the appointment and, having so stipulated, the community exercised its right to terminate immediately at the end of the rabbi's contractual term and not later, a rabbi was entitled to lifetime tenure if he wanted it despite the fixed term written into his contract.

As a matter of contract interpretation, the revised reading is not wholly persuasive. This is particularly true when the contract specifies a term other than the standard three or five years. For example, the city of Poznan appointed a rabbi for six years in 1714, ten years in 1717, and nineteen years in 1796.[23] These terms bear the earmarks of hard bargaining that achieved a result that was meaningful to both sides and was not a mere formality. If rabbis generally were not removed when their contracts ended, it is probably because the communities they served were satisfied with the way they discharged their duties. This refraining from exercising a right to remove should have been distinguished from a lack of legal authority to accomplish that result. Instead, halakhic authorities read into the widespread practice of retention a binding custom never to remove upon the expiration of a contract. As Rabbi Yehiel Epstein noted in his late code of law, "Even when the community writes a contract with the rabbi for so many years [a fixed term], we never remove him, and this is the custom that is widespread in all areas of Jewish settlement."[24]

JOINT APPOINTMENTS

As an alternative to removing an incumbent, some communities or factions within a community sought a partial solution in the joint appointment. They had as a model the arrangement adopted for the return of Rabban Gamaliel as president of the Talmudic assembly of scholars.[25] This arrangement suggested that an incumbent rabbi could accept a colleague to serve at his side without any loss of status or violation of the holiness principle.

The joint appointment found scant support among halakhic authorities, except when an office involved the handling of money. In these cases there was a contrary tradition requiring that a minimum of two officials be appointed, so that one appointee could check the other's accounts.[26] But apart from fiscal appointees, halakhic authorities applied to leadership positions the rule that governed the establishment of biblical monarchy, "Thou shalt surely set over thyself a king" (Deut. 17:15), which they interpreted as a mandate for one king, not two, thus precluding all joint appointments.[27] Common sense dictated the same result both to prevent controversies from erupting between two rivals and to save the community the expense of supporting two people in the same position.[28] Further, most halakhic authorities regarded joining another to an incumbent's post and forcing him to share the dignity, authority, and privileges of his office as a partial demotion in sacred status that did violate the holiness principle.[29] In short, whatever the justification for the arrangement accommodating Rabban Gamaliel's return as a copresident, later halakhic authorities were not prepared to derive a general rule regarding joint appointments from a situation that must have been sui generis.

Interestingly, the rule against joint appointments was relaxed in the case of cantors. Rabbi Hayyim Benveniste recommended joint appointment of two cantors rather than replacing an incumbent with someone who had a more pleasing voice.[30] Although cantors are also entitled to lifetime tenure and cannot be removed without cause,[31] there were practical reasons for distinguishing them from rabbis and permitting joint appointments. The cantor's duties, involving standing and singing without amplification, were much more physically taxing and did not allow any relief on Sabbath and holidays. A joint appointee could bear part of this burden. Further, while rabbis only increased in wisdom as they grew older, it was a sad fact that the cantor's voice tended to deteriorate with age. Since tenure prevented him from being replaced for this reason alone, a partial solution would be a joint appointment with someone whose voice was superior. Since the ultimate result would be *hiddur mitzvah*, the adornment of the prayer service, this might justify a departure from the holiness principle. Finally two cantors, even if they were rivals and their rivalry provoked disputes among their partisans, were unlikely to cause the type of community-wide schisms caused by two rabbis holding contrary opinions and issuing conflicting legal rulings. It is also true that cantors were sometimes viewed as mere congregational employees without much status or authority, again distinguishing them from rabbis and explaining why a departure from the holiness principle might be permitted in their case.

In the end, with fixed-term contracts for rabbis construed restrictively and joint appointments precluded for them, only the custom of rotation in office remained as an acceptable alternative to lifetime tenure.[32] But this was an outmoded custom, suitable only for the smallest Jewish communities and an earlier time, when public service was not a full-time occupation and the functions of office involved simple duties a layman could perform. If any trustworthy burgher could serve as custodian of the charity box for a while,[33] the idea of rotating a rabbinic post among the townsfolk became quite inevitably impracticable. Lifetime tenure had become both the written and the unwritten rule.

Chapter 15

THE COMMUNITY VERSUS THE TENURED RABBI

However elaborate and variegated the justifications for rabbinic tenure and however circumscribed the role of custom, whether a rabbi would maintain his position for life was never certain. Apart from his own willingness to leave when a more desirable post became available to him, it depended on the will of his community and the circumstances of his case. The community was never completely disabled in this regard, wholly apart from its admitted authority to remove an incumbent for cause.[1] The community possessed residual power to challenge the rabbi's continuance in office, a power implicitly acknowledged by the halakhic authorities to whom the communities turned to settle disputes with their rabbis. It is an unstated underlying premise in their responsa that the community has the right, based on its practical control over the rabbi's livelihood and its recognized right to acquiesce in communal leadership, to come forward and raise objections to the rabbi's tenure. Otherwise, the halakhic authorities would not have entertained the communities' petitions, sometimes ruling against the incumbent.

The circumstances under which such a challenge might arise were far from uniform, but in all of the cases the tenor and intensity of community sentiment either for or against the rabbi's removal were important factors in determining the outcome. Where a traditional reading of the responsa might suggest that once a dispute arose, public opinion would play little or no role and the halakhic authority asked to intervene would determine the outcome by applying halakhic principles, our reading suggests the reverse. It suggests that public sentiment played a leading role, for the responsa time and again give the impression that public opinion was assessed first and then appropriate halakhic reasoning brought to bear to effectuate it.

This chapter presents five cases in which a rabbi's tenure was challenged. The disputants turned to eminent halakhic authorities of their day to resolve the disputes. We shall see how in each case the outcome, whether the rabbi was removed from his post or retained, dovetailed precisely with the reported tenor of public sentiment in the matter.

A Community Perplexed

In this celebrated case, the Jews, having been expelled from France more than once in the fourteenth century, were readmitted for a brief period around 1360 by Charles V, who appointed Matathiah ben Joseph as their chief rabbi. He embarked on a program to restore the vital institutions of Jewish life, establishing a yeshivah that attracted many students and ordained many rabbis. Upon his death, his son, Johanan, who filled his father's place in both learning and fear of sin, succeeded him as chief rabbi with the approval of the community and the assent of the king. Five years into his term of office, however, one of his late father's pupils, Rabbi Isaiah Astruc, returned to France from Savoy bearing a writ from the prominent German authority, Rabbi Meir Halevi, that contained several startling provisions. It deposed Johanan as chief rabbi of France, replacing him with Rabbi Isaiah, and excommunicated any French rabbi who practiced without Isaiah's consent. French Jewry, while mindful of Meir Halevi's great stature, doubted he had authority to dictate affairs in another country. Uncertain how to proceed in the face of two rival chief rabbis, they asked the Spanish authority Rabbi Isaac ben Sheshet Perfet (*Rivash,* 1326–1408), to clarify the matter for them.

In his response, Perfet upheld Johanan's entitlement to the post of chief rabbi.[2] Meir Halevi's rulings were obligatory on his students and on the residents of his country only. He lacked the authority to govern the affairs of French Jewry without their consent. But even had he possessed that authority, Perfet wrote, his removal of Johanan from the chief rabbinate was wrongful on four grounds: Johanan was entitled to the post as the qualified heir of his father; having served five years he was established in the post and not subject to being replaced even by a greater scholar; we elevate in matters of holiness but we do not decrease; and "the law of the kingdom is the law," so that the king's assent to the appointment of Johanan is valid under Jewish law so long as the appointee is qualified and the community consents.

Perfet's last point may have been the crux of the dispute. Among Sephardic Jewry, government appointment of rabbis was accepted practice. By contrast, Ashkenazic Jewry had a long-standing tradition against government interference in religious appointments. A German synod prior to 1220 enacted a decree that "no Jew may accept religious office at the hands of the Gentile powers."[3] For Ashkenazic authorities like Meir Halevi, royal approval would have invalidated Johanan's claim to office. He felt authorized to intervene in France to rectify what, in his view, was a religious error committed by both Johanan and his father in accepting a government mandate to serve.[4]

In this instance the challenge to the incumbent was mounted by a colleague and did not issue from the community. Perfet describes French Jewry as perplexed by the unusual situation.[5] The historian Heinrich Graetz claims they were indignant at the interference into their affairs by an outsider.[6] In sum there was no strong public sentiment on the part of French Jewry for Johanan's removal. Consistent with this, Perfet in his responsum marshals all of the doctrines that support rabbinic tenure to ensure his continuance in office.

A Community Stymied

In a town that had several Jewish congregations, the residents agreed to appoint a single spiritual leader to serve the needs of the community as a whole. The town's former rabbi having died without a male heir, the candidate for successor whom most preferred was his grandson through a daughter. But the members of one congregation believed the grandson was either not ready for the task or unwilling to accept its burdens. They therefore broke ranks with their sister congregations and appointed an outsider to be their rabbi. Later, as matters clarified, it appeared that the grandson was both qualified and willing to serve. The breakaway congregation then sought to remove their rabbi and accept the town's overall choice. But an impasse arose, for the rabbi they had appointed refused to relinquish his post. Quite the contrary, he issued a ban of excommunication against anyone who might enter the synagogue to teach or preach without his permission. The congregational leaders, wishing to rejoin the town's other congregations under the leadership of a single rabbi, asked Rabbi Elijah ben Hayyim of Constantinople (*Ranah,* ca. 1530–1610) whether the incumbent's ban was valid and if they could be released from their undertakings to him.

Rabbi Elijah reached a conclusion in favor of removing the incumbent.[7] He pursued two lines of reasoning. First, he held that the assumptions on which were based the congregation's undertakings to the rabbi were false assumptions on two accounts. They would never have appointed him, an outsider, if they had known that the local candidate was suitable, and the congregation would never have taken independent action if they had known how strongly the sister congregations would protest. On both accounts, the undertakings to the rabbi were invalid from the outset.

Second, Rabbi Elijah held, in the course of protesting his removal, the incumbent had made certain statements—that he never sought the appointment and agreed to serve only in the face of importuning by the entire congregation acting as one, that he never intended to accept the post if anyone objected, and that he would not wish to serve in the face of communal opposition. In Rabbi Elijah's opinion, the incumbent's declarations were tantamount to renouncing his appointment and relinquishing his post. He had declared publicly either that his own preconditions for serving as a consensus appointee were violated or that the internal opposition created a change of circumstances under which he no longer wished to serve. This oral release of his post was effective because, at bottom, the congregation's obligation to their rabbi consisted of their duty to honor him as such. When a scholar releases others of this obligation, even orally, the release is valid.[8]

This opinion is cited in halakhic literature for the proposition that renunciation of a rabbinic post is effective.[9] Yet a fair reading of the facts indicates that this was a most peculiar sort of "renunciation," for the incumbent was so desirous of keeping his post that he erected a barricade at the synagogue's entrance, excommunicating whoever came to replace him. We may note that the incumbent's declarations were made in the course of *protesting* his removal. In fact, this is a case of an "involuntary renunciation," a renunciation forced at the instance of the congregation—that is, a removal. With the congregation united against their rabbi and pursuing the laudable goal of reuniting with their sister congregations under a single leader, the balance is tipped quite decisively against the incumbent and in favor of his removal.

A Community Divided

A qualified heir, who had himself served the community for nineteen years, took over the post his father had occupied for forty years. The succession had been ratified during the father's lifetime in a writing signed by a majority of the community. Some who were not signatories sought to replace the son with a candidate whom they regarded as more learned and hence better qualified. This faction proposed that if replacing the incumbent was not possible, their candidate should serve alongside him. Should the request for a joint appointment be denied, they threatened to break away from the majority and form their own synagogue with their candidate as its rabbi. Rabbi Moses ben Joseph Mitrani (*Mabit,* 1550–1580) denied the request in full, holding the incumbent could neither be removed nor forced to share the position with another.[10] He cited the holiness principle, the son's inheritance from his father, and his acquisition of established rights to his post with the passage of time in office. The fact that there was present in the community someone who was arguably better qualified did not affect the result.[11]

As noted, it was a minority of the community who sought to alter the status quo. The majority of the community wanted to abide by the signed agreement, to continue the incumbent in office and not force him to share his position with another. The Mabit's decision tracks the majority's position closely.

A Community Misled

The town's rabbi passed away, leaving a son who wished to assume his post, but the heir was the victim of false accusations that led the community to believe he was unfit to serve. As a result, the townsfolk transferred their allegiance to the court of another scholar and took a solemn oath to be subject to his jurisdiction only. In due course they discovered that the allegations against the heir were unfounded and that he was completely fit to serve as rabbi. They wished to install him in the post and asked the Sephardic scholar Rabbi Yom Tov Algazi (1727–1802) if they could be released from their oath of allegiance to the other rabbi. He replied in the affirmative. Their oath was invalid, either as one sworn in error or sworn to cancel a mitzvah, the obligation to appoint the heir.[12] The stated reasons support the result in full, but we note that the community was united in its desire to switch from one scholar's jurisdiction to the other's and that Algazi's decision affirmed their right to do so.

Another Community Divided

In a town that was served by two rabbis, one Ashkenazic and the other Sephardic, most of the townsfolk, including the Sephardic Jews, preferred the Ashkenazic scholar and took their matters to him, apparently without objection from the Sephardic rabbi. When the latter died, the majority of Sephardim wanted to appoint the Ashkenazic scholar officially as their rabbi rather than accept the Sephardic rabbi's heir, his brother, whom they claimed was unqualified for the post. The heir sought the post by reason of inheritance and offered to study Torah to eliminate any deficiency in his learning. A minority of Sephardim supported his claim and wanted him appointed as Sephardic rabbi of the town.

In resolving the controversy, Rabbi Malkhiel Tenenbaum (1847–1910) cited a number of reasons to deny the heir his inheritance, including the public benefit to be gained from the town's having to support only one rabbi.[13] An important factor in his decision was the status of the Ashkenazic rabbi. Even before his Sephardic colleague had died and by virtue of the fact that most Sephardim were already consulting him, Rabbi Tenenbaum held, the Ashkenazic rabbi had been transformed into the rabbi of the Sephardim. His status was therefore that of an incumbent, in place and serving when the Sephardic rabbi's heir came forward to displace him. This he cannot do, Rabbi Tenenbaum held, because it would violate the holiness principle.[14] Again, we note how the result corresponds exactly to the will of the majority of the Sephardic community.

This line of cases illustrates the suggestion made earlier, that when halakhic authorities were called upon to resolve challenges to incumbent rabbis, adjusting two competing concerns—rabbinic tenure, on the one hand, and communal acquiescence to its leaders, on the other—they did so with due regard to both factors. In this manner they imparted to the community on a case-by-case basis a measure of ongoing control over its spiritual leadership, notwithstanding the general doctrine of lifetime tenure for rabbis.

PART 4

Succession

Chapter 16

"WHEN WILL THESE TWO OLD MEN DIE?"

> Moses and Aaron went first, Nadab and Abihu walked behind them, and all Israel followed, and Nadab and Abihu were saying: "When will these two old men die and we assume authority over the community?"

"Succession" is a universal problem, arising from the need to determine who comes next when a position of leadership falls vacant.[1] "Inheritance" is one possible solution, determining a position's next occupant by identifying and installing the heir of the deceased one. There are any number of alternative solutions, such as combat among rivals, casting lots, consulting an oracle, rotation in office, popular election, and merit-based appointment. Inheritance itself may take many forms. We may designate as heir a direct descendant of the fallen leader or a collateral relation, a son or a daughter, the eldest or the youngest. A society may rely on a combination of procedures to resolve questions of succession.

Aaron's sons, Nadab and Abihu, expected to inherit positions of authority when Moses and Aaron died, but in the course of Jewish history, a number of noteworthy posts were allocated according to principles other than inheritance. The earliest leaders of Israel in the Promised Land, the biblical Judges (*shofetim*)[2] were charismatic warriors who stood down when the crisis that prompted their appointment receded.[3] Selected for their strength, wisdom, and fear of Heaven, the Judges neither acquired office from their fathers nor did they pass their posts on to their sons.[4] When the people requested of Gideon, "Rule over us, both you, and your son, and your son's son also," he declined: "I will not rule over you, neither shall my son rule over you; the Lord shall rule over you" (Judg. 8:22–23).

The priest anointed for war, a religious and military functionary who had the task of rallying the troops before they went into battle (Deut. 20:2–4), required a striking appearance and a high level of oratorical skill to inspire valor and steadfastness for combat.[5] He was selected from among the priests for these qualities rather than for his lineage.[6] His post did not descend to his heir.[7]

Prophets prepared for their calling by perfecting their spiritual and intellectual capacities. The "sons of the prophets" were not their offspring but rather their disciples who through intense discipline and training might prove worthy of receiving a divine revelation.[8]

Judges—ordinary judicial magistrates—whether serving as lower court judges or as members of the Jerusalem High Court, the Great Sanhedrin, had to be extraordinarily well qualified to perform their judicial tasks. For appointment to office they required seven qualifications: wisdom, humility, fear of God, disdain of gain, love of truth, love of fellow, and a good reputation.[9] In addition, High Court judges had to be experts in Torah and other branches of learning with which they were likely to deal as judges, including science, medicine, mathematics, astrology, and idolatry.[10] It was also desirable for them to speak most languages so that the Court could dispense with the services of interpreters.[11] When a vacancy by death occurred and a new member of the Sanhedrin had to be installed,[12] the appointee was not the deceased judge's son but rather the foremost among the students who sat before the court in semicircular rows, each in an assigned place according to his ranking as a scholar.[13]

In citing alternatives to inheritance there is no intention to suggest that the procedures for succession are wholly discretionary under Jewish law. On the contrary, specific verses in the Torah mandate inheritance for king and high priest, and a third verse excludes the priest anointed for war from this principle.[14] Whether the rules regarding rabbinic succession are from the Torah (*mi-d'oraita*) or rabbinic enactments (*mi-derabbanan*) was a matter of dispute, but even those who held the rules are from the Torah conceded that they were not stated expressly but derived by way of midrash. Since no biblical verse expressly speaks to the matter of rabbinic succession, this creates some leeway in establishing the legal principles that should govern it. How and why the authorities of Jewish law came to exercise their rule-making discretion in favor of inheritance is the focus of our inquiry.

Reasoning by analogy could not dictate a definitive answer to the question of rabbinic succession because plausible analogies point in opposite directions. On the one hand, regarding the functions of their office, rabbis resemble the prophets who proclaim God's commandments and exhort the people to perform them. Like the priests anointed for war, rabbis often inspire their congregants to fight the good fight. Like the ancient Judges, rabbis judge Israel according to Jewish law (the halakhah), and in this they differ from kings who administer justice as they see fit according to the needs of the hour (*hora'ath sha'ah*).[15] If these considerations govern, then rabbis should be selected without regard to lineage but solely on their talents and their fitness for their posts. On the other hand, the rabbinic profession is a sacred calling, and appointment to a rabbinic post is deemed to be a sacred appointment. In this rabbis resemble the high priest.[16] In addition, in some communities the rabbi was also a ruler, since he enjoyed supreme authority as its legal decision maker, the master of the place (*mara d'atra*).[17] If these factors govern, then rabbinic posts, by analogy to priesthood and monarchy, should descend by inheritance to heirs.

Inheritance of rabbinic posts may serve a number of salutary purposes. Making the former rabbi's heir his presumptive replacement may reduce disputes over succession and preserve communal peace.[18] Unlike candidates from the outside whose credentials and personal qualities will be unknown, the rabbi's son will be known to the community.[19] If his father has groomed him to succeed, then the heir will be familiar with the community's problems, issues, and personalities and will be able to function effectively very soon after taking office.[20] Transitions in outlook and religious practice will tend to be gradual and moderate, the son having absorbed the attitudes and practices of his father. Further, it has to be conceded that open competitions to fill vacancies will not necessarily guarantee that the best-qualified candidates will be chosen. As common experience demonstrates, any selection process, even one that is ostensibly merit based, is fallible and subject to extraneous influences that may result in inferior candidates taking office.

These possible advantages of inheritance will not be present in every case and should not be overemphasized. If, for example, the heir spends his formative years away from his father and his community, whether studying at a distant yeshivah or living with his out-of-town in-laws, then he will not be well known at home nor familiar with its local problems. The young man is quite liable to have fallen under the influence of the scholar at the head of his yeshivah and to have absorbed his new spiritual mentor's religious outlook and practices, which may differ radically from those of his father.[21] Furthermore, sons might lack the ability, interest, or temperament to become rabbis or scholars or to serve as judges and teachers like their fathers. Whenever Jews lived in societies relatively free of economic restrictions, other callings beckoned them. There was attrition in the ranks of a family's scholars as sons exited the rabbinate and followed other career paths.[22] Thus, it was not always the case that sons wanted to follow in their father's footsteps.

Some communities had a practice of appointing *only* outsiders to succeed their rabbi. They feared that a local candidate with relatives in the town would either be legally disqualified from judging certain lawsuits in which his relatives were parties or would be partial towards them.[23] Rabbi Yair Hayyim Bacharach (*Havvot Ya'ir*, 1637–1702) wrote that his son was rejected as his successor by the leaders of his community, citing this practice.[24]

Whatever the possible advantages, some will always find counterintuitive the notion that rabbis should inherit their positions. Surely, they will argue, a rabbi's successor should be the best candidate, the one most qualified to provide the highest level of Torah scholarship and Torah leadership to the community, whether that person is the rabbi's son or someone else. This was the position of Rabbi Samuel ben Moses De Medina (*Maharashdam,* 1505–1589), who felt that accepting a less qualified heir as the community's rabbi and judge was inconsistent with the biblical injunction "Justice, justice shalt thou pursue" (Deut. 16:20). He wrote:

> A rabbi and leader of the nation of Israel must be an expert in Torah law, whether in monetary matters . . . divorce and marriage . . . or any of the other prohibitions in the Torah. . . for it is written, "Justice, justice shalt thou pursue"—follow a proper court. . . . As our sages said, "There are three crowns [*Yoma* 72b]," and the crown of Torah is not an inheritance. Let anyone who wishes [come] to take it.[25]

The Maharashdam reminds us that the rabbi, in his stewardship of the Jewish community, was first and foremost a judge. Hence making his appointment hinge on a factor, like lineage, unrelated to his Torah knowledge or his ability to administer justice was not a simple error but something more fundamental, a perversion of justice. The result would be wrongly decided cases, miscarriages of justice, and violations of Torah prohibitions.

The idea that Jewish law would prefer lineage over merit and would pass over a better qualified candidate in favor of the decedent's heir seems a striking departure in a tradition that posits both justice and high achievement in Torah learning as paramount values. Yet as we shall see, among the late authorities of Jewish law (the *Aharonim*), a consensus developed favoring this approach to rabbinic succession. How and why this consensus in favor of inheritance developed are the subjects of the following chapters.

Chapter 17

THE CASE AGAINST INHERITANCE
Part One

Aaron's sons, Nadab and Abihu, died without realizing their ambition for high office.[1] Had they survived the deaths of Moses and Aaron, they would have seen their expectations fulfilled in part. Aaron's office of high priest passed by inheritance to his eldest surviving son, Eleazar.[2] Yet Moses was succeeded neither by his own sons nor Aaron's sons but rather by his disciple and faithful servant Joshua.[3]

That his sons failed to succeed him must have disappointed Moses. He sought high office by inheritance for them twice. At the very inception of his career, when God called to him from the burning bush, Moses asked God to make his descendants kings and priests. God denied the request, for, according to God's plan, monarchy belonged to David and his heirs, and priesthood belonged to Aaron and his heirs.[4] Then at the end of his career, just prior to his death, Moses raised succession a second time. In a colloquy with God he argued that his sons should inherit his glory. The Holy One, Blessed be He, replied, "Your sons sat idly by and did not study the Torah."[5] Instead, Joshua was selected as his successor.

The second dialogue was not a repetition of the first. The dialogue at the burning bush settled monarchy and priesthood. Moses' final request before his death was for Torah leadership—rabbinic succession—for his sons. Moses learned that they were disqualified by their lack of Torah learning. In the realm of spiritual leadership, lineage, including descent from Moses himself, will not determine who shall become Israel's next rabbi.

This interpretation of the second dialogue raises a problem of its own, for Joshua was a man of action not known for being learned in the Torah. According to a midrash, some of the people referred to Joshua as a foolish man because he was not well educated in the Torah.[6] How then did he merit to succeed Moses as Israel's rabbi? Rashi explains that Joshua was worthy because he never left the Tent of Meeting.[7] This portable tabernacle that accompanied the Jews on their desert wanderings is regarded in Jewish tradition as the prototypical school. There Torah was studied from morning until night, and Moses, the greatest of all teachers, was the lecturer. A midrash relates that Joshua was the first to arrive in the morning and the last to leave at night, arranging the mats and placing the benches for the scholars.[8] Although not himself a student or scholar but rather an attendant, one may infer from Joshua's continual presence in the Tent that he was able to absorb enough

Torah to qualify as Moses' successor, at least in comparison to Moses' sons, who learned nothing. In fact, the quantum of Torah that Joshua acquired simply by overhearing the lessons while he was arranging the benches, coupled with his unquestioned ability as a warrior, may have made him the ideal "rabbi" to lead Israel during its conquest of the Promised Land. If some of the people thought him a fool, then public opinion in this regard was misinformed.

Joshua's succession is the first case of rabbinic succession in Jewish history. For Rabbi Moses Sofer of Pressburg, the Hatam Sofer, it demonstrated persuasively that inheritance does not apply to rabbinic posts.[9] He regarded it as extremely unlikely that Moses would have asked for his sons to succeed him if he had believed that they were unqualified. That God denied the request and that Joshua succeeded were, for the Hatam Sofer, strong proofs that rabbinic posts do not pass from father to son by inheritance.[10] But others countered this argument by suggesting that Moses was unique in the annals of Jewish history, having himself served in three capacities as priest (during the consecration of the Tabernacle), king, and rabbi, so that no general rules could be derived from the circumstances surrounding the selection of his successor.[11]

It was clear from the Torah that monarchy is hereditary. The rabbis learned this from a biblical verse, "so he may prolong his days in his kingdom, he and his children, in the midst of Israel" (Deut. 17:20). The midrash *Sifre* drew an analogy from this verse in favor of inheritance for all leadership positions in Israel:

> *He and his children . . .*—if he dies, his son will reign in his place. This applies only to kings; whence do we learn that this applies also to all leaders of Israel . . . ? From the verse, . . . *in the midst of Israel*—anyone who is in the midst of Israel, his son will fill his place.[12]

It is important to note that the midrash does not expressly mention rabbis. Although the phrase it uses, "all leaders of Israel" (*kol parnesei yisra'el*), is a broad and inclusive one, all conceded that some positions, including the priest anointed for war and the office of Judge, were not inherited by sons.[13] Hence the phrase "all leaders of Israel" could not have been intended literally to cover every office in Israel.[14] The Hatam Sofer interpreted the midrash in light of its context, a discussion of monarchy. He confined the midrashic rule of inheritance to similar positions of leadership that exercise dominion over Israel.[15] These positions were quite distinct from sacred offices, like those of high priest and rabbi. For the Hatam Sofer, this explained why a second verse was needed to mandate inheritance for the high priest specifically (but not rabbis).[16] Without the second verse one could not derive inheritance of a sacred office from a verse that deals with royal succession.[17]

The rule of inheritance for leadership posts is missing from the Mishnah. The significance of the omission can be debated. On the one hand, the rule lacks the imprimatur of the Mishnah's editor, Rabbi Judah Hanasi, and inclusion in the most important compilation of the oral law. At the same time, many important legal rules of the period are absent from the Mishnah. Often the omitted rules appear in other sources, such as the Tosefta, a legal compendium compiled in the centuries after the Mishnah's completion whose provisions supplement that work. The Tosefta contains the following formulation: "Whoever takes precedence in inheritance takes precedence in positions of authority, so long as he follows the custom of his forefathers."[18] Whether rabbinic posts come within the Tosefta's rule may be questioned, following the Hatam Sofer's view that rabbinic posts are not deemed "positions of authority" but, rather, sacred positions, for purposes of inheritance.

The Talmud relates that Rabbi Judah Hanasi, at the time of his death (ca. 210 C.E.), summoned the scholars to his bedside to make arrangements for succession. Rabbi Judah, a descendant of Hillel and compiler of the Mishnah, was the *nasi*, president of the assembly of scholars in the Land of Israel during Roman times. Rabbi Judah instructed his colleagues that "Simeon my son is wise, [but] Gamaliel my son [shall be the] nasi."[19] The Talmud asks why Rabbi Judah needed to instruct his colleagues that Gamaliel shall succeed, since Gamaliel was his eldest son. It answers that although Simeon exceeded his brother in wisdom, Gamaliel excelled in fear of sin.[20] That one of Rabbi Judah's sons would succeed him was acknowledged by all. The departing leader was merely assessing the qualities by which the selection should be made.

The Hatam Sofer questioned whether this passage deals with rabbinic succession. The nasi's post became hereditary only upon the death of Hillel in 10 C.E. The Hatam Sofer argued that this was an innovation instituted by the sages to commemorate the Davidic monarchy during the periods of Hasmonean and Herodian rule,[21] for the nasi, whom the Roman emperors recognized as ethnarch or patriarch of the Jews, exercised political as well as spiritual authority and traced his lineage to the house of David.[22] Hence inheritance in the case of the nasi was an aspect of the royal crown (keter malkhut) rather than the Torah crown (keter Torah). The basic norm, that inheritance does not apply in the sphere of the Torah crown, was reflected in the practice prior to the death of Hillel when the post of nasi did not pass from father to son.[23]

In the Talmud, the scriptural words on which the midrash *Sifre* bases the rule of inheritance, "in the midst of Israel" (*bekerev yisra'el*),[24] are used as the source for a totally different halakhah, namely, that a king, although himself the son of a king, must be anointed with oil when a dispute arises over his accession to the throne.[25] Whether it is proper to derive two legal rules from the same words in a single biblical verse is open to question. The Sephardic authority Rabbi Joseph ben Hayyim Hazan, in his work *Hekrei Lev,* suggests that the editors of the Talmud may have omitted the midrash deliberately because they rejected its rule of inheritance for "all leaders of Israel," believing inheritance should be confined to the two positions, monarch and high priest, where the Torah expressly requires it.[26] Interestingly, this was the Karaite position, that, based on Scripture, lineage determined succession only for the monarchy and priesthood, not for rabbis.[27]

Hazan's observation leads quite naturally to the following question: If the Talmud rejects the midrash, then what is its approach regarding succession to positions of Torah leadership? One way to fashion an answer is to consider its attitude toward the "heirs apparent," that is, the sons of the sages. The Talmud does not express a high opinion of them. It asks, why is it not common for scholars to have sons who are scholars? There follow five answers: Rabbi Joseph said, "That it might not be maintained, the Torah is their legacy." Rabbi Shisha said, "That they should not be arrogant towards the community." Mar Zutra said, "Because they act high-handedly against the community." Rav Ashi said, "Because they call people asses." And Rabina said, "Because they do not first utter a blessing over the Torah."[28] Thus, the Talmud offers five answers but no dissent from the underlying proposition. It regards a family in which more than three generations are scholars as nothing less than miraculous.[29] This reinforces the importance of Rabbi Yossi's admonition in *Avot*, "Make yourself fit to study Torah, for it is not yours by inheritance."[30] In fact, the entire tractate *Avot* may be read as an argument against hereditary succession in matters of Torah leadership, for by depicting an intellectual genealogy of the sages, it demonstrates that Torah is transmitted from teacher to student, master to disciple, rather than from father to son.

Now it is true that when Moses blessed the Israelites prior to his death, he described the Torah as "an inheritance of the congregation of Jacob."[31] Rabbi Yossi does not dispute this but explains what Moses meant. Just like any legacy that one is fortunate enough to be bequeathed, one has to take possession of it. In the case of Torah knowledge, this requires making oneself fit and studying.

In the Talmudic era, some of the sages regarded being a scholar as a craft and believed their sons were entitled by birth to follow in their footsteps.[32] In practice, however, positions of Torah leadership were not inherited. Thus, according to Rashi, the order of succession to the post of principal (rosh yeshivah) at the academy in Pumbeditha was as follows: Rav Yehuda, followed by Rabbah, Rav Yosef, Abaye, and Rava.[33] These were among the outstanding scholars of their era (3rd–4th c. c.e.), whose merit, rather than lineage, must have been the determining factor in their appointments, for none of their fathers had served as rosh yeshivah before them. Nor did their sons succeed them in office, although some of them left learned sons.[34] The only son of a rosh yeshivah in Babylonia in the Talmudic era who succeeded to the post his father held was Mar, the son of Rav Ashi. There is no evidence of inheritance in a single instance of father-to-son transmission of an office, for it is just as likely in such cases that the son was selected on his own merit as the best candidate available at the time to replace his father. Further, Mar did not become rosh yeshivah at Sura immediately upon Rav Ashi's death (ca. 427 c.e.) but only decades later after two and perhaps three other scholars had occupied the chair.[35] It is questionable whether we should consider as a case of inheritance a son's eventual accession to an office his father once held that, however, is preceded by the service of a number of nonrelated individuals in the post.

The Talmud's approach to the question of succession to Torah leadership positions is better exemplified by its tradition of "the three crowns."[36] God granted the first, the royal crown, to David and his descendants forever. He granted the second, the priestly crown, to Aaron and his descendants forever. And what of the third, the Torah crown? It remains available to anyone who wishes to take it. In some formulations, the Torah crown is referred to as ownerless property (*hefker*),[37] which is not intended to suggest property having no value that is discarded or abandoned by its owner, but rather property that is freely available, in the public domain so to speak, for all who wish to take it.

This characterization of the Torah crown as available to all operates on two levels. On one level, it is simply an invitation to everyone to come and study.[38] In this vein, a midrash asks, "Why was the Torah given in the desert?" It answers, "To teach that just as the desert is ownerless [and available] to all, so the words of Torah are ownerless as to all who wish to learn."[39]

On a second level, however, the tradition of the three crowns has implications for succession to Torah leadership positions. This can be inferred from the context, for the tradition juxtaposes the royal and priestly crowns, on the one hand, with the Torah crown, on the other. While Scripture mandates that monarchy and high priesthood pass by inheritance to the descendants of David and Aaron, respectively, Torah leadership positions remain available to everyone. Rabbi Israel Isserlein stated it this way: "The Torah crown *and its authority* are left ownerless for anyone who wishes to acquire them."[40] Thus, each of the three crowns progressively encompasses a greater portion of the Jewish nation. Monarchy is limited to the descendants of a single family, David's. Priesthood and Levitical service in the Temple are restricted to members of a single tribe, the Levites. But the Torah crown envelops the whole nation—it is the inheritance of the entire congregation of Jacob. When the question is succession to a rabbinic post, let any member of the congregation who is learned in the Torah—whatever his lineage—come and apply.

Chapter 18

THE CASE AGAINST INHERITANCE
Part Two

The last nasi, Gamaliel VI, died without an heir in 425 C.E. Four years later, the Roman emperor Theodosius II abolished the office and appropriated its revenues.[1] Leadership of the Jewish community in Eretz Israel devolved upon the geonim, the principals of the rabbinical college, who considered themselves the nasi's successors, uniting the crowns of Torah and monarchy.[2] The geonim of Eretz Israel were drawn from two prominent academic families. The office passed from father to son for generations, but the father during his lifetime had to buttress the son's right to inherit. The sitting gaon would formally designate his heir as his successor, convene an assembly of scholars to confirm the choice, and seal the succession with curses and bans against anyone who might later contest it.[3]

What was the significance of this buttressing? Some argue it was merely symbolic.[4] In this view, the lifetime designation of sons as successors and the assemblies that ratified the succession were after-the-fact formalities and nothing more. But this is unlikely. In light of the Talmudic principle that "we do not appoint a leader over a community without first consulting it,"[5] the participants would have seen the ratifying assemblies as constitutive of the succession and not simply declaratory or symbolic. Further, the measures taken to buttress the gaon's heir were needed to ensure his succession, for the principle of inheritance in the realm of religious authority (keter Torah) was not established and required heavy-handed support like curses and bans. Sustained internal opposition to succession by the gaon's heir was possible due to continuing doubts as to whether positions of Torah leadership rightfully descend by inheritance. Quite possibly they do not, but since the gaon in Eretz Israel, in place of the deposed patriarch, wore the royal crown (keter malkhut) along with the Torah crown (keter Torah), an arguable case could be made for his son to inherit the post. Still, entrenched opposition had to be countered with assemblies, curses, and bans.

A different situation obtained in Babylonia, one that was even less hospitable to inheritance by the gaon's son. After the Arab conquest, as during the previous neo-Persian period, three officials divided temporal and spiritual leadership of the Jewish community. The "head of the Exile," or exilarch (the resh galuta), exercised temporal authority as an official of the caliph's court. He served as the Jewish community's representative vis-à-vis the government and collected its taxes. The two geonim, principals of the rabbinical colleges of Sura and Pumbeditha, were the joint spiritual heads of the Jewish Diaspora. These officials sometimes cooperated, but just as frequently they vied for jurisdiction, influence, honors, and revenue, involving wealthy partisans in their disputes and appealing to the government when the controversies proved intractable. At some point they reached an accommodation, dividing the Jewish communities of Babylonia (roughly present-day Iran and Iraq) into three "parishes" (*reshuyot*) in which either the exilarch or one of the geonim had the exclusive right to appoint local officials and farm for revenues.[6] When the exilarch Ukba (ca. 900–15) breached the agreement and sought to appropriate revenues coming from Khurasan that had been allocated to the gaon of Pumbeditha, the caliph removed him from office.[7]

The head of the Exile, who exercised temporal authority, wore in Jewish eyes the royal crown, keter malkhut. This had been acknowledged since Talmudic times, when the biblical verse "The scepter shall not depart from Judah" (Gen. 49:10) was understood to refer to "the Exilarchs of Babylon who rule over Israel with sceptres."[8] Accordingly, the post was hereditary, passing directly from father to son in most but not all cases.[9] Thus, after Ukba was removed from office, the post remained vacant for four years until his nephew, David ben Zakkai, was appointed. Court intrigues, the pleadings of special interests, and the preferences of the geonim would naturally be factors in the accession of a high official like the resh galuta.[10] His appointment required the caliph's confirmation. Yet for more than four centuries the office remained the exclusive possession of the members of a single extended family that traced its descent from the house of David on the male side.

By contrast, the Babylonian geonim exercised spiritual authority and wore the Torah crown, keter Torah. Some claimed descent from the royal house of David, and others intermarried with the exilarch's family, but the authority of their office was grounded in Torah learning, not lineage. The geonim and their institutions possessed authentic traditions regarding the interpretation of Torah and Talmud, traditions formulated and passed down to them by the generations of scholars who preceded them in the colleges they now headed. These ancient and revered traditions formed the basis of a corpus of jurisprudence that the geonim promulgated and applied to solve everyday legal problems. The geonim exercised a measure of temporal authority also, such as appointing local officials and collecting taxes. Financial necessity required them to cultivate a dedicated source of revenue to support the scholars in their schools, and they needed judges and local officials to execute their rulings and enforce discipline in the communities under their control. But this temporal authority was secondary to their main focus on Torah and Talmud, interpreting, teaching, and judging.[11]

In Babylonia, did the post of gaon pass from father to son by inheritance? Some have answered the question in the affirmative while, at the same time, qualifying their answers by terming the succession "quasi-hereditary"[12] or acknowledging a notable measure of flexibility in the order of inheritance.[13] As we shall show, the evidence supports an entirely different conclusion.

Ninety men served as gaon of Sura or Pumbeditha during a period lasting more than four centuries, beginning some time before the Arab conquest in the middle of the seventh century and ending in the middle of the eleventh century with the disintegration of the Baghdad caliphate.[14] All of the geonim were drawn from the same six or seven prominent families.[15] However, with one exception, son never followed father directly into office. Before the son became gaon, there was an interlude during which scholars from other families occupied the post. Sometimes the office would transfer from an incumbent to his brother.[16] On occasion a scholar trained in one academy was called to serve as gaon in the other. According to one reckoning, five scholars of Sura were appointed gaon of Pumbeditha, and two from the latter school received appointment to be gaon of Sura.[17]

The time between a father's death and his son's installation as gaon varied in duration. It could be as brief as four years or as long as seventy-one years.[18] The wide variations in waiting time can be seen in the experience of one family. Nahshon (d. 879) became gaon of Sura some fifty-five years after the death of his father, Zadok (d. 818); in the interim, seven individuals from other families served as gaon. By contrast, Nahshon's son, Hai, became gaon just six years after his father died. Interestingly, during this brief time span, two individuals from other families completed their terms as gaon.[19] Professor Grossman notes that brief tenures were characteristic of geonic succession; because of the long wait, the scholars were often elderly men when they took office.[20] Short tenures, elderly incumbents, and the occasional unqualified appointee were only some of the problems engendered by the pattern of succession that governed in the Babylonian schools. It also fostered an atmosphere of passive learning and lack of motivation among the majority of students who did not have the correct lineage to ascend to high office.[21]

How were the gaon's sons occupied during the interlude between their father's reign and their own accession? At the colleges, there was a hierarchy of academic and administrative posts.[22] Prior to being installed in the top position, that of gaon, the son had to serve an academic and administrative apprenticeship in a string of secondary posts.[23] The same prominent academic families whose sons became gaon staffed these lower positions as well.[24] Some of the scholars, having obtained appointment to their post upon the death of the prior incumbent, quite commonly their father, would then remain in their post for life and, perhaps, be succeeded in turn by their son. For others, the lower posts were stepping-stones to higher office. These upwardly mobile sons served in a variety of posts successively. In the course of their career they moved up the ladder of positions, advancing in rank each time. Advancement depended on a vacancy in a higher position, most often caused by the incumbent's death and sometimes by his resignation, at which point the next in line moved forward.

The prominent academic families comprised an academic oligarchy that possessed lineage, credentials, and influence. They would have been keenly interested in the staffing of the lower positions, involving, as it did, the sensitive issues of the nature and status of the academic careers their sons would be allowed to pursue. All of their sons—at least those with scholarly inclination and ability—would have to be placed. The families would want to be certain that the total number of posts would be allocated equitably among the total number of families. It would be unacceptable for a single family to be overrepresented in the academic ranks by a disproportionately large number of appointments for its sons. Also, since certain positions were stepping-stones to the gaonate—that of the vice principal, *av beth din* (lit. "father" or "head of the court") and also the scribe of the academy (*sofer ha-yeshivah*)[25]—who would be elevated to occupy these offices, and when they would ascend would have been subjects of very special concern. Adjusting all of the relevant factors to staff the lower posts could not have been an easy task, given the variations in age and ability among the sons who were vying for positions, the need to satisfy the aspirations of families who produced many sons alongside other families with just one or a few sons, and the obvious inability to control or predict when deaths or resignations would occur to create openings.

It is unlikely that the families would have delegated these sensitive, complex matters solely to the discretion of one of their number, the sitting gaon.[26] Rather, the staffing of the lower positions would have been subject to consultation, bargaining, and negotiation among the families and the gaon, having due regard to the families' valid expectations, assessments of the available candidates' academic potential, the overall needs of the institution, and principles of fairness governing the allocation of posts. In general, the yeshivahs operated on the basis of consultation and consensus and not by the gaon's fiat.[27] There is no reason to believe that they operated differently when the question was that of filling the lower positions. Since there were many posts to allocate and none carried the prestige, prerogatives, and income of the top position, most appointments were not controversial and proceeded without much debate. The settled expectation that a qualified son would follow in his father's footsteps could be honored most of the time. No doubt the appointment itself would be issued in the gaon's name, for the appointees would serve as his subordinates in an academic hierarchy that he headed. In that limited sense, he "appointed" them. But the gaon's final official act, sealing the appointment, must have been preceded by a consensus-building process of consultation in cases where there was any disagreement over who should receive the post.

What determined which candidate was next in line to succeed the gaon and when he was ready and suitable to be elevated to the post? Before addressing the question, we must acknowledge the possibility that it may be the wrong question to ask. Since it was normally the vice principal, the av beth din, who was elevated to the gaon's chair, it could be the case that the actual succession debate for the position of gaon took place when the academy needed to select a new *av beth din*.[28] In choosing the new second-in-command, everyone understood they were in all likelihood selecting a future gaon as well. Having the succession debate take place at this time would make enormous sense from an institutional point of view. It would give the sitting gaon a voice in the selection of his probable successor. It would assist in making transitions between geonim relatively smooth, for the new av, once appointed, could concentrate during the gaon's declining years on preparing to assume his office. It would reduce the gap in time between a gaon's death and his successor's installation, since the successor was already designated. For the same reason, it would permit the gaon's death to be an occasion for mourning rather than politicking, an important consideration in a community of religious scholars.[29]

To determine whose turn it was to serve in the top positions, av beth din and gaon, the prominent academic families kept track of each family's entitlements by some complex or shifting formula that has not been ascertained. The order of succession, based on factors that were likely to vary over time, was subject to external pressures, bargaining, and negotiation. In Goitein's view, the geonim were not elected but followed each other according to a complicated system of precedence.[30] In Brody's formulation, the scholars made the choice of gaon by consensus, based in principle on intellect and leadership qualities, with seniority and family alliances playing a role.[31] We may accept this list of factors with a caveat and an addition, for the crucial question concerns the basis for the consensus. The two factors Brody mentions last—seniority and family alliances—may have been more important than the two factors he mentions first—intellect and leadership qualities. At any point in time there were likely to be many learned individuals at the academy who were qualified to become gaon. At the same time, individuals were elevated to the post who did not possess the necessary qualifications. Thus it appears the essential consensus the scholars needed to achieve to select the next gaon concerned *which family* was entitled to occupy the office again. Which family's wait in the wings had lasted long enough; which family was now entitled to enjoy again the prestige, benefits, and patronage of the office? Once consensus was achieved on these questions, someone from the family—hopefully not lacking in qualifications or too elderly, but if not, no matter—could be found to receive the appointment.

Thus what governed the selection of gaon was not the Torah-mandated order of inheritance but an extralegal arrangement created and implemented by the families to serve their own purposes, the most important of which was power sharing. By rotating the post among the families, they spread the authority, prestige, and benefits of office to a small group of families rather than allowing the power and perquisites of office to become concentrated in a single family, as happened in the case of the exilarch. Incumbency as gaon shifted from one family to another in turn, so that no single family monopolized the post and enjoyed its rewards to the exclusion of the others. For the same reason, son did not follow father directly into office but had to wait his—or perhaps more accurately, his family's—turn.

The system was political and hardly ironclad. A variety of circumstances—an unusual order of deaths, atypical longevity on a gaon's part, an upheaval in family alliances, a temporary closure of one of the schools, or a breakdown of consensus over the formula—might prevent the right candidate, the consensus choice, from being in place as av beth din when the gaon died. A dispute over the succession would result. Factions formed inside and outside the schools, jockeying to advance or retard candidacies.[32] The scholars at both academies, the resh galuta, community leaders, and wealthy Jewish merchants and bankers, as well as the caliph and members of his court, all had an interest in who would become the next gaon and wanted to participate in the decision. Occasionally, when the factions disputing succession were evenly balanced, the succession could not be agreed upon. Two individuals, a gaon and a countergaon, might be installed and officiate simultaneously until one of them died or resigned.[33]

Two notable deviations from the usual pattern illuminate the nature of geonic succession. When the next-to-last gaon of Pumbeditha, Sherira, retired in 998, he was succeeded immediately by his son, Hai. The colleges at this time were in a period of decline that would soon lead to their closing. Their demise paralleled the disintegration of the Baghdad caliphate occurring at the same time. Sherira had taken pains to carefully groom Hai as his successor, allowing him to cosign his correspondence and making him known to everyone who counted.[34] It is possible that when Sherira retired, the pool of suitable candidates to be gaon had run dry and the only qualified candidate was Hai. At Hai's death in 1038, there was no scholar fit to succeed him, and no gaon was appointed. The exilarch, Hezekiah ben David, assumed the post and served for two years until he was deposed in 1040. Hai's accession to be gaon immediately after his father Sherira left office is the single instance of direct father-to-son succession among the Babylonian geonim. If inheritance governed the order of succession, then we would expect cases of direct father-to-son transmission of the office to be common. They were not. Further, it is questionable whether the Sherira-Hai succession represents a case of inheritance since it occurred while Sherira was still living.

A second notable deviation from the pattern of succession occurred when Saadiah ben Joseph became Sura's gaon in 928. Saadiah, born in Egypt, was an outsider who did not belong to one of the prominent academic families of Babylonia.[35] Of course, Saadiah's father was never gaon; it seems his father was a simple laborer. Much concerning Saadiah's early life is unknown, including the identity of his teachers and the reason he left Egypt.[36] His travels took him first to the Land of Israel, then to Aleppo, and finally to Baghdad, arriving in 921. Just seven years after his arrival he was installed as gaon of Sura. How did this come about?

In 922, the principal of the Jerusalem academy, Aaron ben Meir, announced that the upcoming Passover holiday would begin on a Sunday that year. The Babylonian sages, however, setting the Jewish calendar according to their traditions, determined that Passover would commence on the following Tuesday. For centuries world Jewry had observed the annual cycle of holidays according to calculations embedded in the calendar. The ancient and exclusive prerogative of the Jerusalem sages to fix the dates by astronomical observation had long before fallen into disuse. Ben Meir's stunning announcement, suddenly reasserting the standing of the Jerusalem sages to resolve a case of dispute over the calendar, challenged the primacy of the Babylonian scholars in a crucial sphere of Jewish life.[37] It threatened to split the Jewish world on this single but extremely important point of observance.

Letters seeking reconciliation went back and forth but were unsuccessful. The threat of a schism between the branches of world Jewry was real. Jewish communities in Babylonia and the Land of Israel celebrated Passover and the Jewish New Year on different days in 922. Since each of the academies had adherents spread around the world, it seems that Jewish neighbors living in a single city or town observed the festivals, with their various prohibitions on work and food, on different dates, a situation unprecedented in Jewish history and untenable as a matter of Jewish solidarity.[38] All acknowledged that uniformity had to be restored, but neither side would concede.

Just as the calendar controversy was unfolding, Saadiah arrived in Baghdad. Upon investigating the matter he concluded that the Babylonian sages were right and wrote a tract supporting their position. The quality of his arguments impressed the Babylonian authorities, who decreed that the tract be read publicly on the Sabbath in all synagogues under their jurisdiction. The reading marked a turning point in the dispute. Aaron ben Meir and the Jerusalem scholars lost ground, and the controversy receded. Thanks largely to Saadiah, public opinion shifted in the direction of the Babylonian sages. The calendar they supported resumed its status as authoritative for world Jewry.

The same year Saadiah wrote his tract, the authorities granted him an appointment as instructor (*resh kallah* or *aluf*) at Sura. In effect, they invited him to join the academic hierarchy although he was an outsider lacking proper family connections. Was Saadiah's appointment a recognition of his outstanding intellectual abilities—or a reward for his decisive support in the calendar controversy? No doubt it was both. Six years later, when the presidency of the college at Sura became vacant, the exilarch, David ben Zakkai, proposed Saadiah for the post. Naturally there was opposition from supporters of the candidate with proper lineage, Zemah ben Shahin, who came from a "good" family.[39] In the end, Saadiah's supporters prevailed and he was installed as gaon of Sura in 928. It is hardly conceivable that Saadiah would have deprived Ben Shahin of his due if the latter had been entitled to the post by Torah-mandated right of inheritance. Although Saadiah's treatise on the laws of inheritance, *Sefer Hayerushot,* devotes chapters to the inheritance of types of property that are difficult or impossible to divide, such as fields, vineyards, houses, and sacred books, it contains no mention of inheritance of office.[40]

The pattern of geonic succession in Babylonia was fundamentally different from inheritance.[41] Geonic succession was characterized by (1) the need to serve a lengthy apprenticeship in secondary positions before being installed as gaon; (2) the fact that some of the men elevated to be gaon were unfit to serve; (3) the rotation of the post among several families; (4) instances in which a gaon was chosen from the pool of scholars at the sister school; (5) instances in which two incumbents served for a period simultaneously; (6) the gap in time between a father's death and his son's accession;[42] (7) the fact that sons from other families occupied the office during the interlude; and (8) the possibility of admitting a new family to the inner circle whose sons would thereafter be in line to succeed. None of these factors are present in cases of inheritance of office under Jewish law. If this be "inheritance," then Jewish law recognizes two orders of inheritance—one that applies exclusively to the geonim of Babylonia, in which sons never follow their fathers immediately into office, and one that applies in all other cases, in which—except in the case of minors—sons succeed immediately upon their father's death. But the Torah mandates a single order of inheritance, not two, and it applies to both property and offices that pass by inheritance: "Whoever takes precedence in inheritance [of property] takes precedence in positions of authority."[43] Further, according to the midrash *Sifre,* when a high official dies and his post descends by inheritance, "his son will fill his place"[44]—not someone else's son, as was the case with the Babylonian geonim.

It was precisely because hereditary succession was *not* the rule in the realm of keter Torah (the Torah crown) that these arrangements were possible in the Babylonian schools. If the lower posts passed normally from father to son, it was not because Jewish law required it but because this pattern of succession was agreeable to the prominent families. It suited their needs because it satisfied their aspirations for their sons. By the same token, lineage played a role in geonic succession, of course, but it was only one factor in the oligarchical equation. Lineage made one a member of an eligible family, and first-born status made one the scion of the family and heir apparent; but when a candidate would ascend to the top was determined not by his father's death but by the accepted understanding that fixed the duration of an apprenticeship and when it was each family's turn to occupy the highest office again. Into this arrangement an outsider could be admitted when the new family strengthened the group and furthered its collective interests, as in the case of Saadiah who proved his usefulness to the oligarchy during the calendar controversy.

Inheritance of office is not a power-sharing arrangement but the opposite. Inheritance makes an office the exclusive preserve of a single family in perpetuity. Monarchy and priesthood are the paradigms. They belong exclusively and forever to the families of David and Aaron, respectively. Even the offspring of Moses cannot be admitted.[45] The Torah's order of inheritance cannot be altered at will to benefit outsiders and admit a new family to the order of succession. Kings of Israel not from the house of David rule as a temporary expedient. Their dynasties will not endure. In time dominion will be wrested from them and the monarchy restored to David's heirs.[46] Single-family exclusivity was the rule for the patriarch in the Land of Israel after Hillel and the exilarch in Babylonia, both of whom wore the crown of monarchy (keter malkhut). Their positions never passed back and forth among the descendants of half a dozen families but remained always the entitlement of a single family. Even when the office passed to a brother or nephew, it remained within the family, for collateral relatives share with the deceased officeholder descent from a common ancestor. By contrast, the hallmark of geonic succession was an interlude between father and son when individuals drawn from other families occupied the post. Thus it is clear that inheritance did not govern geonic succession in Babylonia. Rather, the prominent academic families that controlled the colleges allocated positions, including the top one, according to a power-sharing formula they devised, one that was acceptable to them and served their needs.

Chapter 19

FORGING A NEW CONSENSUS FOR INHERITANCE

As the center in the East declined, new centers of Jewish population and culture developed in the West. The earliest Jewish communities in pre-Crusade Europe were small. Many began their existence as large extended families, formed when a local ruler granted residence rights to a Jewish trader or banker and allowed him to settle in the ruler's domain with family members and retainers. A small community might consist of one hundred persons; a medium-sized community held several hundred. The French town of Troyes had some one hundred Jewish families in 1040 at the time of Rashi's birth.[1] Few Jewish communities outside of Spain exceeded one thousand in number.[2]

Demographic and social factors naturally affected issues of communal leadership and patterns of succession. Temporal leadership gravitated to the patriarch of the leading family and his sons. If they were learned, they might possess religious authority as well. If the town had a rabbi, the rabbi's sons would be reared in a home suffused with the spirit of learning and possessing scarce manuscripts for study. The rabbi would strive to produce learned sons, just as any father would wish to pass down his trade or craft to his offspring. This made the rabbi's son a natural candidate to succeed him. In a small community he might be the only candidate to succeed his father. In such cases the son inherited by default since there was no other suitable candidate to replace the departed scholar.

In a responsum by the thirteenth-century Ashkenazic authority Rabbi Moses ben Hasdai Taku, we observe social and demographic factors operating in favor of a son's succession:

> Our Masters, our brethren in Magdeburg, request that we settle a dispute that has arisen among them. While I am unworthy to instruct them, it is warranted to lament the passing of the righteous Rabbi Jacob.... Leaving good behind him in life and in death, he left offspring learned in Torah. Although the son has not attained the level of his departed father's wisdom, he too is worthy to intercede between Israel and their Heavenly Father. Those who fought the Lord's fight, to do right by the son as they did by his father, performed a good deed, since there is no one else with sufficient wisdom available and fit to assume the father's post. But just as he [the son] is ready to intercede

between Israel and their Heavenly Father, so it is lawful and correct [*shurat hadin vemishpat*] that he appease the community members. The young man, the son of the [former] rabbi, must knock on every door, to mollify and to appease, to make himself beloved and pleasant in his acts whether to great or small, distant or close.³

Here the son acquires the office by dint of his own merit and availability as the sole qualified replacement, provided he can obtain the community's consent. Significantly absent from the responsum is any reference to a Torah-mandated *right* of the son to inherit his father's post or to any corresponding legal duty on the community's part to appoint him.

Surveying succession of spiritual leaders in the early Jewish communities of Europe and North Africa, Professor Abraham Grossman notes the social and demographic factors as well as the fact that information is sparse. Still he is able to distinguish between patterns of succession in different locations.⁴ In Spain and North Africa, positions of religious authority did not descend from father to son by inheritance. If there were instances of father-to-son transmission of office, as when early in the eleventh century leadership of the Kairawan schools passed upon death from Hushiel to his son Hananel and from Jacob to his son Nissim, they were sporadic episodes, for here father-to-son transmission did not continue in the following generations. More typical was the case of the renowned Rabbi Isaac Alfasi (1013–1103), who nominated his student, Rabbi Joseph ibn Migas (1077–1141), to succeed him as rabbi of Lucena, Spain, although Alfasi left a learned son. By contrast, in Italy, there were dynasties of scholars and "hints" of inheritance in the spiritual realm. In the important German communities of Worms and Mainz, seven families (two in Worms and five in Mainz) provided spiritual leadership on a rotating basis for five generations. In northern France, spiritual leaders came from three families, although Rashi, who founded a yeshivah in Troyes, did not belong to one of them. In Narbonne, where the rosh yeshivah was styled "gaon," the post appears to have passed to sons by inheritance. Grossman acknowledges the impact of social and demographic factors on succession, and he accords due weight to the small size of the early communities. At the same time he surmises that in those localities where family lineage played the greatest role in succession of spiritual leaders (Italy, Germany, and southern France), one can discern the impact of traditions of inheritance that originated under the geonim in the Land of Israel and Babylonia.⁵

The surmise extends the available evidence in an unwarranted way. Social and demographic factors are sufficient to explain the natural occurrence in this period of lineaged families, scholarly dynasties, their near dominance of religious authority in small communities, and instances of father-to-son transmission of rabbinic posts. Thus, in a study of religious succession in North Africa during the ninth through eleventh centuries, Menahem Ben-Sasson found different patterns, depending on whether the Jewish community was large or small.⁶ In a small town like Kabis (Gabès), one family supplied the yeshivah leadership. But in a large community like Kairawan, the heir did not automatically succeed his father in office. Since many scholars resided there, choice was possible. In these communities, the pattern of succession to religious leadership was a function of population size and the presence or absence of a pool of candidates from which a real choice could be made.

Further, since it is doubtful that the geonim recognized a principle of inheritance in the realm of spiritual leadership (keter Torah),[7] it is equally doubtful that such a tradition stemming from them would be reflected in Europe and North Africa. Sons did not inherit their father's post as gaon in Babylonia where geonim wore the Torah crown only. In the Land of Israel, where sons did inherit, the geonim exercised both temporal and spiritual authority. There inheritance of office found its source in the gaon's custody of the royal crown (keter malkhut), not the Torah crown (keter Torah).

A strikingly similar pattern can be discerned in the communities Grossman surveyed. In Mainz, Worms, and Narbonne, where sons inherited their father's positions of spiritual leadership, rabbis united religious and temporal authority in their communities.[8] By contrast, in Spain, where generally sons did not inherit positions of spiritual leadership, court Jews, not rabbis, exercised temporal power.[9] Thus, religious authority and temporal authority were divided. Grossman is correct to highlight this factor among his conclusions.[10] The result, however, is to eliminate the evidence of inheritance in the realm of spiritual leadership per se during this period. We may regard the practice of father-to-son succession in early Germany and France, even cases lasting for generations, as inheritance in the realm of temporal authority (keter malkhut) rather than spiritual leadership (keter Torah), just as the Hatam Sofer regarded father-to-son transmission of the nasi's office in the four centuries following Hillel.[11]

This interpretation of the evidence affords an answer to a question left unanswered in Grossman's study. He asks why inheritance in the realm of spiritual leadership, as an innovation in early Ashkenaz, did not elicit express opposition from those excluded from high posts because they did not descend from lineaged families.[12] He doubts that criticism expressed later, in the fourteenth and fifteenth centuries, is a delayed reaction to conditions three or four centuries earlier. In our view, the criticism of the practice arises later because the phenomenon being criticized appeared later than Grossman posits. What existed in early Ashkenaz was not inheritance in the realm of spiritual leadership (keter Torah)—an innovation to which some would surely have objected both orally and in their writings—but inheritance in the realm of temporal authority (keter malkhut). This was a practice analogous to one the sages instituted in ancient times when the nasi united temporal and spiritual authority in a single office. This practice, dating from the time of Hillel, was hoary and unobjectionable.[13] Further, it was well suited to the conditions that existed in the early Ashkenazic communities.

Was a right to inherit a religious post recognized by the halakhic authorities of the period, the *Rishonim*? Rabbi Joseph ben Hayyim Hazan, in his work *Hekrei Lev*, surveyed the sources and found a mixed picture.[14] The rule regarding inheritance of rabbinic posts is absent from the works of many early authorities—he mentions Rabbi Isaac Alfasi (*Rif*), Rabbenu Asher ben Yehiel (*Rosh*), his son, Rabbi Jacob ben Asher (*Tur*), and Rabbi Joseph Karo (*Beit Yosef*). By contrast, the rule appears in the works of Maimonides[15] and Rabbi Solomon ibn Adret of Barcelona (*Rashba*),[16] and in *Sefer Hahinukh*.[17] We shall look at each of them in turn.

Maimonides cites the rule of inheritance twice in *Mishneh Torah*. In "The Laws of Kings" he writes:

> When a king is installed, he is anointed with anointing oil. . . . As soon as he is anointed, he acquires the office for himself and his children forever. The right thereto is transmitted as a legacy. . . . But not only the office of king but every position or appointive office held by the father descends to his son and son's son in perpetuity, provided that the son is entitled to fill the vacancy by reason of wisdom and piety.[18]

In "The Laws of Temple Vessels" Maimonides states the rule as follows:

> When a king or a High Priest or one of the other appointees died, his son or his proper heir was appointed in his stead. The one who preceded in inheriting the property of the deceased also preceded in inheriting his office, provided he could replace him in wisdom, or in piety if not also in wisdom. For it is said concerning the king: *he and his children, in the midst of Israel* (Deut. 17:20); teaching us that the kingdom is inherited. And the same law applied to every office in the midst of Israel: namely, that he who attained office did so for himself and for his children.[19]

Neither ruling mentions rabbis.

The question arises why Maimonides stated the rule twice since each time he states it broadly enough to cover all offices in Israel. Further, the rule does not appear a third time in the treatise dealing with Torah sages, *Hilkhot Talmud Torah*. From this pattern one may argue that Maimonides accepts the rule of inheritance only for "the royal crown" (keter malkhut) and "the priestly crown" (keter kahuna), hence its inclusion in his treatises dealing with kings and priests, but he rejects the rule for "the Torah crown" (keter Torah), thus explaining its absence from his treatise on Torah sages. The broad language he used in the cited passages ("every position or appointive office," "every office in the midst of Israel") may be attributed to Maimonides' merely having adopted the wording of the midrash *Sifre*, on which the rulings are based, without intending by such language to include rabbinic posts, just as the post of priest anointed for war is excluded.[20] It is possible that Maimonides did not consider rabbinic posts an "office," "position," or "appointment" as those terms are used in his code.[21] However, based on the two passages in *Mishneh Torah*, halakhic authorities generally cite Maimonides as one of the early authorities who apply the rule of inheritance to rabbinic positions, as the *Hekrei Lev* cites him here.[22]

The rules in *Mishneh Torah* provided a legal basis in Morocco for *serarah*—the principle that religious posts and their corresponding remuneration are the hereditary right of a small number of families in each town.[23] The families were prominent families of Spanish origin whose ancestors arrived in Morocco as émigrés after the Jews' expulsion from Spain in 1492. The newcomers brought to Morocco their leadership credentials and a tradition of scholarship that they nurtured and passed to their offspring. They acquired religious leadership in town after town.[24] In their responsa, Moroccan halakhic authorities implemented the rule of hereditary succession with respect to a broad array of religious personnel, including rabbis, judges, scribes, cantors, *mohelim* (ritual circumcisers), and *shohetim* (ritual slaughterers).[25] Scholars have cited various factors to explain the dominant role inheritance played in religious appointments in Morocco. These include the community's gratitude to the Spanish émigrés who reestablished Jewish scholarship in Morocco;[26] the value that Moroccan Jews—who venerated ancestors as saints and prayed at their graves —ascribed to *zekhut avot,* the "merit" or "privilege" of ancestors;[27] and the influence of the surrounding Muslim culture.[28] Approaching serarah from the perspective of a social anthropologist, Shlomo Deshen notes that the legal sources on which serarah was based, such as *Mishneh Torah,* were available to halakhic scholars in all localities, "but the sages of Morocco in particular placed unique emphasis on them, considering them relevant to the problems of their society and extended their application creatively."[29] Whatever the underlying causes, Morocco remained until the middle of the twentieth century, when its Jewish community departed for Israel, a unique and isolated island of certainty in a sea of uncertainty regarding the question whether rabbinic posts descend by inheritance to heirs.

Sefer Hahinukh's discussion comes under the heading of Commandment 497, "To Appoint a King of Israel." In summarizing aspects of the commandment, the author states the king's son (but not daughter) is entitled to inherit provided he fills his father's place in fear of Heaven. An elder son takes precedence over a younger son, and so on through the order of inheritance of property. If the son is a minor at his father's death, the monarchy is held for him until he attains majority. These rules of inheritance apply not just to monarchy but also to all offices and appointments in Israel that confer honor upon the incumbent. There is no sentence in the discussion that either includes or excludes religious posts (keter Torah) from the stated rules, although surely a rabbinic post is one that confers honor on the officeholder.

The Rashba's Responsum no. 300 involved an elderly cantor who wished to appoint his son as his assistant. Some in the community opposed the son's appointment, claiming his voice was not suitable. The Rashba held that the cantor's right to name whomever he wished as his assistant was expressly granted to him in his contract of appointment and it was fitting for a father to turn to a son for assistance. Further, every lifetime appointee has the implied right to name an assistant, even when his contract is silent, for surely he will on occasion become ill or need to travel and hence require a temporary substitute. Now there may come a time when because of the father's age or infirmity, he will never be able to resume his duties and his replacement will be permanent rather than temporary. In such a case, the Rashba writes, the correct rule (*shurat ha-din*) gives the son priority, and this is the custom (*minhag*) in many communities respecting cantors—sons follow their fathers in office. This practice is consistent with an important principle (*kelal gadol*) of the sages—that in all matters of appointment, if the son is qualified, he has priority over all others, including those who are equal to him in ability and even those who are greater.

In this responsum, the Rashba treats three separate issues: first, appointing a temporary replacement and second, appointing a permanent replacement—both while the father is still alive; and third, succession to the post upon the father's death. Only the first issue was involved in the situation presented to the Rashba. His views on the second were offered gratuitously, and his brief comment on the third provided support for his position on the second, namely, that it is proper to appoint a son when a father needs a permanent replacement. Thus, although the Rashba acknowledges the principle that sons have priority in matters of appointment if qualified, the responsum does not specify how he might weigh all the various factors involved in applying the principle in a given situation. The "important principle" (*kelal gadol*) is a *general* principle. Whether the Rashba would include rabbinic appointments within the general rule or exclude them as exceptions cannot be learned from his tract dealing with an elderly cantor.

There is another difficulty in ascertaining the Rashba's view, arising from the references in his responsum to both law (*din*) and custom (*minhag*). Later authorities were at a loss to explain why he mentioned both and offered a variety of possible explanations. According to the Maharsham, R. Shalom Schwadron, by law inheritance applies to positions of authority only, like that of the king; by custom it applies to positions that lack communal authority, such as cantor or slaughterer.[30] In the *Hekrei Lev*'s reading, it is custom to permit a son to replace his father while the father is alive, but it is law for a son to succeed his father at his death.[31] The Hatam Sofer explained that by law, inheritance applies to the offices of king and high priest; by custom it applies also to the posts of rabbis and cantors.[32]

To the Hekrei Lev's enumeration of authorities who cite the rule of inheritance for rabbinic posts we must add Rabbi Isaac ben Sheshet Perfet (Rivash). When Rabbi Meir Halevi of Vienna sought to unseat the chief rabbi of France and replace him with one of his students, the Rivash ruled in favor of the incumbent who was the son of the prior chief rabbi.[33] The son was entitled to the post, the Rivash wrote, because he had inherited it from his father, he had received the assent of both the French monarchy and the Jewish community, and he was qualified to serve.[34] In his response, the Rivash treats inheritance of rabbinic posts in a straightforward way as settled law based on midrashic sources.

The rule of inheritance for rabbinic posts is absent from *Arba'ah Turim,* the fourteenth-century legal code of Rabbi Jacob ben Asher of Toledo, Spain, and from *Beit Yosef,* the halakhic compendium written in the first half of the next century by Rabbi

Joseph Karo of Safed. Likewise, the rule is missing from the text of Karo's code, the *Shulhan Arukh*. By contrast, Rabbi Moses Isserles (Rema), in his glosses appended to Karo's text, states a rule that favors the inheritance of rabbinic posts by qualified heirs while acknowledging the continuing validity of alternative customs. In this manner the *Shulhan Arukh* mirrors the differing practices that existed in early Sephardic and Ashkenazic communities, mentioned previously.

The Rema's ruling concerns a rabbi who is established in a town:

> Even his son and his son's son forever have priority over others as long as they fill their fathers' place in fear of Heaven and are somewhat learned. But in a place where it is the custom to appoint a rabbi for a fixed term or where it is the custom to appoint whomever they wish, they have the right to do so.[35]

The Vilna Gaon cites three sources for the Rema's ruling—the midrash in *Sifre*, the Tosefta, and the Talmud's discussion of succession at the death of Rabbi Judah Hanasi.[36] As noted previously, the Hatam Sofer, who held that inheritance by the nasi's heir was an aspect of the royal crown, not the Torah crown, doubted whether any of these passages deal with the question of *rabbinic* succession.

Two requirements qualify the right to inherit a rabbinic post under the Rema's rule. First, the community's consent to the appointment is required.[37] No compulsion is applied to force them to consent, but they remain under a legal obligation to appoint the heir.[38] Second, the heir must possess certain minimum qualifications— fear of Heaven and a little learning.[39] If he possesses those qualifications, he is entitled to the post even if there is a better qualified candidate.[40] Some authorities carve out an exception to this rule where the differences in scholarship between an heir and a rival candidate are so vast that the heir is not even in the same league as the other candidate. They hold that in such cases the community is free to reject the heir and to appoint the greater scholar.[41] All agree that where the heir is unfit to serve because he lacks learning or fear of Heaven, his right to inherit lapses as a matter of law.[42]

Given the need to establish his qualifications and to obtain the community's consent, some construe the heir's right to be a preference (*zekhut kedimah*) rather than an inheritance (*yerushah*).[43] The Rema formulates the rule in terms of a priority rather than outright inheritance: "Even his son and his son's son forever have priority over others."[44] The heir is preferred over other candidates and has a right to be considered ahead of them but not necessarily to obtain his father's post in all events.

While the early authorities (the *Rishonim*) presented a mixed picture in the debate over inheritance, after the Rema's ruling there was a notable shift in sentiment. The later authorities (the *Aharonim*) achieved a consensus in favor of the rule that regards religious posts as the inheritance of qualified heirs. They continued to debate the precise source of the halakhah, whether the rule was from the Torah (*mi-d'oraita*) or a rabbinic enactment (*mi-derabbanan*) based on custom originating with Hillel.[45] But the upshot of even this dispute was a practice that, in case of doubt, favored the heir's inheritance over another candidate on the following logic: Jewish law requires stringency in applying a law that is possibly from the Torah (*safek d'oraita le-humra*). Under this principle, if there is genuine doubt concerning who is entitled to succeed to a post—the heir or someone else—the heir should be appointed, for if he is denied the appointment when he is in fact entitled to it, a possible Torah norm will have been violated.[46]

In a celebrated case of disputed succession in the sixteenth century, the rule of inheritance was applied in the following manner. A community's rabbi died and left a son who was a minor. The townsfolk settled on a prominent scholar, Rabbi Moses Alsheikh (ca. 1505–1584), as their new rabbi. However, another scholar, Rabbi Solomon Alkabetz (d. ca. 1593), argued that they should wait until the prior rabbi's son came of age and then appoint him. In support of his view he cited a ruling by Maimonides that when a king dies leaving a minor heir, we hold the kingdom for him until he comes of age.[47] By analogy, he reasoned, the same procedure should apply to rabbinic appointments. His argument carried the day and the decision to appoint Rabbi Alsheikh was rescinded.[48]

Later authorities interpreted the outcome of the controversy in different ways. Some cited it with approval to support the notion that an heir is preferred even when a greater scholar is available, for surely Moses Alsheikh was more learned than the young child who displaced him.[49] In another view of the matter, the community's conduct went beyond the letter of the law (*lifnim meshurat ha-din*). Although it was under no legal obligation to hold the post for the heir until he came of age, it quite properly of its own accord wished to do so.[50] Still others denied that a community may choose to wait for a minor to come of age. In this view, we hold the throne for a minor only because the Torah specifically requires it in the case of kings. In the case of rabbis, the community should appoint someone else immediately, for there is no assurance that the minor will grow up to be a qualified scholar.[51] Nor may the community leave the father's post vacant in the interim. If this community could do so, it was only because the town was an extraordinary place where many qualified scholars resided. They could handle halakhic matters while waiting for the heir to mature.[52] Rabbi Yom Tov Algazi recommended that a community appoint a temporary rabbi while the heir is a minor and then, when he comes of age, install the heir if, but only if, he has become a qualified sage.[53] What united all the disparate views of the incident was the consensus that a qualified heir is entitled to inherit his father's rabbinic post. The disagreements concerned only whether and how to apply the rule when the heir is a minor at the time of his father's death.

The strength and breadth of the consensus can be seen in the work of a single latter-day authority, the Hatam Sofer. In an early legal opinion, *Orah Hayyim* no. 12, he argued from biblical and midrashic sources that rabbinic positions do not pass to heirs by inheritance.[54] In a second legal opinion penned some ten years later, *Orah Hayyim* no. 13, he reversed his position.[55] He said he was doing so in deference to the Rema's ruling that supported priority for the rabbi's heir. Sofer's stated rationale for reversing course was a belated acknowledgement of changes in the function and status of rabbinic office. If in days of yore occupying a rabbinic chair was a purely sacred calling, in the modern era rabbis serve communal needs and receive salaries. The rabbinate has lost some part of its sacred trappings and become a form of public service. Like the king, the rabbi is subordinated to the needs of his community. Hence the analogy drawn from royal succession has been rendered apt by the times, for the modern rabbinate serves the nation's needs just as the ancient monarchy once did. By the same token rabbinic posts in the modern era, like monarchy in former times, should pass to heirs by inheritance.[56]

Of course both the Rema's ruling and the functions performed by contemporary rabbis were known to the Hatam Sofer at the time he wrote the first responsum, no. 12. One wonders if, after it appeared, he felt any pressure from his rabbinic colleagues to conform to the consensus permitting their sons to inherit. As the Maharam Shik commented after Sofer's change of position became known, "It is hard to deflect a widespread ruling."[57]

Sofer never conceded to the consensus view when the question was succession to the post of chief rabbi of a country. There he continued to maintain that lineage does *not* determine succession.[58] At first blush this is perplexing. One might think that the analogy to monarchy was most applicable in such cases, for surely the chief rabbi ruled his colleagues like a king. But Sofer refused to apply the analogy here, for he rated other factors higher when the post of chief rabbi is involved. A chief rabbi must be a greater scholar than the country's other rabbis, who look to him for guidance. Lineage cannot serve as a substitute for Torah learning nor can it guarantee wisdom. Where *superior* Torah scholarship is an essential requirement of a rabbinic post, succession must be governed by an assessment of the candidates' merits, not their lineage.[59] This was always true in the case of the *gadol hador,* the recognized greatest halakhic authority of his generation to whom other rabbis turned to answer their most intractable legal questions. This position, although an informal one, possessed a high degree of authority in the Jewish legal system, but no one argued that it could or should pass by inheritance.

According to his son, Rabbi Shimon Sofer, once the Hatam Sofer accepted the consensus, he steadfastly applied it. When Rabbi Shimon Sofer learned that elders of Cracow's Jewish community were relying on his father's first legal opinion to challenge an heir's right to inherit a rabbinic post, he wrote to ask them why they did not consult his father's second opinion. Like his father, they should follow the Rema's ruling "as my father did in all of Hungary at the end of his days,"[60] thus pointedly reminding them how his father, the author of a well-reasoned legal tract raising many arguments against inheritance of rabbinic posts, had in the end joined the prevailing consensus of his colleagues in favor of inheritance by their sons.

Chapter 20

EXPLAINING THE NEW CONSENSUS
Rabbinic Posts as Property

The late-developing consensus in favor of inheritance of rabbinic posts is noteworthy in light of the paucity of support from the Mishnah, Talmud, geonim and many *Rishonim*. Further, it runs counter to the trend towards professionalization of the rabbinate, which stresses, among other things, the fitness of the candidate for his post based on objective merit-based criteria, certified independently by a reliable ordination (*semikhah*). Can we suggest a reason for the development of the consensus in this fashion and at this time? It is possible to do so provided we take into account the developments regarding rabbinic compensation, competition, and tenure, surveyed in parts 1, 2, and 3, that were occurring at the same time.

We have seen how Jewish law by the fifteenth century had undergone a sea change on the propriety of rabbis' accepting compensation, departing from the traditional position that one's Torah knowledge should be placed at the community's disposal free of charge. It is true that Rabbi Zadok's hoary admonition never to use the Torah as a spade for digging, along with Hillel's comment that anyone who derives a profit from the Torah will perish from the world,[1] were still studied whenever *Pirke Avot* was read in the synagogue, school, or home. So too the Talmud's tradition concerning Moses, who instructed the elders to teach Torah without compensation just as he was privileged to learn it from God at Mount Sinai.[2] In his works Maimonides argued across the generations for the continuing validity of the traditions, describing the ideal scholar as one who labors in the Torah without compensation while toiling at a secular trade to earn a living.[3] But the harsh realities of Jewish life in the Middle Ages conspired against the classic ideal. In straitened economic circumstances, no one was willing to serve as a religious functionary without compensation. In addition, if the ancients possessed the ability to study Torah and toil at a trade and succeed at both endeavors, people feared that contemporary scholars who tried to combine the two would succeed at neither. Left to the attention of part-time scholars who interrupted their studies each day for trade, there was the danger that the Torah would be forgotten. Jewish communities required the services of a full-time rabbinate to minister to their pressing needs. This would be possible only with a salaried rabbinate that, forsaking the earnings to be gained from commence, looked instead for their livelihoods to the Jewish communities they served.

Once rabbis began to receive salaries and fees, they began to compete for lucrative appointments. In the fifteenth century, for the first time, rabbis leveled the charge of trespass, *hasagat gevul,* against colleagues who invaded their economic territory, a charge previously reserved for merchants and tradesmen complaining about newcomers who opened competing business concerns in their town. Yet as time passed, rabbinic compensation became entrenched. Generation by generation, the initial embarrassment over accepting fees dissipated. Halakhic authorities, acknowledging the change of circumstances, raised the status of rabbinic compensation to the level of a legitimate livelihood entitled to legal protection against encroachers. Rabbi Moses Sofer wrote that in modern times, when communities hire a rabbi as an employee and are obligated to pay him a salary, anyone who siphons off his fees is an evildoer.[4]

At the same time, it was widely argued in halakhic literature that a rabbi, once appointed, was entitled to retain his position for life. Lifetime tenure complemented halakhic developments in relation to compensation and noncompetition, for once a rabbi's salary was legally sanctioned and insulated from competition, tenure guaranteed him the ability to enjoy the benefits of office for the longest possible time—the remainder of his life.

With the material profile of the rabbinate contoured in this fashion, inheritance of positions became the logical next step. Inheritance extended the benefits of rabbinic office beyond the incumbent's life to the next generation by passing the post to his heir at his death. Instead of engaging in ordinary trade or commerce and building up a large estate with accumulated wealth that they could bequeath to their heirs, rabbis bequeathed their positions. The Maharam Shik put it this way: "This is part of the compensation of leaders in Israel—they benefit in that their sons will be leaders after them."[5]

In sum, once the rabbinate had become associated with property through the receipt of salaries and fees, rabbinic positions acquired some of the characteristics of property, such as descendibility to the next generation. Something that began as *hefker,* ownerless property, free for all to acquire, became in the end a sort of quasi property, for a property interest developed in the rabbinic appointment itself.

The term "quasi property" is used to suggest that halakhic authorities never completely equated rabbinic positions with ordinary property. For example, they ruled an incumbent could not transfer his post to a third party by sale or gift.[6] If early authorities sometimes drew broad parallels between property and office for purposes of inheritance,[7] later authorities tended to be more guarded in their statements. They perceived that the rules governing inheritance of office and property would differ in some respects. This was clear from the Torah itself, for if succession to office was to be treated exactly the same as inheritance of property, then the laws that govern the inheritance of property would have sufficed for both. There would have been no need for additional verses in the Torah to specify inheritance for king and high priest.[8]

It became a recurrent theme in the responsa of the later authorities to delineate the differences between the two types of inheritance. A broad and interesting list of differences emerges from their efforts:

Property—the decedent's heirs divide it; office—one heir acquires it to the exclusion of all the others.[9]

Property—daughters will inherit where there are no sons; office—a daughter never inherits.[10]

Property—even an evil-doer will inherit; office—to qualify to inherit a rabbinic post, the heir must be a righteous person who fears Heaven.[11]

Property—the heirs' rights arise upon their father's death; office—the heir's right to succeed arises at the moment his father is appointed to his post.[12]

Property—no one can oppose the rightful heirs' inheritance; office—community opposition will vitiate an heir's right to succeed.[13]

Property—even a minor or a fool inherits; office—heir must be qualified to serve as rabbi and of age in order to inherit his father's post.[14]

These differences underscore the fact that an inherited office may never be treated exactly the same as inherited property.

But the fine distinction between property and quasi property could be lost on the heirs who sometimes attempted to take the notion of office as property to what seemed to them its logical conclusion. For example, since a decedent's property is divided among his heirs, while his office passes to just one of them, the excluded heirs might claim monetary compensation from the one who received the appointment. This happened when a town official died and his sons did not want his post. His son-in-law accepted the appointment. The sons did not object to this but sought damages as compensation for not assuming their father's office. Asked to resolve the matter by the town council, Rabbi Catriel F. Tecoresh rejected the sons' claim for damages, reasoning that office, unlike property, passes to just one heir, and that the excluded heirs succeed to nothing—neither the office nor any right to compensation as a substitute.[15]

In a similar vein, where none of the heirs wish to follow their father in office, they still might wish to receive the fees he customarily collected or demand a payment from the new appointee, claiming they were entitled to a monetary equivalent as their inheritance in place of the office they declined. In one instance, upon the death of a rabbi who supervised the compliance of the community's butchers with Jewish dietary laws (kashrut), his heirs had no desire to serve in his post. However, after their father's death, they claimed the right to continue to collect his customary fees as part of their inheritance. In the meantime the community hired someone else to perform the supervisory functions. Rabbi Shneur Zusha Reiss expressed displeasure at the heirs' conduct, stating that he had never heard of a similar case in which the heirs lived elsewhere, declined to perform the functions of office, and still wished to collect the fees. He advised the heirs to submit the matter to religious adjudication (*din Torah*) or binding arbitration to prevent the Divine name from being profaned by their actions (*hillul ha-Shem*).[16]

In advancing claims of this sort, the heirs were treating their deceased father's position exactly as property, seeking to divorce the emoluments of the office from its functions and to inherit the former or a monetary equivalent while declining the latter. The halakhic authorities who considered their claims properly rejected them as overreaching by the heirs. Yet it is possible to see their claims for a cash substitute for the office as a direct and perhaps inevitable extension of the notion that office is a sort of property that descends from one generation to the next like an inheritance.

Chapter 21

INHERITANCE IN THE MODERN ERA

Emancipation, the Enlightenment and reform, scientific progress and political change, the Holocaust and Israel's statehood, all impacted on the Jewish people and their spiritual leadership in countless ways. The rabbinate splintered in modern times into traditional and progressive branches with dissimilar beliefs, allegiances, and career aspirations. As a result, today's rabbis differ in their self-image, their observance of the halakhah, and even in their gender in ways that were unimaginable in prior eras. A history of the modern rabbinate would chart the development of each movement and trend and their impact on the people's religious authorities. A sociology of the modern rabbinate would describe the results of two centuries of continuous change in the recruitment and training of rabbis, their functions and status within their communities, and the overall conduct of their professional lives. By comparison, the goal of this final chapter is modest. We consider two trends, one in the Diaspora and the other in Israel, that in the modern era are affecting the inheritance of rabbinic posts with markedly contrasting results.

Under the prevailing pattern in the Diaspora, the rabbinate has acquired the trappings of a modern profession. Typically rabbis no longer serve for life as "rulers" of their towns, provinces, or countries.[1] A rabbi's community has been reduced to the single congregation whose board of directors interviews, hires, and employs him pursuant to contract. The board, in negotiation with the candidate for a rabbinic post, will fix his duties, compensation, benefits, and length of service. Seminary graduates will learn of vacant positions from the placement office of the school or movement to which they belong. Within the congregation, the rabbi will function less as a judge of halakhic matters and more as a modern clergyman who counsels individuals and families, leads religious worship, delivers sermons, celebrates life's events, administers synagogue and school, and participates as a public figure in community affairs.

In addition, modern rabbis, similar to their counterparts in other professions such as medicine and law, tend to specialize in their vocation.[2] While some continue to serve synagogues and congregations, others turn to teaching or find employment as campus, military, or hospital chaplains. Some rabbis become social workers, while others join the staffs of Jewish communal agencies. Some serve as judges (*dayyanim*) on rabbinic tribunals, and others supervise the observance of dietary rules in institutions and plants. Each specialization requires its own program of training and certification in a yeshivah, kolel, or seminary to acquire knowledge and skills that quite obviously cannot be inherited. Nor can the personal preference that led to an individual's career choice, whether to become a congregational rabbi, teacher, social worker, or the like, be passed down to an heir. In sum, the professional environment in which today's rabbis function has altered in ways that make inheritance an inappropriate way to fill vacancies.

The changed circumstances of the profession have halakhic implications. They tend to undermine the principle that a rabbi, upon appointment to a post, acquires for his descendants a right to succeed him, for unlike the leaders of Israel whose offices descend to heirs, the ordinary hired worker occupies a post that is not inheritable under Jewish law. There is a long-standing debate among halakhic authorities concerning which communal religious functionaries are to be regarded as "leaders of Israel" whose offices pass to heirs and which are merely employees or "hired workers" whose posts are not inherited. For example, cantors and religious slaughterers are often, but not always, assigned to the second category.[3] Officials in the second category may be accorded inheritance rights by custom, if not by law.

That rabbis in recent times have become mere employees of their congregations, schools, and agencies and should now be assigned to the second category are conclusions halakhists are understandably reluctant to reach, particularly in light of the hard-won consensus among *Aharonim* that rabbis should be equated with monarchs for purposes of inheritance. But that equation is not fixed for all time and becomes increasingly untenable as the rabbinate continues its modern transformation in plain sight. Candid assessments of the current situation appear in halakhic literature. In this vein, commenting on the Rema's ruling dating from the sixteenth century that gave the rabbi's heir priority in appointment, Rabbi Yehiel Epstein in his late code of law, *Arukh Hashulhan,* published at the end of the nineteenth century, wrote: "It appears to me that the son has no priority [to succeed as rabbi], even where he fills his father's place [in learning and fear of Heaven], *for it is the father that they wanted to employ and not the son.*"[4] Rabbi Epstein concludes the passage somewhat wistfully: "Still, if the son fills his father's place in Torah and fear [of Heaven], why should he be less preferable than anyone else?"[5]

The author of the *Mishnah Berurah,* the greatly respected *Hafetz Hayyim,* Rabbi Israel Meir Hakohen Kagan (1838–1933), summarizes the halakhah today as follows: "There are those who say in the case of a sage who is appointed to be rabbi (*marbitz Torah*) or judge, we do not give the son priority; and some disagree with this."[6] This bare-bones restatement of the law is interesting because typically the position the author states first is his assessment of the better or majority view. Thus, the *Mishnah Berurah*'s formulation hints that in modern times, the halakhic consensus has shifted or is shifting again, this time away from granting the son priority in matters of succession.[7]

This shift in the consensus will be meaningful to the segment of today's rabbis that is orthodox in belief and practice. If, from their reading of traditional texts, they entertain any vestige of the notion that sons should succeed in office by dint of Torah law, they will look to recognized halakhic authorities to explain why the principle does not operate in the congregational rabbinate today. At the same time, other contemporary rabbis who are not orthodox in their outlook harbor no expectation, halakhic or otherwise, that their sons will inherit their posts, nor do the congregations, schools, and agencies that employ them anticipate that the rabbi's heir will succeed him in office.

The heads of the Hasidic rabbinic dynasties remain exceptions to these observations. The Hasidic *rebbe* passes his position as leader of his movement to his heir. The Hasidic rebbe cannot be equated with the rabbis who are the subjects of our study and whose authority is based on their yeshivah training and Torah scholarship. The Hasidic movement introduced a new type of spiritual leader whose rabbinic authority was based on personal charisma and lineage rather than erudition in Talmud and codes.[8] As Menahem Freedman expressed the difference, the Hasidic rebbe intercedes between his followers and Heaven, while the traditional rabbi mediates between his congregation and the halakhic literature.[9] It is interesting to note that hereditary succession was not an original feature of the Hasidic movement.[10] Its eighteenth-century founders bequeathed their positions to their foremost pupils, not to sons.[11]

With the establishment of the State of Israel and the creation of a host of official positions staffed by members of the rabbinate, the rule of inheritance is experiencing something of a renaissance. The state and its municipalities employ cadres of rabbis to serve the communal needs of the Jewish population in all parts of the country and in the military. The rabbis' fixed terms of office and compulsory retirement ages, stipulated in their employment contracts or in the ordinances creating their posts, tend not to be insisted upon by their employers, an important factor that played a role in the outcomes of both of the rabbinical court cases discussed below. Rabbinic appointments in Israel thus become de facto appointments for life, recalling the historical model of lifetime tenure for rabbis. When a rabbi dies while in office, the circumstances are ripe for his heir to come forward and claim the vacant post by right of inheritance. In two recent cases where the community demurred, the disappointed heirs sought a resolution of the matter in the rabbinical courts, where they achieved a measure of success.

In the first case, *Religious Council of Tel Aviv-Yaffo v. Rabbi "A,"*[12] the father had served until his death as head of the Sabbath and Sabbath Boundaries Department of the local rabbinate. Upon his death, his son wished to succeed him. The Israeli Chief Rabbinate certified the son as qualified for the post. However, the local religious council wanted to hold an open competition to fill the vacancy. It claimed that the son was not qualified and further, that the position was not one that passed by inheritance.

A three-judge panel of the Rabbinical High Court of Jerusalem decided the case with a split verdict. Two members of the panel held for the son.[13] On the issue of qualifications, they ruled the heir must be deemed presumptively fit based on the Chief Rabbinate's certification. The local religious council has the burden to prove the heir unfit, a burden it had not yet met at the time the case was heard.[14]

The majority also held that the post in question was one that passed by inheritance. The local religious council had argued that although the father was a rabbi, his function was that of an administrator, supervising his department, checking the Sabbath boundaries, and making sure that no labor was performed in violation of the Sabbath. The son countered that in addition to his administrative duties, his father had functioned as a rabbi, deciding halakhic questions relating to Sabbath observance and Sabbath boundaries (*eruvin*).

The majority was satisfied that the father had exercised rabbinic functions in deciding halakhic questions relating to matters within the purview of his department. But even if he had not, they held, his post would pass to his heir, for inheritance is the rule that governs succession to all offices in Israel. It is not limited to positions of authority but applies equally to offices that accord honor but not authority to the incumbent.[15]

One member of the panel, Rabbi Saul Israeli, dissented. While he agreed with his colleagues that the father had exercised rabbinic functions, he believed this fact was inimical to the son's claim. In his view, to the extent the father engaged in halakhic decision making, he wore the Torah crown (keter Torah). But the Torah crown does not pass by inheritance.[16] Now if, in modern times, according to the Hatam Sofer, rabbis, in addition to deciding halakhic matters, act also for the public welfare as public servants and leaders of their communities and in this capacity acquire also the royal crown (keter malkhut), then surely inheritance will apply only to the post of rabbi of a town who indeed rules his community. By contrast, the post of someone like the claimant's father, a functionary, not a leader, who lacked communal authority and in deciding religious questions wore the Torah crown only, does not pass by inheritance.[17]

The two-person majority was itself split on the issue of altering the rule of inheritance by adopting a new regulation. Rabbi Elijah held the town religious council may change the rule prospectively by properly enacted rabbinic regulation so that all future appointments could be limited to the incumbent and not pass to heirs.[18] Rabbi Goldschmidt questioned whether the town's religious council, even acting with the addition of all the local rabbis and rabbinical judges, was sufficiently representative of the community to exercise the authority to alter its customs by enacting a new regulation.[19] There was no need for them to resolve the question because both agreed that any such regulation could only operate prospectively and would not affect the outcome of the case.

The second case, *"A" v. Selection Board for the Ashkenazic Chief Rabbi of City "B" and the Religious Council of City "B,"*[20] was decided three years later by the district rabbinical court of Petah Tikvah. Here the father had served as chief rabbi of a city for thirty years prior to his death. A son claimed he was entitled by right of inheritance to appointment as his successor. He sued in the district rabbinical court to enjoin the town's religious council and its selection board from appointing anyone but him to fill the vacant post. Further, he sought an order enjoining any other candidates from even stepping forward to offer themselves for consideration.

The court held that little discussion was necessary to establish an heir's right to succeed to his father's rabbinic post in view of the consensus among the *Aharonim* on this point, provided the heir is qualified.[21] In this case, where the father had served for life, upon appointment he acquired the post as an inheritance for his descendants in perpetuity. The court cited the statement of the rule in Maimonides' code, *Hilkhot Melakhim* 1:7, and noted the consensus interpreting this passage to encompass rabbinic positions (keter Torah).[22] Still, the heir's right to inherit the post was dependent upon the community's consent to his appointment.[23] The attorney for the respondents had argued that a majority of the community did not consent. In reviewing the submissions in the case, the court found evidence of opposition to the heir but no evidence of local support. The heir characterized the opposition as merely political or emanating from persons unworthy of determining who is fit to serve as a rabbi. The court rejected this characterization, for there was opposition from the members of the religious council and the selection board, and surely they were qualified to make this judgment.[24]

But the court went further, holding that even if the opposition were "merely political," as the heir claimed, it would block his appointment.[25] It derived its conclusion from a close reading of a passage in the *Maharam Shik*.[26] He states there is no right to inherit a post where a community does not consent, and no legal compulsion is used to force it to consent, but a community should consent to the succession of a rightful heir, and so long as it does not, it is not acting properly under Torah law. Regarding the Maharam Shik's comment that in such a situation the community "is not acting properly under Torah law," the court reasoned as follows. He cannot be referring to a case where the community rejects for legitimate reasons, for example where the heir is in fact *not* qualified to serve, for such an individual is not entitled to the post by Torah law and the community acts correctly when it rejects him. Rather, the Maharam Shik's comment must be addressed to the community that rejects a fully qualified heir, refusing to consent to his appointment "for reasons of its own," including purely political reasons. In such a case, since the heir is entitled to the post under Torah law, the community is not acting properly. Still, its opposition vitiates the right of inheritance, and the town is free to appoint another.[27]

Since the case involved appointment as chief rabbi of a city, the court had to consider the position of the Hatam Sofer. He denied that the rule of inheritance applied to the post of chief rabbi of a country, for the occupant of such a post must be greater in learning than his colleagues, and lineage alone cannot ensure this.[28] The religious council claimed that there resided in its town rabbis and scholars whose stature and attainments were greater than those of the heir. The court held this fact would not alter their decision.[29] As they read the Hatam Sofer, his position is limited to a case where the chief rabbi commands a rabbinic hierarchy that he heads. In such a case the chief must be greater than his subordinates who are obligated to follow his directives. But this principle has no application to the chief rabbi of a town who is not in a direct chain of command with respect to other rabbis who live in the town. The heir's right to inherit is not impeded by the fact that greater scholars reside in the town, for they do not take orders from him.

Apparently the heir did not live in the town and was not well known to the residents. The court ruled he should make an attempt to become known to them and secure their consent to his appointment. It ordered the religious council to make arrangements for a visit by the heir and gave him two months to appear. If the heir failed to appear, or if after the visit the opposition persisted, his claim to inherit the post would be dismissed. Whether the heir was qualified for the post and whether the opposition emanated from "a majority" of the community were questions to be decided by a competent *beth din* (rabbinical court) convened for this purpose.[30]

The decisions in these two cases demonstrate the continuing vitality in Israel of both the consensus view that rabbinic positions pass by inheritance and the minority view that they do not, at least where the rabbi wears the crown of Torah only. It is equally clear that an heir may never assume his father's office without first obtaining the community's consent to his appointment. Further there appears to be some scope for the community's power to abrogate the rule of inheritance prospectively by regulation, provided it is enacted by a religious body that is sufficiently representative of the community as a whole. Taken together, the decisions in these two cases achieve a rather surprising result. They suggest that the rule of inheritance for rabbinic posts can be revived in Israel in a manner that is consistent with the aspirations of the State to be both Jewish and democratic: Jewish, by honoring the rule that the halakhah has bequeathed, and democratic, first, by requiring the community's consent to the heir's accession and second, by allowing the community's duly constituted representatives to legislate the rule's demise if and when they deem it advisable.

EPILOGUE

Jewish law insisted in antiquity on an ideal of uncompensated teaching of the Torah by learned men who engaged in labor to support themselves. It progressed over time to a rabbinate that was salaried, insulated from competition, secure in office for life, and able to pass their positions to qualified heirs at death. In reviewing the vast distance Jewish law has traveled from its origins, at first blush it may seem that a measure of cynicism is warranted. In defining the material contours of the rabbinate, as they did in the legal codes they authored and the rulings they issued, the rabbis themselves were not disinterested parties. The conclusions they reached were not inevitable nor were they compelled by the halakhic sources they cited, as shown by their many disagreements over interpreting the sources. Yet here were issues, namely, their own compensation, job security, and inheritance rights, concerning which the rabbis, who on other issues could be quite inflexible, instead found ways to overcome traditional strictures and institute a radically different regime.

In fairness, such an appraisal is to a degree unwarranted. In the first place, the communal need that underlay the rabbis' action regarding their compensation was profound and undeniable. For their very survival in the dark years of Exile, the Jewish people required the services of a full-time rabbinate to minister to their needs. Their problems were not part-time problems. Since rabbis were universally men with families who required a livelihood to support themselves and their dependents, that support could only be drawn from the communities they served.

Second, in devotion to Torah, which in one sense required the scholar to build a wall between his pursuit of a livelihood and his pursuit of Torah, lay the very factor that in the end made this separation impossible. Devotion to Torah is a demanding commitment that does not readily permit the practitioner to break away temporarily, even if he should wish to do so. Scholars, who are commanded to meditate on the Law day and night, invariably through their love of Torah come to desire this. Maimonides' attempt to endow secular employment with a degree of religious sanctity did nothing to accommodate the scholar's deep yearning for a life completely devoted to Torah studies. His approach had little resonance among scholars, for the best and the brightest drawn to Torah as a vocation would be the least willing to interrupt their studies for trade, even for the minimal three hours a day he recommended. If earning a living is not deemed a complete "waste of time"[1] in relation to Torah studies, it is at best a necessary evil. Once compensation became available to rabbis, toiling at a trade was no longer necessary. Then, given the alternatives, a rabbinic post could be regarded as the best way to devote one's entire life to study and scholarship, or at least that part of one's waking hours not spent ministering to the needs of congregants and engaging in public affairs on their behalf.[2] In the end complete devotion to Torah demanded compensation, where initially the two were considered incompatible.

That halakhic authorities were able to base the new approach on authentic Jewish legal sources is a tribute to their own legal acuity and to the immense flexibility of Jewish law. The halakhah possesses an innate ability to change in light of changing historical conditions when the rabbis themselves recognize and appreciate the need for change. On the whole, halakhic authorities mostly did appreciate the need for change in this case that struck so close to home and resonated on a personal level. Noteworthy is the degree to which they resorted to policy arguments to justify reversing course on compensation. Arguing that no one would be willing to come forward and serve as a rabbi without compensation, that the Torah would be forgotten if committed to the care and custody of part-time scholars, and that the public would never heed the admonitions of religious leaders whom they observed engaging in trade or menial labor, halakhic authorities employed policy arguments very effectively to counter Talmudic dicta against compensation.

It is less clear whether the times also required that rabbis be insulated from competition, enjoy lifetime tenure, and have the ability to pass their posts at death to their heirs, but these issues have to be evaluated with regard to their social and historical contexts. In general in premodern Jewish communities, the value of unrestricted economic competition was questioned. Once the rabbinate acquired an economic component, its development naturally would track that of other trades and professions where new entrants could be excluded.

As to tenure and inheritance rights for his heir, a given rabbi's ability to enjoy them varied from time to time and place to place. As we have seen, a community that wished to replace its rabbi had the power to challenge his tenure and, when strong public sentiment favored removal, might succeed. The same held true when the question was his heir's inheritance of the post. The community's consent was required, and community opposition vitiated the right to inherit. The majority could reject the heir for good reason or for no reason. At the same time, rabbis also claimed the right to leave their posts early to assume office in larger communities with higher salaries and more prestige. Rabbinic tracts arguing for lifetime tenure and inheritance rights were legal briefs advocating a position rather than accurate reflections of uniform contemporary practices. Thus, what has to be weighed is not the reality of lifetime tenure for rabbis and succession for their heirs but most rabbis' yearning for them, and that is completely understandable.

The heir's right to inherit his father's rabbinic post was a late and it seems temporary development in Jewish law. Over the course of Jewish history, halakhic authorities debated whether the Torah crown (keter Torah) should pass from father to son by inheritance. For the most part they resisted this notion, for it was evident to them that the qualities most essential to the rabbinic vocation—fear of Heaven and a little learning—are not inherited traits. It was only in the latest period, after the rabbinate became salaried and rabbinic posts were associated with property, that a consensus developed in favor of inheritance. Still, each generation called forth a prominent dissenter, such as Rabbi Israel Isserlein in the fifteenth century, Rabbi Samuel De Medina (the Maharashdam) in the sixteenth, Rabbi Moses Sofer (the Hatam Sofer) two centuries later, and Rabbi Saul Israeli in recent times, who argued that high achievement in Torah learning and not lineage must determine who shall wear the crown of Torah and exercise its authority over the community.

Descent alone never guaranteed the heir's succession. He needed to demonstrate his own fitness for the post—his fear of Heaven and a little learning—and obtain the community's consent to his appointment. Still, his status as heir conferred some advantages. He had a right to be considered first among the candidates for a post. He was preferred in cases of doubt and where the candidates were equal. Even when the candidates were unequal, the community rested under an obligation to accept the heir although he might be the lesser scholar. These preferences based on descent, which may induce a community deliberately to appoint a less qualified individual as its rabbi, we regard as a singular anomaly in a tradition that in most other contexts places Torah learning at the apex of its scale of values.[3]

In the modern era, the changing nature of the rabbinate presents a challenge to the notion that rabbinic positions should descend by inheritance, at least in communities where a rabbi is considered an employee of his congregation. By contrast, in the State of Israel, in response to the claims of heirs seeking official posts their fathers held until death, rabbinical court judges have revived the rule of inheritance. As this dichotomy of approaches suggests, new chapters in the struggle over rabbinic inheritance rights are sure to be written.

It may be that Jewish law arrived at the best of all possible solutions. The classic ideal of uncompensated Torah service remained always as an ideal. It was never discredited, and the new regime never supplanted it entirely. The ideal of uncompensated service therefore tends to restrain any tendency to view the rabbinate as just another profession, a mere means to earn a living. Anyone inclined to utilize his position primarily for this purpose is subject to the charge of using the Torah as a spade for digging. This in turn will moderate to a degree the material demands advanced by the rabbinate and also have an impact on determining those who will be drawn to the profession. In the end, wherever traditional halakhic concepts are honored, the *Tur*'s admonition, "Heaven forbid that the Lord's work should ever be a mere trade!"[4] will always, on some level, be taken to heart.

NOTES

CHAPTER 1

1. Num. 27:15–23; see chap. 17, below.
2. *Sanhedrin* 13b.
3. For an account of the reemergence of ordination in the second half of the fourteenth century, see Breuer, *The Rabbinate in Ashkenaz,* 19–21. The title conferred was *morenu ha-rav,* "our teacher, the rabbi."
4. On the first seminaries (in Padova, Italy, 1829, and Metz, France, 1830), see Schwarzfuchs, *Concise History,* 88–91.
5. On these terms, see the articles collected in Gammie and Perdue, *Sage in Israel.*
6. *Avot* 1:2.
7. Ibid., 1:4, 1:17.
8. Ibid., 1:6, 1:16.
9. *Bekhorot* 4:6.
10. Heller, *"Tosafot Yom Tov,"* *Bekhorot* 4:6.
11. *Avot* 4:5.
12. Ibid.
13. Heller, *"Tosafot Yom Tov,"* *Avot* 4:5, point 16.
14. *Nedarim* 37a; Maimonides, *Mishneh Torah, Talmud Torah* 1:7.
15. For a survey of the trades and occupations of Talmudic rabbis, see Aberbach, *Labor, Crafts,* 38–90.
16. *Berakhot* 28a.
17. See Urbach, *The Sages,* 1:601. On the relationship between the patriarchs and the rabbis of their time, see Levine, *Rabbinic Class,* 134–62, 186–91.
18. *Bava Batra* 174b. For a discussion of the legal underpinnings of this case, see Shilo, "Circumvention of the Law," 338–39.
19. Maimonides, *Mishneh Torah, Talmud Torah* 1:12. See chap. 2, below.
20. Goldin, *The Fathers according to Rabbi Nathan,* 26. For the suggestion that the Hebrew text of Beth Shammai's statement should contain the word *kasher* (fit) in place of *ashir* (rich), see Alon, *Jews, Judaism,* 440n12.
21. Goldin, *The Fathers according to Rabbi Nathan,* 26.
22. *Bava Batra* 7b-8a ("R. Nahman b. R. Hisda levied a poll tax on the Rabbis. Said R. Nahman b. Isaac to him: You have transgressed against the Law, the Prophets and the Writings").
23. Ibid., 7b–8a, 22a.
24. *Bava Metzi'a* 33a.
25. *Ketubbot* 96a ("All manner of service that a slave must render to his master a student must render to his teacher, except that of taking off his shoe").
26. *Shevu'ot* 30a–b.
27. *Ketubbot* 105a; *Yoma* 72b.
28. *Berakhot* 34b.
29. *Pesahim* 53b.
30. *Berakhot* 34b.
31. *Pesahim* 49a.

32. Obadiah of Bertinoro, commentary on the Mishnah, *Avot* 4:5 (end); Sirkes, *Responsa*, no. 52.

33. Maimonides, *Commentary on the Mishnah, Avot* 4:7 (Kapah ed., 291). The obligation to contribute half a shekel annually to a fund for the upkeep of the Temple service is imposed by Exodus 30:11–16 on "every man"; there is no express exemption for priests. The priests, however, claimed they were exempt from this obligation (Mishnah, *Sheqalim* 1:4). In his code, Maimonides ruled against the priests on this point, but he also ruled, "for the sake of peace," that their property, unlike the property of ordinary Israelites, was exempt from distraint for failure to make a timely contribution (Maimonides, *Mishneh Torah, Sheqalim* 1:7, 1:10). Priests could, however, be dunned regularly until they paid (ibid.). Apart from the half-shekel levy, priests were exempt from taxes at least from the period of Ezra (ca. fifth century B.C.E.) and onward under a mandate of the Persian king Artaxerxes recorded in the Bible: "Also we announce to you, that touching any of the priests and Levites . . . it shall not be lawful to impose tribute, impost, or toll upon them" (Ezra 7:24). Persian policy was generally tolerant of native cults, and the tax exemption for priests was one aspect of this policy. See Bright, *History of Israel,* 343–44, 370–71. The tax exemption for scholars recognized by Jewish law may have its origins in this provision, with scholars succeeding to some of the functions and privileges of the priests after the destruction of the Temple in Jerusalem in 70 C.E. (Heller, "*Tosafot Yom Tov,*" *Avot* 4:5, point 18).

34. Levine, *The Rabbinic Class,* 71.

35. Maimonides, *Commentary on the Mishnah, Avot* 4:7 (Kapah ed., 291).

36. *Ketubbot* 96a.

37. *Ketubbot* 111b.

38. *Nedarim* 37a.

39. Ibid.

40. *Ketubbot* 105a.

41. Rashi, *Ketubbot* 105a.

42. *Ketubbot* 105a.

43. Ibid., 106a.

44. *Bekhorot* 4:6.

45. *Avot* 4:5.

46. See *Talmud Yerushalmi, Nedarim* 4:4.

47. Rashi, *Ketubbot* 105a, s.v. "*notlin sekharum*"; *Tosafot, Ketubbot* 105a, s.v. "*gozrei gezerot.*"

48. See Rheins, "Professionalization of the Rabbinate," 30–32.

CHAPTER 2

1. Ginzberg, *Geonica,* 1:53.

2. The text of the Talmud available at this time consisted of a definitive oral recension. The work's structure was essentially fixed, but the precise wording of the passages remained fluid (Brody, *The Geonim,* 156–62). Brody dates the earliest known written copies of the Talmud to the eighth or ninth centuries (ibid., 163, 171). According to Salo Baron, written copies of the Talmud were available after about 650 C.E. but were still rare for another century (Baron, *Social and Religious History,* 6:19).

3. Ibid., 111.

4. Ginzberg, *Geonica,* 1:6. On this point and its significance, see Grossman, "From Father to Son," 195. Although the gaon consulted the scholars who surrounded him in the academy, there is no way to determine how much they influenced the contents of his rulings. This probably varied with the gaon's personality and ability. There is no evidence that legal questions were put to a vote or that rulings were decided by majority (Brody, *The Geonim,* 61–62, 186).

5. The title *gaon* is derived from the phrase *gaon ya'akov*, "the excellency of Jacob," in Psalm 47:5: "He shall choose our inheritance for us, the excellency of Jacob whom he loved."

6. See chap. 18, below. The last gaon of Sura died in 1034, and the last gaon of Pumbeditha was deposed in 1040. See Brody, *The Geonim*, 344–45.

7. Ginzberg, *Geonica*, 1:13. On the gaon's sources of income, see Brody, *The Geonim*, 39.

8. Twersky, *Introduction*, 83.

9. Abraham ibn Daud (b. Toledo, c. 1110–1180), *The Book of Tradition (Sefer Ha-Qabbalah)*, 65–66. *Sefer Ha-Qabbalah* dates to about 1161.

10. Ibid., 66.

11. Brody, *The Geonim*, 11.

12. Stillman, "Aspects of Jewish Life," 56–61.

13. Brody, *The Geonim*, 132; on the rulers of Muslim Spain, see Hitti, *History of the Arabs*, 493–504.

14. Goitein, *A Mediterranean Society*, 2:11–14. The support took several forms, including fixed annual assessments, special collections, private donations, and bequests. It was also common to stipulate a payment to the yeshivah as the penalty for breach of contract (ibid., 14).

15. Ibid., 85, 121–26, 211.

16. Maimonides, *Mishneh Torah, Talmud Torah* 3:10.

17. Minkin, *World of Moses Maimonides*, 36.

18. Ibid., 44.

19. Maimonides, *Mishneh Torah, Talmud Torah* 1:9.

20. Maimonides, *Commentary on the Mishnah, Avot* 4:7 (Kapah ed., 288–91).

21. Maimonides, *Mishneh Torah, Talmud Torah* 3:11.

22. Ibid., 3:7.

23. Ibid., 3:6; see Mishnah, *Avot* 6:4.

24. Maimonides, *Mishneh Torah, Talmud Torah* 3:11.

25. Maimonides, *Commentary on the Mishnah, Avot* 4:7 (Kapah ed., 289).

26. Ibid., 290.

27. See chap. 1, above.

28. Maimonides, *Mishneh Torah, Talmud Torah* 5:1, 6:10.

29. Ibid., 1:7. Maimonides here presents the view that the Mosaic stricture against accepting a stipend for teaching excludes the teaching of Scripture, construing Moses' reference to the "statutes and ordinances" he learned from God gratis as a reference to the Oral Law and not the Written Law (the Pentateuch). See Talmud Yerushalmi, *Nedarim* 4:4: "Statutes and ordinances [i.e., the Oral Law] must you teach without pay, but you need not teach Scripture and translation without pay" (Neusner, *Talmud of the Land of Israel: Nedarim*, 80). The parallel passage in the Babylonian Talmud, *Nedarim* 37a, continues with a query, "Then should not Scripture too be unremunerated?"—for Moses also learned the Written Law at Sinai. There follow two answers, "Rab said: The fee is for guarding [the children]. R. Johanan maintained: The fee is for the teaching of the accentuation [of the biblical text, which is post-Mosaic]." Many authorities cite these answers as rationales for permitting teachers of young children to receive salaries (for example, Rabbi Obadiah of Bertinoro, commentary on the Mishnah, *Avot* 4:5; see above, chap. 1, note 39 and accompanying text).

30. Maimonides, *Commentary on the Mishnah* (Kapah ed., 291).

31. See chap. 1, above.

32. *Ketubbot* 105a.

33. Maimonides, *Commentary on the Mishnah* (Kapah ed., 289).

34. *Ketubbot* 105a.

35. See Rashi, *Ketubbot* 105a.

36. Kapah suggests Maimonides might have had a different text of the Talmud (Maimonides, *Commentary on the Mishnah,* Kapah ed., 289).

37. Maimonides, *Mishneh Torah, Sanhedrin* 23:5.

38. Joseph Karo (1488–1575) noted the omission and rectified it in his commentary on this passage (*Kesef Mishnah, Talmud Torah* 3:10).

39. Maimonides, *Commentary on the Mishnah, Avot* 4:7 (Kapah ed., 288).

CHAPTER 3

1. The letter was published around the year 1260 by Rabbi Isaac ben Moses of Vienna (ca. 1200–1270) in his compendium of halakhic commentary, rulings, and correspondence known as *Or Zaru'a. Or Zaru'a,* no. 113.

2. Marcus, *Piety and Society,* 15, 90, 114, 138. For a discussion of their beliefs, see Scholem, *Major Trends,* 80–118 and Ben-Sasson, *History,* 545–53.

3. Isaac ben Moses of Vienna, *Or Zaru'a,* no. 113.

4. Exod. 30:11–16.

5. Isaac ben Moses of Vienna, *Or Zaru'a,* no. 113.

6. See chap. 2, above.

7. "The Testament of Judah Asheri," in Abrahams, *Hebrew Ethical Wills,* 2:163–200, at 169.

8. Ibid., 2:166–67, 2:189–190.

9. Ibid., 2:189–190.

10. Ibid., 2:190.

11. Ibid., 2:167, 2:180–82, 2:190.

12. Ibid., 2:179.

13. Ibid., 2:191.

14. Ibid. We note the great disparity between Judah's estate and his father's. It may be that Asher lost significant property upon his flight from Germany and received a salary in Toledo that just matched his expenditures, including his outlays for charity. We know that Asher tithed 10 percent of his income both in Germany and in Spain (ibid., 2:192–93).

15. Ibid.

16. Ibid., 2:181, 2:195–96.

17. Ibid., 2:181–82.

18. Ibid., 2:192–93.

19. Ibid., 2:194.

20. Ibid., 2:198.

21. Ibid., 2:191–92. This section precedes two annexes, one setting forth the terms of the tithing agreement and the other the terms of Judah's will.

22. Ibid., 2:171–72, 2:195, 2:197.

23. See also ibid., 2:184.

24. Ibid., 2:181.

25. Ibid., 2:182, where he writes, "Had I been willing to accept more, they would have given it, as is expressly stated in their letter (which I still possess) of the year 1341." The congregation's letter would have been written some seven or eight years prior to the time of Judah's writing. Assaf believes this letter was actually Judah's contract, which is sometimes referred to as a letter, *k'tav rabbanut* (Assaf, *Lekorot Harabbanut,* 45).

26. They would also learn it is easier to leave town, if it became necessary to earn a livelihood elsewhere, if they married a relative—a member of their grandfather's family—rather than a local woman, because then no one would raise objections about her having to move away from her relatives to remain with her husband (Abrahams, *Hebrew Ethical Wills,* 2:184–85).

27. Ibid., 2:182.

28. Ibid., 2:191. He did not specify the nature of the requests.

29. Ibid., 2:181.

30. Ibid., 2:185, 2:196.

31. Ibid., 2:196, 2:200. The names of the two witnesses are Moses son of R. Benjamin of Rome and Isaac son of R. Abraham Maimon.

32. Ibid., 2:180.

33. Ibid., 2:194.

34. Ibid., 2:182–83, 2:191.

35. Ibid., 2:165.

36. Ibid., 2:170.

37. Ibid., 2:174.

38. See ibid., 2:164–65, 2:173–74, 2:177, where the following teachings appear in quotation or paraphrase: Those who emulate the deeds of their fathers are called the friends of God (*Avot* 6:1); Who is rich? He who rejoices in his portion (*Avot* 4:1); Do your tasks faithfully and faithful is your Employer who will pay your wages (*Avot* 2:14); When three have eaten at a table and spoken words of Torah, it is as if they have eaten from God's altar (*Avot* 3:3); I have not found anything better for a person than silence (*Avot* 1:17).

39. Hillel's maxim "He that makes use of the crown shall perish," which appears independently in *Avot* 1:13 and as an addendum to Rabbi Zadok's maxim in *Avot* 4:5, made an appearance in Judah's letter in a context other than earning one's livelihood from Torah. When Judah advised his children against the sin of pride—for majesty is God's garment—he warned them that "he that makes use of the crown shall perish" (Abrahams, *Hebrew Ethical Wills,* 2:177).

40. Ibid., 2:195.

41. Ibid., 2:173.

42. Ibid., 2:195–96.

43. Ibid., 2:195.

44. Ibid., 2:170.

45. Compare Abrahams, who notes that Judah was writing "at the transition period, when the Rabbi was passing out of the category of voluntary to salaried official" (*Hebrew Ethical Wills,* 2:164).

46. We may regard as close to certain that Judah knew the arguments of R. Eliezer of Bohemia and R. Judah Hahasid in their controversy over communal collections for the cantor's fund, even apart from the publication of Eliezer's letter in *Or Zaru'a*. Judah's grandfather, Rabbi Yehiel, was a prominent rabbinic scholar in Germany around the time of Judah Hahasid and was, perhaps, within the circle of Hasidei Ashkenaz. Judah Hahasid's teachings would have been passed down from Rabbi Yehiel to his son Asher and from Asher to his son Judah.

CHAPTER 4

1. Simon ben Zemah Duran, sometimes referred to by the Hebrew acronym *Tashbetz*, lived from 1361 to 1444.

2. I. Epstein, *Responsa of Rabbi Simon b. Zemah Duran,* 7–9.

3. Ibid., 12.
4. Ibid., 35.
5. *Tashbetz*, 1:142–48.
6. Karo, *Kesef Mishnah, Talmud Torah* 3:10.
7. *Tashbetz*, 1:147.
8. Karo, *Kesef Mishnah, Talmud Torah* 3:10. In defense of Maimonides' position, it is equally hard to reconcile Hillel's statement that one who makes a worldly profit out of the words of the Torah will perish from the world (Mishnah, *Avot* 4:5) with the supposition that he himself accepted compensation for imparting his Torah knowledge to others.
9. *Tashbetz*, 1:142.
10. Ibid.
11. *Yoma* 18a; *Horayot* 9a.
12. *Tashbetz*, 1:142.
13. *Ketubbot* 105b.
14. *Tashbetz*, 1:142.
15. *Nedarim* 37a.
16. *Tashbetz*, 1:147.
17. *Gittin* 60b.
18. See Rashi, *Gittin* 60b.
19. Ibid.
20. *Tashbetz*, 1:142.
21. Ibid. ("The custom of Israel is Torah"); and Karo, *Kesef Mishnah, Talmud Torah* 3:10 ("In a case where the halakhah you have received is unclear, follow the custom").
22. *Tashbetz*, 1:147, based on *Berakhot* 35b: "See what a difference there is between prior generations and later ones. Prior generations made their Torah study fixed and their work occasional and succeeded at both; later generations made their Torah study occasional and their work fixed and succeeded at neither." Duran conceded that Maimonides himself was a rare exception.
23. *Tashbetz*, 1:147.
24. Karo, *Kesef Mishnah, Talmud Torah* 3:10.
25. *Tashbetz*, 1:148; see also Abrabanel, *Nahalat Avot* 4:6 (Chill trans., 246–47); Obadiah of Bertinoro, commentary on the Mishnah, *Avot* 4:5; and Sirkes, *Responsa*, no. 52.
26. Maimonides, *Commentary on the Mishnah, Avot* 4:7 (Kapah ed., 289).
27. *Tashbetz*, 1:147; Abrabanel, *Nahalat Avot* 4:6 (Chill trans., 246–47).
28. *Tashbetz*, 1:147; Karo, *Kesef Mishnah, Talmud Torah* 3:10; Sirkes, *Responsa*, no. 52.
29. *Avot* 4:5; see Sirkes, *Responsa*, no. 52.
30. *Tashbetz*, 1:147; Karo, *Kesef Mishnah, Talmud Torah* 3:10.
31. *Nedarim* 62a.
32. *Tashbetz*, 1:147.
33. Karo, *Kesef Mishnah, Talmud Torah* 3:10.

Chapter 5

1. Baron, *The Jewish Community*, 2:81.
2. See chaps. 2–3, above.
3. Ben-Sasson, *Hagut Vehanhagah*, 160.
4. See Meir ben Isaac Katzenellenbogen (*Maharam Padua*, 1482–1565), *Responsa*, no. 40 (end), denying claim to past compensation on the suspension fee rationale where claimant had no known secular work in his town and hence his losses could not be proven.

5. Saperstein, *Jewish Preaching*, 48.

6. Etkes, for example, cites the case of a rabbi who went on strike when his salary was suspended for forty weeks, refusing to issue halakhic rulings until payments were resumed ("Institution of the Rabbinate," 117–19). Etkes believes rabbinic strikes for nonpayment of salary were common. See Etkes, *The Gaon of Vilna*, 219. The following anecdote told of a rabbi in the first half of the nineteenth century, Rabbi David of Novaredok, is worth repeating. The rabbi was asked how much he earned, and he replied, "This week three rubles." When his questioner asked why he responded "three rubles *this* week" instead of "three rubles *a* week," the spiritual leader of Novaredok replied, "In a week when they pay I receive three rubles, and in a week when they don't pay I earn nothing" (Etkes, "Institution of the Rabbinate," 117). See also Greg Myre, "Israel: Rabbis Strike," *New York Times*, March 11, 2004, sec. A, p. 8: "Rabbis protesting salary delays went on strike across Israel, threatening to disrupt services varying from marriages to funerals to the ritual slaughter of livestock. The strike involves more than three thousand people, including many rabbis, who work at municipal rabbinates and religious councils. The protesters say the government has failed to pay their salaries for months, and in some cases up to a year."

7. Assaf writes that rabbis in large communities were given more than they wanted, while rabbis in small communities suffered poverty (*Lekorot Harabbanut*, 46, 48). Baron observes that small and insecure salaries were typical but notes that "the smallest rabbinic income . . . compared favorably with the extremely low median income of the masses" (*The Jewish Community*, 81–82, 92).

8. Finkelstein, *Jewish Self-Government*, 354. There is no evidence that the decree was ever implemented prior to the Jews' expulsion from Spain sixty years later (ibid., 103).

9. Bonfil, *Rabbis and Jewish Communities*, 163.

10. Etkes, "Institution of the Rabbinate," 115–16.

11. Etkes, *The Gaon of Vilna*, 217.

12. Schwarzfuchs, *Concise History*, 59.

13. On the activities of Jewish scribes, see Baron, *The Jewish Community*, 110–13.

14. Saperstein, *Jewish Preaching*, 45; see also M. Cohen, *Autobiography*, 103 ("Some young men organized an academy and [study] society, and to fill my pockets, I would teach them each weekday, and on the Sabbath [give them] words of Torah and a sermon. In this way I accumulated more than 260 scudi a year").

15. See chap. 10, below.

16. Etkes, *The Gaon of Vilna*, 226.

17. Maimonides, *Mishneh Torah, Talmud Torah* 1:12.

18. Zemer, *Rabbi Hayyim ben Bezalel*, 11.

19. Baron, *The Jewish Community*, 81.

20. Karo, *Shulhan Arukh, Yoreh De'ah* 243:4 and Rema, *Hoshen Mishpat* 156:5.

21. Etkes, "Institution of the Rabbinate," 120 (citing salt and yeast monopolies).

22. Assaf, *Lekorot Harabbanut*, 33.

23. Karo, *Shulhan Arukh, Yoreh De'ah* 243:2. Asher ben Yehiel limited the tax exemption to scholars who made Torah study their profession, engaging in a secular trade only to meet their subsistence needs. *Rosh, Bava Batra* 7b, point 26.

24. Baron, *The Jewish Community*, 80; see Karo, *Shulhan Arukh, Yoreh De'ah* 243:2.

25. See Baron, *The Jewish Community*, 82–83 (citing also a fee schedule mandating graduated payments for other rabbinic functions such as arranging a divorce, administering an oath to a widow, and delivering a sermon).

26. Kober, "Documents," 45–46. Schwarzfuchs published a useful English translation of the contract (*Concise History*, 20–21). The author labels this the oldest extant rabbinic contract.

27. Ibid., 51–54.

28. Obadiah of Bertinoro, commentary on the Mishnah, *Bekhorot* 4:6.

29. Assaf, *Lekorot Harabbanut*, 47n144.

30. Baron cites the fees paid to rabbis in Hamburg as eight schillings for the examination of each witness and four marks for rendering judgment, payable one-half by each party (*The Jewish Community*, 84). Rabbi Spira's contract provided that each of the parties would give the rabbi one gulden when he presided in court. Rabbi Loeb's contract, which referred to him throughout as "the head of the court" (*av beth din*), provided he would receive forty-five sous from both sides for hearing testimony relating to insults and injuries (Schwarzfuchs, *Concise History*, 20, 51).

31. On the origins and enforcement of this prohibition, see Elon, "Sources and Nature," 524–27.

32. Baron, *The Jewish Community*, 84.

33. Ben-Sasson, *Hagut Vehanhagah*, 186–87.

34. Twersky, *Rabad of Posquières*, 6, 30–33.

35. Ben-Sasson, *Hagut Vehanhagah*, 164–65.

36. Assaf, *Lekorot Harabbanut*, 47.

37. Katz, *Tradition and Crisis*, 176, 334n15; Assaf, *Lekorot Harabbanut*, 46–47.

38. Katz, *Tradition and Crisis*, 135.

39. M. Cohen, *Autobiography*, 5, 43, 102, 133–34, 156–58. Talmudic sages and later rabbinical authorities tended to be less approving of gambling than Modena. Maimonides ruled gambling was a waste of time and a form of robbery prohibited by the sages if not by Scripture (*Mishneh Torah, Robbery and Lost Property* 6:7, 10–11). Judah ben Asher, in his ethical will, admonished his descendants to "play no game for money, for that, too, is a form of robbery" (Abrahams, *Hebrew Ethical Wills*, 2:176).

40. M. Cohen, *Autobiography*, 102, 135, 158.

41. Adelman, "Leon Modena," 44–45.

42. M. Cohen, *Autobiography*, 160–62.

43. Ibid., 41–42.

44. Ibid., 36, 42.

45. Assaf, *Lekorot Harabbanut*, 47.

46. Katz, *Tradition and Crisis*, 74–75. For some students of the rabbinate, the impact of compensation on public perceptions of the rabbinate was not positive. In this vein, Schwarzfuchs writes, "From the moment the rabbinate became professionalized and salaried it lost much of its prestige and could no longer claim leadership of the community" (*Concise History*, 19). This assessment is overblown. Clearly, rabbis who engaged in abuses relating to their compensation discredited themselves, and some notable battles between rabbis competing for the same post impacted quite negatively on the communities involved. Etkes is closer to the mark when he writes, "It is clear that *this competition* affected the status and prestige of the rabbis" ("Institution of the Rabbinate," 121; emphasis added). It was not compensation per se but the manner in which some rabbis sought to obtain it that brought dishonor to some. Further, given its intimate association with Torah scholarship and Jewish law, the traditional rabbinate as a whole could never lose its claim to leadership of the Jewish community, whatever might be the shortcomings of individual rabbis.

47. See chap. 4, above.

48. Etkes, "Institution of the Rabbinate," 111–16.

49. Etkes, *Gaon of Vilna*, 210–16.

50. Goldberg, *Between Berlin and Slobodka*, 32. The sense of the term *kolel perushim* is "collective of those who separate themselves" for study. The term was borrowed from Jewish settlers in Palestine at the time who used the term *kolel* to describe their collective enterprises.

51. See Bomzer, *The Kolel in America*, for more on the history of the institution and a survey of some forty schools in the United States. The author found a mean stipend of $750 per month, which the students supplement with payments for academic work such as tutoring, support from parents, spousal earnings, and state and federal programs. The average stay in a kolel lasts three to five years, and a career as a rabbi, teacher, or social worker is presumed but not required (ibid., 24, 140).

52. See Katz, *Tradition and Crisis*, 74, 94, 99, 305n2, 307n20 (citing eras of intense economic competition among rabbis and their striving for appointment in lucrative divorce cases and litigations).

53. Ibid.

54. Assaf, *Lekorot Harabbanut*, 30. To prevent this, local councils fixed a number of years of study that must pass after a candidate's marriage before he could be ordained.

55. Baron, *The Jewish Community*, 80.

56. Ben-Sasson, *Hagut Vehanhagah*, 162. Local rulers also accepted payments from Jewish communities that wished to purchase the right to appoint their religious leaders without interference from the government (Assaf, *Lekorot Harabbanut*, 34–40).

57. Saperstein, *Jewish Preaching*, 49.

58. Assaf, *Lekorot Harabbanut*, 39.

59. Katz, *Tradition and Crisis*, 74.

60. Assaf, *Lekorot Harabbanut*, 37–38; Schwarzfuchs, *Concise History*, 56–57; Etkes, *Gaon of Vilna*, 224.

61. Schwarzfuchs, *Concise History*, 57; Etkes, "Institution of the Rabbinate," 121; Assaf, *Lekorot Harabbanut*, 54.

62. Schwarzfuchs, *Concise History*, 51.

63. See chap. 3, above.

64. Hershman, *Rabbi Isaac Ben Sheshet Perfet*, 25.

65. Feuchtwanger, *Righteous Lives*, 90–91.

66. Assaf, *Lekorot Harabbanut*, 33, 61.

67. See Goodblatt, *Jewish Life in Turkey*, 68.

68. Etkes, *Gaon of Vilna*, 217.

69. For examples, see Zimmer, *Harmony and Discord*, 123–28. In his study of the Lithuanian rabbinate in the nineteenth century, Etkes found "sharp, and at times, unrestrained, competition over rabbinic offices in general, and over those which were considered prestigious and lucrative in particular" ("Institution of the Rabbinate," 121). For the rivalry between Rabbis Judah Sarfati and Isaac Arama in Salonika in 1541, see chap. 11, below.

70. Etkes, "Institution of the Rabbinate," 121–23.

71. Karo, *Shulhan Arukh, Orah Hayyim* 53:24.

Chapter 6

1. For a discussion of the electoral process as it related to rabbinic appointments, see Katz, *Tradition and Crisis*, 72–74; and Schwarzfuchs, *Concise History*, 69–70.

2. Assaf, *Lekorot Harabbanut*, 27–28; Katz, *Tradition and Crisis*, 73; Schwarzfuchs, *Concise History*, 24, 56.

3. Tama, *Transactions,* 182–83.

4. See, for example, Schwarzfuchs, who cites short-lived attempts by government officials in sixteenth-century Poland, Russia, and Lithuania to influence the choice of rabbis (*Concise History,* 56). For a discussion of the official rabbis appointed by the Holy Roman Emperors in the sixteenth century, see Zemer, "Rabbi Hayyim ben Bezalel," 18–23.

5. Assaf, *Lekorot Harabbanut,* 35–36; Ben-Sasson, *Hagut Vehanhagah,* 161–62.

6. *Sanhedrin* 5b; Maimonides, *Mishneh Torah, Talmud Torah* 5:3; Karo, *Shulhan Arukh, Yoreh De'ah* 242:3; see also Isaac ben Sheshet Perfet (*Rivash*), *Responsa,* no. 271.

7. On the rules governing the student-teacher relationship, see Roth, "Responding to Dissent," 75–84.

8. Isserlein, *Terumat Hadeshen, Pesakim u-Ketavim,* no. 128.

9. Ibid.

10. See chap. 1, above.

11. Weil, *Responsa,* no. 151.

12. Ibid.

13. See below, chap. 10.

14. Marx, "Glimpses," 605, 609.

15. Ibid., 609–14.

16. Meir ben Isaac Katzenellenbogen, *Responsa,* no. 40 (end).

CHAPTER 7

1. Katz, *Tradition and Crisis,* 49, 88.

2. See Rema, *Shulhan Arukh, Hoshen Mishpat* 156:7.

3. Rabinowitz, *The Herem Hayyishub,* 13.

4. Tamari, *With All Your Possessions,* 114.

5. Mordecai ben Hillel, *Sefer Mordecai, Bava Batra,* sec. 519.

6. Rema, *Shulhan Arukh, Hoshen Mishpat* 156:7.

7. Rabinowitz, *The Herem Hayyishub,* 13; see Karo, *Shulhan Arukh, Hoshen Mishpat* 156:7 (end).

8. Rabinowitz, *The Herem Hayyishub,* 10.

9. See Finkelstein, *Jewish Self-Government,* 13–14; on the work of Rabbenu Gershom, see ibid., 20–35.

10. *Bava Batra* 21b.

11. See, for example, *Tosafot, Bava Batra* 21b, s.v. *"Peshita";* and *Rosh, Bava Batra* 21, no. 12.

12. Maimonides, *Mishneh Torah, Laws of Neighbors* 6:8; Karo, *Shulhan Arukh, Hoshen Mishpat* 156:5.

13. Tamari, *With All Your Possessions,* 113.

14. Ibid., 68–76.

15. See Isaac ben Moses of Vienna, *Or Zaru'a,* sec. 146 (quoting letter of Rabbi Moses ben Hasdai Taku, who heard it from Rabbenu Tam); see also Falk, *Sefer Me'irat Einayim, Hoshen Mishpat* 156:7, sec. 26 (citing position of Rabbenu Tam). For a discussion of his position, see Finkelstein, *Jewish Self-Government,* 14.

16. See Baron, who cites for the collapse of the residence ban widespread pogroms in 1648–49 that turned entire Jewish communities into refugees, causing the system of exclusion to break down, and the subsequent Emancipation of the Jews that rendered all forms of internal Jewish communal controls largely ineffective (*The Jewish Community,* 7).

17. Karo, *Shulhan Arukh, Hoshen Mishpat* 156:5–7.

18. See chap. 8.

19. Compare Karo, who discusses the tax exemption of a scholar who trades only to meet his subsistence needs and not to become wealthy, and spends the rest of his time engaged in study (*Shulhan Arukh, Yoreh De'ah* 243:2).

20. Hershman, *Rabbi Isaac ben Sheshet Perfet,* 36.

21. See Schwarzfuchs, who cites examples of tax resisters who objected to the tax exemption for scholars (*Concise History,* 18). Depending on local practice, the tax exemption might be extended to all scholars residing in the community or just some of them. For evidence of the latter practice, see Bonfil, *Rabbis and Jewish Communities,* 80–82, 170 (rabbis were taxed like anyone else unless appointed to a position of communal leadership). See chap. 5, notes 23 and 24, above.

Chapter 8

1. *Bava Batra* 21b.
2. See chap. 1, above.
3. *Bava Batra* 21b–22a.
4. Tamari, *With All Your Possessions,* 117.
5. See chap. 1, above.
6. Maimonides, *Mishneh Torah, Talmud Torah* 2:7.
7. Karo, *Shulhan Arukh, Yoreh De'ah* 245:22.
8. Rema, *Shulhan Arukh, Yoreh De'ah* 245:22 (end).
9. Heb. *ketzat,* lit. "somewhat" or "a little."
10. See, for example, Rema, *Shulhan Arukh, Yoreh De'ah* 245:22 (parenthetical note).
11. Chap. 6, above.
12. See chap. 6, above.
13. Rema, *Shulhan Arukh, Yoreh De'ah* 245:22 (end).
14. Ibid.
15. Mishnah, *Avot* 1:5; see chap. 1, above.
16. See chap. 7, above.
17. Shalom Mordecai Schwadron (*Maharsham*), *Responsa,* part 5, no. 15.
18. The *Shulhan Arukh* of Rabbi Joseph Karo was first published in Venice in 1564–65. An edition that included the glosses of Rabbi Moses Isserles was printed in Cracow in 1580 (Passamaneck, "Towards Sunrise," 339–40).
19. See chap. 5, above.
20. See Breuer, *The Rabbinate in Ashkenaz,* 20–21, noting that the charge of *hasagat gevul,* trespassing against another's economic boundaries, was never leveled by one rabbi against another until they began to receive salaries and fees, and that such accusations were most prevalent during the fifteenth century, when accepting compensation became the norm. On the concept of economic trespass, also known an "descending into the midst of a neighbor's trade" (*yored letokh amanuto shel havero*), see Krauss, "Hasagath Gvul," 5–29.
21. See Schwadron, *Responsa,* part 5, no. 15.

Chapter 9

1. Shabbetai ben Meir Hakohen, "*Siftei Kohen,*" commentary in Karo, *Shulhan Arukh, Yoreh De'ah* 245, sec. 16.
2. Schwadron, *Responsa,* part 5, no. 15.
3. Shabbetai ben Meir Hakohen, "*Siftei Kohen,*" commentary in Karo, *Shulhan Arukh, Yoreh De'ah* 245, sec. 16; Y. Epstein, *Arukh Hashulhan, Yoreh De'ah* 245:28.

4. Hatam Sofer, *Responsa*, vol. 6, *Hoshen Mishpat*, no. 21.

5. On informal versus formal appointment as rabbi, see chap. 6 above.

6. Ibid.

7. Chap. 6, above.

8. Y. Epstein, *Arukh Hashulhan, Yoreh De'ah* 245:28; accord, Tenenbaum, *Divrei Malkhiel*, vol. 4., sec. 82.

9. Y. Epstein, *Arukh Hashulhan, Yoreh De'ah* 245:28.

CHAPTER 10

1. Maimonides, *Mishneh Torah, Talmud Torah* 2:7.

2. Karo, *Shulhan Arukh, Yoreh De'ah* 245:22. Whether the difference in our printed texts is the result of the author's deliberate or unintentional alteration or, indeed, scribal or printing error cannot be stated with certainty. See also Tur Y. D. 245 (end).

3. Some communities exempted schoolteachers from taxes (Assaf, *Lekorot Harabbanut*, 50n167).

4. Marx, "Glimpses," 611–14.

5. See chap. 6, above.

6. M. Cohen, *Autobiography*, 90.

7. Ibid., 214.

8. On the rabbi's duty to supervise elementary instruction in his town, see Assaf, *Lekorot Harabbanut*, 52.

9. For surveys of Jewish education, see Maller, "Role of Education," 1234; and Greenberg, "Jewish Educational Institutions," 1254. On Jewish elementary education, see, for example, Katz, *Tradition and Crisis*, 159–63. For a defense of instruction in the *heder*, see Ginzberg, "The Jewish Primary School," in *Students, Scholars and Saints*, 1–34.

10. The term *heder*, which means "room," was first used in the thirteenth century to denote the room in the synagogue set aside for the instruction of youngsters. It later came to denote the elementary classroom, wherever it was located, most often in the teacher's house (see *Encyclopedia Judaica*, s.v. "Education," 6:381–466). The children of wealthy families were tutored at home.

11. Maimonides, *Mishneh Torah, Talmud Torah* 2:4.

12. Goitein, *Mediterranean Society*, 2:188. Goitein found that competition among school teachers in large cities was keen. He cites the case of one teacher who sought to influence a judge to send orphans to his school rather than a rival's. Ibid., 186–87.

13. Zborowski and Herzog write of the *melamed* in the small rural European hamlet, the shtetl: "The teacher . . . barely manages to live on the meager tuition fees he receives from their parents, so that he and his family are chronically underfed" (*Life Is with People*, 89). For the orphans and children of the truly poor, whose parents could not afford to pay a private teacher, the community ran a free school, the *Talmud Torah*.

14. Maimonides, *Mishneh Torah, Talmud Torah* 2:6 ("A child may be transferred from one teacher to another who is more competent in reading or grammar"); Karo, *Shulhan Arukh, Yoreh De'ah* 245:16 (ibid.).

15. See Zborowski and Herzog, *Life Is with People*, 97.

16. Katz, *Tradition and Crisis*, 161.

17. See chap. 12, below.

18. Schwarzfuchs cites a Lithuanian ordinance that withheld ordination from anyone who had studied less than eleven years after his marriage (*Concise History*, 57). Leon Modena came to

Venice in his early twenties hoping to be ordained. Although he received the preliminary title *haver* soon after his arrival, he was not ordained until just prior to his fortieth birthday (Adelman, "Leon Modena," 22). Setting a high age for ordination served two purposes. It tended to ensure the candidate's qualifications while at the same time restricting the entry of new rabbis into limited markets.

19. Carlton and Weiss's study of the problem is flawed by their mistaken perception that rabbis and schoolteachers were members of the same profession; hence, they believe, when the rabbis opened school teaching to free competition, they acted against self-interest. "It is particularly remarkable," they write, "that the scholars [rabbis]—who were in large part in control of Jewish law—generally chose not to close *their profession* [Torah education—i.e., school teaching] or enact restrictions on entry but instead chose to keep competition thriving in *their profession*" ("Competition in Torah Education," 272; emphasis added); see also ibid., notes 42–43.

A rabbi who engaged in school teaching would quite naturally be subject to the rules that governed schoolteachers. But insofar as their rabbinic practices were concerned, the situation was quite different. With the correct understanding of the rabbinate and school teaching as two separate professions, what becomes remarkable is how the rabbis restricted competition quite severely within their own professional sphere of the rabbinate, while leaving school teaching open to vigorous competition. That Jewish education benefited from this competition is quite possible; still, the rabbis' oxen were (generally) not being gored by it.

20. See chap. 9, above.

Chapter 11

1. On removal for cause, see chap. 12, sec. 2, below.

2. See chap. 5, above.

3. Hatam Sofer, *Responsa, Orah Hayyim* 205–6; Y. Epstein, *Arukh Hashulhan, Yoreh De'ah* 245:28.

4. Chap. 5, above.

5. Hebrew: *mipne darkei shalom*. See Mishnah, *Gittin* 5:8; and Karo, *Beit Yosef, Orah Hayyim* 53 (end) (citing *Rashba*).

6. In his study of medieval Jewish communities, Baron found that where rabbis did not have lifetime tenure, they tended to curry favor with the electors. On the other hand, rabbis who had lifetime tenure tended to become autocratic (Baron, *The Jewish Community,* 2:94). Saperstein notes that where tenure was lacking, for example, in the case of itinerant preachers who were hired for a single speaking engagement, those invited to speak were reluctant to jeopardize their fees by delivering sermons that criticized their hosts (*Jewish Preaching,* 49, 58). Itinerant preachers pandered to their employers and refrained from rebuking the wealthy, instead complimenting them on their righteousness. There were intensifying complaints against preachers that "economic dependence produced moral cowardice" (ibid., 49).

7. When a rabbi obtained his position informally by gaining over time the community's recognition that he was qualified to serve, there was necessarily a probationary period of three or five years before he was deemed to be "established" in his post. See Schwadron, *Responsa,* part 3, no. 73 (citing *Mabit* for the three-year rule and *Rivash* for the five-year rule). On formal versus informal appointment to a rabbinic post, see chap. 6, above.

8. Or even earlier. See Isserles, *Responsa,* no. 50, holding that the community ordinarily cannot rescind its appointment of a rabbi during the period prior to the date on which he takes office and commences service.

9. See chaps. 5 and 6, above.

10. Etkes, "Institution of the Rabbinate," 119. Leon Modena's autobiography was not written for publication. Intended for his students and descendants, it did not appear in print until centuries after his death (M. Cohen, *Autobiography,* xviii, 19, 75). On the paucity of rabbinic autobiography, see, for example, Schacter, "History and Memory," 428–29. Compounding the problem is the fact that some rabbinic autobiographies, like that of Rabbi Moses Hagiz (1671–1751), have been lost in the course of time. See Carlebach, *Pursuit of Heresy,* 3.

11. Zimmer, "R. David b. Isaac of Fulda," 220–23.

12. Tenenbaum, *Divrei Malkhiel* 4:82. See also Feinstein, *Iggerot Moshe, Hoshen Mishpat,* part 1, no. 38. Here members of a congregation broke away from their rabbi to found a synagogue of their own. Their former rabbi protested because their action reduced his income and the value of his synagogue building, which he owned. Rabbi Feinstein held that the breakaway faction (whose reasons for separating he did not regard as legitimate) had impermissibly deprived the rabbi of his livelihood. However, he conceded that if they closed their new synagogue and prayed instead at a service at an established congregation in a distant location, they would no longer be guilty of invading the complaining rabbi's territory, either economic or geographic.

13. *Berakhot* 55a.

14. How the community's consent should be ascertained, whether in a direct fashion or through a representative body like a local board of electors, and who is entitled to participate in the deliberations, are issues that were debated by halakhic authorities and subject to local practices. See Elon, *Principles of Jewish Law,* 645–53.

15. Rashi, *Rosh HaShanah* 2b.

16 *Berakhot* 55a.

17. See, for example, Rabbi Shalom Schwadron, who cites the rule that the community must consent to the rabbi's appointment and holds that even where a board of electors selects a rabbi, the majority of the community must ratify its choice (*Responsa,* vol. 3, no. 73). See also Rabbi Moses Sofer, who faults a rabbi who obtained government authorization but lacked communal consent to his appointment (*Responsa, Hoshen Mishpat,* vol. 6, no. 21).

18. Isserles, Responsa, no. 123.

19. See Goldman, *Life and Times,* 192.

20. *Radbaz, Responsa,* no. 953/518 (1882 ed., 64).

21. *Yoma* 12b.

22. For an explanation for why priests must consent to high priest's appointment, see Solti, "Behirat Rabbanim," 26, 31.

23. For an attempt to deal with the passage from this perspective, see Rabinowitz-Teomin, "Ma'alin Bekodesh," 59–66. He interprets the passage in *Tosafot* as referring to removal for cause only.

Chapter 12

1. On the monarchy, see Deut. 17:20 and the midrashic comment in *Sifre, Piska* 162; on the priesthood, see Lev. 16:32 and the midrashic comments in *Sifra, Tsav,* chap. 5, sec. 2, and *Aharei Mot,* chap. 8, sec. 5.

2. Moses Mitrani, *Responsa,* part 3, no. 200.

3. Ibid.

4. Isaac ben Sheshet Perfet, *Responsa,* no. 271; Rema, *Shulhan Arukh, Yoreh Deah* 245:22; see part 4, below.

5. Moses Mitrani, *Responsa,* part 3, no. 200.

6. Mishnah, *Avot* 4:13; Talmud, *Yoma* 72b; Maimonides, *Mishneh Torah, Talmud Torah* 3:1.

7. See S. Cohen, "Keter," 39, 51.

8. See S. Cohen, describing "exegetical transfer," whereby rabbis removed from their contexts biblical provisions relating to the offices of monarch and high priest and applied them to rabbinic positions (*The Three Crowns*, 237–41).

9. Maimonides, *Mishneh Torah, Temple Vessels* 4:21 ("One was never removed from an office in the midst of Israel unless he acted offensively"); and Benveniste, *Knesset Hagedolah* 53 (ibid.).

10. Maimonides, *Mishneh Torah, Temple Vessels* 4:22 and *Sanhedrin* 17:8.

11. A charge of heresy (*minut*) was leveled against Rabbi Joseph of Arles in the sixteenth century, apparently by a single student who attended his yeshivah. Although he was initially removed from his post as rabbi in Bologna, a rabbinic synod that investigated the matter found the charge unsubstantiated and reinstated him (Marx, "The Removal of Rabbi Josef," 171–84).

12. The official charge against Rabbi Samuel ben Avigdor of Vilna was "not studying the Torah sufficiently," but it seems certain that the communal elders who sought his ouster had other reasons for opposing him, related to communal governance. See Assaf, *Lekorot Harabbanut*, 58; and Fuenn, *Kiri'ah Na'amanah*, 25, 141. The matter remained unresolved at the time of Rabbi Samuel's death.

13. For a brief summary of the controversy, see Margolis and Marx, *History*, 593–94. On Jacob Emden, Eybeschutz's accuser, see Schacter, "History and Memory," 428–52.

14. On Levi Isaac's career, see Dresner, *Levi Yitzhak of Berdichev*, 26–35.

15. Meyer, *Without Wissenschaft*, 11.

16. See, for example, Judah Mintz (*Mahari Mintz*, ca. 1408–1508), *Responsa*, no. 10 (removal of Rabbi Gershon Bonofaso); Joseph ben Solomon Colon (*Maharik*, ca. 1420–1480), *Responsa*, no. 83 (removal of Rabbi Moses Capsali of Istanbul); see also Assaf, "Responsa of R. Azriel Dayyena," 113–19 (removal of Rabbi Benjamin Za'ev).

17. Colon, *Responsa, Shoresh* 83.

18. Karo, *Beit Yosef, Orah Hayyim* 53 (end).

19. Kook, "Hasagat Gevul Berabbanut," 285, 286.

20. Ibid.

21. For a discussion of the concept of holiness in Judaism, see Chief Rabbi Hertz's commentary on this verse in Hertz, *Pentateuch and Haftorahs*, 497.

22. Heb. *ma'alin bekodesh velo moridin*.

23. Maimonides, *Mishneh Torah, Temple Vessels* 4:21.

24. Mishnah, *Menahot* 11:7 (order of removal of Shewbread); Talmud, *Shabbat* 21b (ascending number of Hanukah candles); *Menahot* 39a (order of winding white and blue threads on fringes) and 79a (when blemished animal may not be taken down from the altar).

25. Mishnah, *Yoma* 1:1.

26. Talmud, *Yoma* 12b–13a and *Megillah* 9b.

27. Berakhot 27b–28a.

28. The arguments are surveyed in a rabbinic court case, "*A*" v. *Selection Board of the Ashkenazic Chief Rabbi in City "B*," 11 P.D.R. 97, 109 (5735).

29. Ibid.

30. Tenenbaum, *Divrei Malkhiel*, part 4, no. 82.

31. See chap. 14, sec. 3, below.

32. See, for example, Hatam Sofer, *Responsa, Orah Hayyim* 12 (holding appointment of rabbi, unlike that of king, is a sacred appointment, *minui kedusha*); and Abraham Bornstein (1839–1910),

Avnei Netzer, no. 312, part 34 (disagreeing with Hatam Sofer as to king but not as to rabbi and holding both are sacred appointments).

Chapter 13

1. Leiter, *"Worthiness, Acclamation, Appointment,"* 156 ("This is the paradox of appointment: When one attains office he is endowed with the necessary qualities. His deficiencies are made up by his induction").

2. *Midrash Tanhuma, Emor* 4; on this and the following *midrashim,* see Leiter, *"Worthiness, Acclamation, Appointment,"* 155–57.

3. *Yalkut Shimoni, Ps.* 45:3.

4. *Bava Qamma* 66b.

5. Rema, *Shulhan Arukh, Yoreh De'ah* 245:22.

6. See Moses Mitrani, *Responsa,* part 3, no. 200 (denying request of some community members to replace their rabbi who had served nineteen years with a person who, they claimed, was better qualified than the incumbent), discussed in chap. 15 below.

7. See, for example, Nathanson, *Shoel U-Masheev,* part 2, no. 17 (stating Heaven will assist heir who inherits his post to acquire knowledge and achieve a level comparable to his father's); and Vais, *Rabanut Ukehila Bemishnat Maran Hahatam Sofer,* 47 (citing Rabbi Moses Sofer for the view that it would be impossible for any rabbi to conduct even the smallest community's affairs without divine help).

8. Rema, *Shulhan Arukh, Yoreh De'ah* 245:22.

9. Joseph ben Meir Halevi ibn Migas, *Responsa,* no. 114.

10. Ibid.

11. Isaac ben Sheshet Perfet, *Responsa,* no. 271; Amarillo, *Sefer D'var Moshe, Orah Hayyim, Hilkhot Shatz,* sec. 1.

12. Isaac ben Moses of Vienna, *Or Zaru'a,* no. 113 (stating impoverished Jewish communities in Central Europe have to accept whatever intelligent person they can find to serve as cantor, teacher, and preacher); see chap. 3, above.

13. See Rosensweig, "Emergence of Professional Rabbinate," 22, 28.

14. Katz, *Tradition and Crisis,* 198, 500n52 (citing Rabbi Sheftel Horowitz, who praised the rabbis of Poland who excommunicated those who purchased a rabbinic office).

15. Assaf, *Lekorot Harabbanut,* 28. In the aftermath of the Black Death, the Church confronted similar problems, having suffered significant losses in the ranks of the clergy, and it responded by ordaining the minimally qualified. See Tuchman, *A Distant Mirror,* 118 ("To fill vacant benefices the Church ordained priests in batches. . . . Many were barely literate, 'as it were mere lay folk' who might read a little but without understanding"). On the uprisings against the Jews, see ibid., 112–16.

16. Abramsky, "Crisis of Authority," 15.

17. David ben Hayyim Hakohen of Corfu, *Responsa,* no. 22, sec. 11.

18. *Berakhot* 63a.

19. See chap. 12, sec. 3, above.

20. David ben Hayyim Hakohen of Corfu, *Responsa,* no. 22, sec. 11.

21. Ibid.

Chapter 14

1. See Elon, *Principles of Jewish Law,* 91–110.

2. See ibid., 107–9.

3. Katz, *Tradition and Crisis*, 92, 173.

4. Agus believes that high levels of education and lifelong devotion to study greatly multiplied the number of the erudite in pre-Crusade Ashkenazic communities, obviating the need for a professionalized rabbinate (*Heroic Age,* 259). Although Agus may exaggerate the extent of Torah scholarship in the general Jewish population, his point, that communities typically contained more than one person learned enough to exercise spiritual leadership, is plausible. See, for example, Baer, who writes of "the justified assumption that the majority of the community [in tenth- and eleventh-century Ashkenazic Jewry] were learned men; where reality did not match this ideal, it was understood that the 'small obey the great'" ("Origins of Jewish Communal Organization," 59, 76).

5. Assaf, *Lekorot Harabbanut,* 29.

6. For the arguments for and against rotation in office in relation to nonrabbinic posts, see Ben-Sasson, *Hagut Vehanhagah,* 245–47.

7. Karo, *Shulhan Arukh, Orah Hayyim* 53:26; and Karo, *Beit Yosef, Orah Hayim* 53 (end) (citing *Rashba*).

8. Rema, *Shulhan Aruhh, Yoreh Deah* 245:22 (end).

9. Assaf, *Lekorot Harabbanut,* 57–58.

10. Yom Tov ben Abraham Ishbili, *Hidushei Ha-Ritva, Maccot* 13a (removal for cause is the sole basis for removal only in the case of a contract in which no fixed term of appointment is prescribed); Benveniste, *Knesset Hagedolah* 53 (community can remove rabbi either for cause or at end of term fixed in his contract of appointment); see also Hazan, *Hekrei Lev, Orah Hayyim,* part 1, no. 18 (congregation may appoint temporary cantor for fixed term and remove at end of term with no violation of holiness principle).

11. See chap. 12, sec. 3, above.

12. See ibid. Rabbi Rabinowitz-Teomin argues that one cannot reason from the case of the substitute high priest or president (*nasi*) of the Sanhedrin that removal of a rabbi at the end of a fixed term will violate the holiness principle. The offices of high priest and president are unique. Once the incumbent is removed, he cannot obtain a similar post of equivalent sacred status anywhere else. By contrast, a rabbi appointed for a limited term and removed at its expiration can secure another post as rabbi in another location with no loss of sacred status. Thus for purposes of applying the holiness principle, the cases of high priest and president of the Sanhedrin, on the one hand, and rabbi, on the other, are not analogous (Rabinowitz-Teomin, "*Ma'alin Bekodesh,*" 63).

13. Rema, *Shulhan Arukh, Hoshen Mishpat* 333:3 (three years); Hatam Sofer, *Responsa, Orah Hayim,* no. 205 (six years).

14. See Exod. 21:2–11; and Deut. 15:12–18.

15. Based on Lev. 25:55, "For unto Me the children of Israel are servants; they are My servants whom I brought forth out of the land of Egypt"; see *Bava Metzi'a* 10a ("They are My servants but not servants to servants").

16. Based on Deut. 15:18 ("The double of a hire of a hireling hath he served thee six years"); and Isa. 16:14 ("Within three years, as the years of a hireling").

17. Karo, *Shulhan Arukh, Hoshen Mishpat* 333:3 and *Shakh,* ad loc.

18. Hatam Sofer, *Responsa, Orah Hayyim* 205–6.

19. For example, *Horayot* 10a ("If you believe I am endowing you with leadership, I am endowing you with slavery").

20. Rashi, *Horayot* 10a.

21. Hatam Sofer, *Responsa, Orah Hayyim* 206.

22. Rabinowitz-Teomin, *"Ma'alin Bekodesh,"* 64; see part 4, below.

23. Katz, *Tradition and Crisis,* 292n43.

24. Y. Epstein, *Arukh Hashulhan, Yoreh De'ah* 245:28; see also Israel Meir Hakohen Kagan of Radin, *Mishnah Berurah* 53:86 ("In our day [when] it is not the manner to remove [at the expiration of a contract] without suspicion [of wrongdoing] then certainly we should not dismiss for no reason at all in order not to create suspicion"); and Feinstein, *Iggerot Moshe, Hoshen Mishpat,* part 2, no. 34 (holding that a fixed term in a rabbinic contract "is nothing, and in the 40-plus years I have been in America it has never happened that the directors [of a synagogue] should of their own accord remove the rabbi").

25. See chap. 12, sec. 3, above.

26. See Mishnah, *Sheqalim* 5:2 ("We do not establish authority over the community in relation to money with less than two"); and Nariyah, *"Serrarah al Ha-Tzibur,"* 128–29 (interpreting the Mishnah in broader terms by dropping the phrase "in relation to money" [*bemamon*] from his quotation of the Mishnah).

27. Moses Mitrani, *Responsa,* part 3, no. 200; but see Abraham ben Mordecai Halevi, *Ginat Veradim* 3:8 (where rabbi established himself in his post and never received the formal appointment of the community, then after his death, community can join another rabbi to his heir).

28. Tenebaum, *Divre Malkhiel,* 4:82.

29. Ibid.

30. Benveniste, *Knesset Hagedolah* 53 (in the name of the *Ralnah*).

31. Karo, *Shulhan Arukh, Orah Hayyim* 53:25.

32. Rabbi Moses Sofer strained to read this result into a ruling by the Rema that is worded more broadly. Where the Rema writes, "And in a place where it is the custom to accept a rabbi for a fixed term . . . they have authority to do so" (*Shulhan Arukh, Yoreh Deah* 245:22 [end]), Sofer suggests he never meant to endorse fixed-term contracts in general but only the ancient custom of rotation in office in a community where there are many individuals who are qualified to hold office (Hatam Sofer, *Responsa, Orah Hayyim* 206).

33. Karo, *Shulhan Arukh, Orah Hayyim* 53:26.

34. See Baron, *The Jewish Community,* 88 (permanency of tenure became unwritten law); see also Bleich, *Contemporary Halakhic Problems,* 2:193 ("Under existing practice, a rabbi cannot be dismissed through failure to renew his contract").

CHAPTER 15

1. On removal for cause, see chap. 12, sec. 2, above.

2. Isaac ben Sheshet Perfet, *Responsa,* no. 271.

3. Finkelstein, *Jewish Self-Government,* 60.

4. Zeitlin, "Opposition to Spiritual Leaders," 287, 294. Later Ashkenazic authorities endorsed government appointment of rabbis based in part on the Sephardic precedents and in part on the biblical model of Ezra and Nehemiah, appointed by the Persian monarch Cyrus to their religious offices in Judea (Isserles, *Responsa,* no. 123). The Rema incorporated his conclusion in this regard in the *Shulhan Arukh,* stating the rule in a fashion that contains a veiled reference to Meir Halevi's action in France: "But as to anyone whom the congregation has accepted over them [as their rabbi], and all the more so where they acted with the consent of the government, no great personage has the authority to prevail against him and remove him from office" (Rema, *Shulhan Arukh, Yoreh De'ah* 245:22 [end]). But a rabbi who receives a government appointment and serves without also obtaining the community's consent "in the end will be destined to answer

in Judgment" (Isserles, *Responsa,* no. 123; see also Hatam Sofer, *Responsa, Hoshen Mishpat,* vol. 6, no. 21 (faulting rabbi who obtained authorization from the government but lacked consent of community to his appointment and displaced qualified heir of former rabbi).

5. Rivash, *Responsa,* no. 271.
6. Graetz, *History of the Jews,* 4:153.
7. Elijah ben Hayyim (*Ranah*), *Responsa,* no. 98.
8. Ibid.
9. See, for example, Medini, *Sedei Hemed, Hazakah be-Mitzvot* 7:61. That one may relinquish a sacred position cannot be regarded as self-evident under the holiness principle. Renunciation, as a voluntary reduction in sacred status, would seem to be precluded for the same reason dismissal from a post is forbidden—"We elevate in matters of sanctity, but we do not decrease." Why should this maxim apply to the congregation but not the officeholder himself? Now it is true that a scholar may disclaim the honors due to him as such (Maimonides, *Mishneh Torah, Talmud Torah* 5:11). The Ranah cites this principle in support of permitting a rabbi to renounce his office, characterizing a congregation's obligation to its rabbi as essentially the duty to honor him as a scholar, which he may renounce. But the scholar who renounces the *honors* due to him remains a *scholar,* having given up only some of the perquisites of his position. By contrast, a rabbi who renounces his post demotes himself, stripping away his status as an officeholder. Hence, a problem arises under the holiness principle. The answer may lie in the Ranah's reference to the Hebrew slave who can be freed by the oral declaration of his masters in front of witnesses. If a rabbi could not renounce his post, he would be no better than a Hebrew slave, obligated to serve out his term until his "masters" release him. To prevent this, we permit a rabbi to relinquish his post, although such action is not entirely consistent with the holiness principle. Interestingly, a king, once he ascends the throne, may not abdicate. See Aaron Halevi, *Sefer Hahinukh,* no. 497 (citing *Kedushin* 32b).
10. Moses Mitrani, *Responsa,* part 3, no. 200.
11. Ibid. On tenure versus merit, see chap. 13, above.
12. Algazi, *Simhat Yom Tov,* no. 6.
13. Tenenbaum, *Divrei Malkhhiel,* 4:82.
14. Ibid.

Chapter 16

1. *Midrash Rabbah: Leviticus* (*Achare Mot*) subdivision 20, sec. 10 (Israelstam trans., 260–61).
2. As used in this connection, the term "Judge" (*shofet*) has a broad connotation akin to "ruler" or "governor." After the Israelites established a monarchy and governmental roles became specialized under a central royal administration, the term acquired a narrower sense relating specifically to the administration of justice. See Whitelam, *The Just King,* 52, 59.
3. Bornstein, *Avnei Netzer, Yoreh De'ah,* no. 312, sec. 52. By contrast, in his introduction to the book of Judges, Isaac Abrabanel states his belief that there was no break in continuity between the Judges (*Perush al Hatorah*).
4. Abrabanel, *Perush al Hatorah,* introduction to the book of Judges. According to Moses ben Joseph Schick (*Maharam Shik*), upon appointment a Judge agreed specifically to a proviso that his son would not inherit the post although Torah law would have allowed the inheritance. The Judge relinquished the right out of respect for Moses, whose sons had not inherited leadership from him (Schick, *Responsa, Yoreh De'ah,* no. 228).
5. Aaron Halevi, *Sefer Hahinukh,* no. 526.

6. Abraham ben Mordecai Halevi, *Ginat Veradim, Yoreh De'ah* 3:8.
7. *Sifra, Tsav,* chap. 5, sec. 1; and *Yoma* 72b–73a.
8. Maimonides, *Mishneh Torah, Yesodai Ha-Torah* 7:1–5.
9. Maimonides, *Mishneh Torah, Sanhedrin* 2:7 (Hershman trans., 8).
10. Ibid., 2:1.
11. Ibid., 2:6.
12. See Obadiah of Bertinoro, commentary on the Mishnah, *Sanhedrin* 4:4, s.v. *"hutzrehu lismokh."*
13. Mishnah, *Sanhedrin* 4:4; see also Maimonides, *Mishneh Torah, Sanhedrin* 1:7–8.
14. The verses are Deut. 17:20 regarding the king—see *Sifre, Piska* 162 and *Horayot* 11b; Lev. 6:15 and 16:32 regarding the high priest—see *Sifra, Tsav,* chap. 5, par. 2, and *Aharei Mot,* chap. 8, par. 5; and Exod. 29:30 regarding the priest anointed for war—see *Sifra, Tsav,* chap. 5, par. 1, and *Yoma* 73a.
15. See the discussion infra, chap. 19.
16. See Abravanel, *Perush al Hatorah,* introduction to the book of Judges.
17. Hatam Sofer, *Responsa, Orah Hayyim,* no. 12 (holding appointment of a rabbi, unlike that of a king, is a sacred appointment, *minui shel kedusha*), and Bornstein, *Avnei Netzer,* no. 312, sec. 34 (disagreeing with Hatam Sofer as to king but not as to rabbi and holding both are sacred appointments).
18. Hatam Sofer, *Responsa, Orah Hayyim,* no. 13; Bornstein, *Avnei Netzer, Yoreh De'ah,* no. 312, secs. 51–55 ("Rabbis today have the law of a king").
19. Abraham ben Mordecai Halevi, *Ginat Veradim, Yoreh De'ah* 3:8 (citing *Rashba, Kol Bo,* and *Beit Yosef*).
20. See the responsum of Rabbi Saul ben Rabbi Heschel involving application of a *takkanah* that imposed stricter requirements on rabbinic appointees from outside the community whose impartiality as judges vis-à-vis their relatives in the town could not be known. The responsum was published by Asher Ziv in his edition of the Rema's responsa. See Isserles, *She'elot Uteshuvot Harema,* 518–19.
21. See Elijah ben Hayyim (*Ranah*), *Responsa,* no. 98, stating community would never have appointed an outsider as its rabbi if it had known that the incumbent's son, who was familiar with the community and its affairs, was qualified to succeed his father.
22. On the development of the important yeshivahs and the way their leaders challenged the halakhic authority of the local rabbinate, see Freedman, "Fundamental Problems," 140–42.
23. See, for example, Goitein, *A Mediterranean Society,* 2:91.
24. See Katz, *Tradition and Crisis,* 129.
25. Bacharach, *Responsa,* introduction to *Kelalei Etz Hahayyim,* printed in the 1834 edition following no. 238; see Hoenig, "Filial Succession," 21.
26. Samuel ben Moses De Medina (*Maharashdam*), *Responsa, Yoreh De'ah,* no. 85.

CHAPTER 17

1. See Lev. 10:1–2 and 16:1.
2. Num. 20:22–29.
3. Num. 27:15–23.
4. *Midrash Rabbah, Exodus (Shemoth),* subdivision 2, sec. 6 (Lehrman trans., 57); see also *Zevahim* 102a.
5. *Midrash Rabbah, Numbers (Pinchas),* subdivision 21, sec. 14 (Slotki trans., 840–41).
6. *Yalkut Shimoni, Mishlei* 21:20.

7. *Rashi* on Num. 27:16, referring to Exod. 33:11: "And the Lord spoke unto Moses face to face, as a man speaks unto his friend. And he would return into the camp; but his minister Joshua, the son of Nun, a young man, departed not out of the Tent."

8. *Midrash Rabbah, Numbers (Pinchas)*, subdivision 21, sec. 14 (Slotki trans., 841); Heiman, *Yalkut Shimoni Al Hatorah, Sefer Be-Midbar, Pinchas*, 546. For an attempt to interpret the midrashic passages in relation to social and political trends of their time, see Beer, "Hereditary Principle," 149–57.

9. Hatam Sofer, *Responsa, Orah Hayyim*, vol. 1, no. 12.

10. Ibid.

11. Tenenbaum, *Divrei Malkhiel*, part 4, no. 82; Bornstein, *Avnei Netzer, Yoreh De'ah*, no. 312:40–42.

12. *Sifre, Piska* 162 (Hammer trans., 194–95).

13. See chap. 16, above.

14. See Reiss, "*B'inyan Yerushat Hezkat Rabanut*," 10–11.

15. Hatam Sofer, *Responsa, Orah Hayyim*, no. 13 (citing *Magen Avraham, Orah Hayyim*, sec. 53, par. 25).

16. In rabbinic literature, two verses are cited for inheritance of the priesthood, Lev. 6:15 and Lev. 16:32.

17. Ibid. In a later responsum, the Hatam Sofer concluded that in the modern era, rabbinic posts should pass by inheritance to qualified heirs. See chap. 19, below.

18. *Tosefta, Sheqalim* 2:15.

19. *Ketubbot* 103b.

20. Ibid.

21. Hatam Sofer, *Responsa, Orah Hayyim*, no. 12 (stating view that inheritance in the case of the *nasi* should be considered an aspect of *keter malkhut*, the royal crown, rather than *keter Torah*, the Torah crown); see also Gumbiner, *Magen Avraham, Orah Hayyim* 53:25 (stating view that inheritance did not apply to *keter Torah* as a matter of law but, after Hillel, only as a matter of custom).

22. *Ketubbot* 62b (Rabbi Judah Hanasi was a descendant of one of David's sons).

23. See Mishnah, *Hagigah* 2:2. By contrast, according to the Maharam Shik, the basic norm is reflected in the practice *after* Hillel when the post of nasi was inherited (*Responsa, Yoreh De'ah*, no. 228). The rule of inheritance was suspended prior to that time, perhaps out of respect for Moses, whose sons did not inherit. In his view, in the generations immediately following the death of Moses, the appointment of the biblical Judges was made subject to an express proviso that their sons would not inherit when their terms expired.

24. Deut. 17:20.

25. *Horayot* 11b, *Keritot* 5b.

26. Hazan, *Hekrei Lev, Orah Hayyim*, part 1, no. 15.

27. See Hoenig, "Filial Succession," 15, citing Solomon ben Yeruham.

28. *Nedarim* 81a.

29. *Bava Metzi'a* 85a ("R. Parnakh said in the name of Rabbi Johanan: One who is a sage whose son is a sage and whose grandson is a sage—the Torah will not cease from his descendants forever," citing Isa. 59:21 as a prooftext).

30. *Avot* 2:12.

31. Deut. 33:4. The Hebrew *morashah* may be translated as "inheritance," "heritage," or "possession." This biblical verse is the first verse a father is instructed to teach his child (Maimonides, *Mishneh Torah, Talmud Torah* 1:6).

32. Alon, *Jews, Judaism*, 436–57; see also Baumgarten, "The Politics of Reconciliation," 213, and S. Cohen, *The Three Crowns*, 240–43.

33. Rashi, *Gittin* 60b.

34. Tenenbaum noted that Rav Yehuda, Rabbah, and Abaye left sons who were scholars but did not become *roshei yeshiva* (*Divrei Malkhiel*, part 4, no. 82).

35. Strack lists as Rav Ashi's immediate successors as principal of the Suran academy Meremar (417–32 C.E.), R. Idi bar Abin II (432–52 C.E.), and Rab Nahman bar Rab Huna (452–55 C.E.), followed by Mar, the son of Rav Ashi, who served ca. 455–68 C.E. (Strack, *Introduction*, 133).

36. *Yoma* 72b; see also Mishnah, *Avot* 4:4; Goldin, *The Fathers according to Rabbi Nathan*, chap. 41; *Midrash Tanhuma, Parshat Va-Yakhel*, sec. 8; Maimonides, *Mishneh Torah, Talmud Torah* 3:1.

37. For example, Isserlein, *Terumat Hadeshen, Pesakim Uketavim*, sec. 128.

38. Tenenbaum interprets the passage as an invitation to study; since appointment to office requires the community's consent, it would be inappropriate to say of communal office, "Let anyone who wishes come and take it" (*Divrei Malkhiel*, part 4, no. 82).

39. *Midrash Tanhuma, Parshat Va-Yakhel*, sec. 8.

40. Isserlein, *Terumat Hadeshen, Pesakim Uketavim*, sec. 128 (emphasis added).

Chapter 18

1. Grant, *Jews in the Roman World*, 287.

2. Grossman, "From Father to Son," 196. Historical sources regarding the geonim in Eretz Israel during this period are incomplete. Most date from the ninth century and later. For a survey of the evidence concerning the academy in Eretz Israel, its location and its activities, see Brody, *The Geonim*, 102–11. He notes that the surviving letters of the geonim of Eretz Israel concern mostly administrative matters, while those of the Babylonian geonim focus primarily on religious questions, suggesting the greater involvement of the former in matters of temporal governance (*keter malkhut*) (ibid., 105).

3. Grossman, "From Father to Son," 191–92, 196–97.

4. Ibid., 192n6.

5. *Berakhot* 55a.

6. The tenth-century chronicler Nathan Habavli mentions the division of Babylonia and nearby countries into three parishes. See Ginzberg, *Geonica*, 2:14. Baron says the date of the division is unknown (*The Jewish Community*, 1:180). Grossman places it after 825 C.E. ("From Father To Son," 197). On the geographical boundaries of the three parishes, see Brody, *The Geonim*, 59–60, 123–28, 339–40. In his view, only the exilarchate was recognized by the caliph's government. Hence the division into three parishes represents an internal Jewish redistribution of power, reflecting the growing prominence of the geonim at the expense of the exilarch. The territory covered by the *reshuyot* was never extended beyond Babylonia to include all the lands of the Arab conquest, leaving those lands free to choose their allegiances and suggesting the division may have had its origins in the Sasanian period (ibid., 340).

7. The incident is related in the medieval historical chronicle *Seder Olam Zuta* (The Smaller Order of the World) (Neubauer, *Medieval Jewish Chronicles*, 2:68–88).

8 *Sanhedrin* 5a.

9. Baron writes: "The caliph's choice was clearly restricted to the immediate relatives of the deceased or deposed exilarch and, except for periods of inner dissension, it followed the usual hereditary succession" (*The Jewish Community*, 1:173).

10. See Bashan, who writes: "Although the position of exilarch was hereditary, it was not always the firstborn who was chosen, but rather the member of the family who was most suitable and accepted by the academy heads and the important merchants who wielded influence in the court of the caliph" ("Exilarch," 1027).

11. In a nice symmetry, the exilarch, like the geonim, maintained an academy and a court, but his activities in these venues were secondary to his temporal functions as an official in the caliph's administration (Brody, *The Geonim,* 72–74).

12. Ginzberg, *Geonica,* 14.

13. Grossman, "From Father to Son," 192, 196; see also Grossman, "Social Structure," 1–20. Grossman holds the gaon's post began to pass by inheritance in the middle of the ninth century when the *resh galuta*'s power declined and the geonim acquired some temporal authority. The order of succession was an intricate one in which a son acquired the post eventually but not immediately upon his father's death. The heir's qualifications for office (many were unqualified) did not affect the succession, a factor that for Grossman marks the practice as inheritance ("From Father to Son," 193). This conclusion seems off the mark since Jewish law requires that the heir be fit to serve in order to inherit an office. If the heir is unqualified, his right to inherit is canceled. See, for example, Maimonides, *Mishneh Torah,* Kings and Wars 1:7, and the discussion in chap. 19, below.

14. The number ninety is taken from "Chronological List of the Geonim of Sura and Pumbedita," prepared by Simha Assaf and Joshua Berend for the *Encyclopedia Hebraica,* 10:135–36. In their synchronistic list, A. Eckstein and W. Bacher name eighty-seven incumbents with dates that differ in some respects (*The Jewish Encyclopedia,* 5:571). Brody prepared a chronological list of ninety-three individuals, fifty as Pumbeditha's gaon and forty-three as Sura's gaon, including individuals who served for one month or half a year, others whose appointments were disputed and headed splinter academies, and one exilarch who also served as gaon (Brody, *The Geonim,* 344–45).

As these variations indicate, the details of geonic history are not well established. The primary source is a tract by the late-tenth-century gaon of Pumbeditha, Rav Sherira (*Iggeret Le-Rav Sherira Gaon,* ca. 986). Neubauer published two recensions of the work (*Medieval Jewish Chronicles,* 1:3–46). Sherira refers to all the principals of Sura and Pumbeditha after the Arab conquest as geonim, although it seems that the title was first applied to Sura's principal in the seventh century and to Pumbeditha's principal in the ninth century. The older term was *rosh yeshivah* (Hebrew) or *resh metivta* (Aramaic). For a survey of the historiography of the geonic period, see G. Cohen, "Reconstruction." Traditionally, the geonic period is said to have ended in 1040 with the deposition of Hezekiah ben David, who served as both gaon and exilarch. The title "gaon" continued to be used by prominent Jewish scholars in Baghdad, Damascus, and Egypt for centuries, but henceforth the holders of the title were local communal authorities rather than leaders of world Jewry. See Assaf and Berend, "*Gaon, Geonim*"; Baron, *The Jewish Community,* 1:184; see also Goode, "Exilarchate." The last known exilarch was Samuel ben David, ca. 1240–70.

15. Assaf and Berend, "*Gaon, Geonim,*" 133 (six or seven families); Ben-Sasson, *History,* 424 (six families); Brody, *The Geonim,* xx ("a small number of families").

16. Ginzberg, *Geonica,* 11.

17. Ibid., 43.

18. Dosa, the son of Rav Saadiah Gaon (d. 942), became gaon of Sura in 1013, seventy-one years after his father's death. According to some reckonings, he was eighty-three years old at the

time. Part of the delay in his elevation may have been caused by the fact that the Suran academy closed for forty-five years shortly after Saadiah's death. Dosa served as gaon for four years.

19. Assaf and Berend, "*Gaon, Geonim,*" 135.

20. Grossman, "From Father to Son," 201.

21. Ibid., 201–4.

22. For a description of the posts, see Brody, *The Geonim*, 48–50.

23. Compare Goitein, who writes: "Scions of a number of gaonic families would accede to the office after having served for many years in other capacities" (*A Mediterranean Society*, 2:14).

24. Ginzberg, *Geonica*, 11.

25. See Brody, *The Geonim*, 50. According to Goitein, the geonim groomed their sons for succession by using their services as scribes of the academy to formulate responsa and countersign official correspondence, thus making them known to important personages and demonstrating their value to the institution (*A Mediterranean Society*, 2:15).

26. Contra, Brody, *The Geonim*, 50–51: "It would appear that appointments below the rank of Av Beth Din were made at the discretion of the Gaon." For support he mentions a passage from the account of Nathan the Babylonian that mentions four factors that played a role in appointments—lineage, knowledge, the gaon's prerogative, and the availability of stipends to mollify candidates who were disappointed. By what equation these factors were weighed and by whom is not set forth. Nathan mentions the gaon's prerogative to appoint in connection with one particularly difficult case, where the heir apparent and another candidate were closely matched in intellect. Here, Nathan writes, "it is the prerogative of the head of the academy to appoint as head of the row whom he pleases" (Brody, *The Geonim*, 51). In these difficult, vexing cases, where opinions would naturally be divided, perhaps the gaon served as final arbiter or tiebreaker. But it would be too broad a reading of Nathan's account to assert that *in general* appointments were at the gaon's discretion.

27. Brody argues persuasively that the geonim did not and could not run their academies in an authoritarian manner. They had few sanctions to deploy against resisting scholars, other than an adjustment of stipend, and no mechanism to expel anyone. Indeed, they were fearful of a mass exodus of scholars who might transfer to the sister school or open a rival one (Brody, *The Geonim*, 147–49). We may add another factor, the gaon's certain knowledge that treating others peremptorily would create a reservoir of ill will that might, after he left the scene, haunt his heirs. The defining activity at the academies was consultation among the scholars, even on halakhic rulings that ultimately would issue in the gaon's name alone. We may extrapolate from all this that appointments were decided in a similarly collegial fashion.

28. Compare Graetz: "Next to the president [gaon] came the chief judge [av beth din], who discharged the judicial duties and was, as a rule, his successor in office" (*History of the Jews*, 3:96–97).

29. Almost no information concerning how the av beth din was selected has come down to us (see Brody, *The Geonim*, 51). From this fact it is tempting to infer that the deliberations were a sensitive and highly private matter, taking place behind closed doors, so to speak, and leaving no trace in the documentary evidence. They would not have been revealed to or discussed with an outsider like Nathan the Babylonian.

30. Goitein, *A Mediterranean Society*, 2:14.

31. Brody, *The Geonim*, 52–53.

32. According to Goitein, many successions were hotly contested, and sometimes lay leaders or the community at large tipped the balance in favor of the winning candidate (*A Mediterranean Society*, 2:15–16).

33. For an interesting account of the countergeonim, see Bacher, "*Gaon,*" 569. On one occasion, when Joseph ben Hiyya and Abraham ben Sherira were both serving as gaon of Pumbeditha, the former thought better of the arrangement and voluntarily resigned, resuming the post of av beth din.

34. Goitein, *A Mediterranean Society,* 2:15.

35. Rav Sherira Gaon put it this way, discussing Saadiah's lineage in his famous letter: "He was not from the sons of the Rabbis of the Mesivta [academy], but was from Egypt, and was known as [al-]Fayumi" (Rabinowich, *Iggeres of Rav Sherira Gaon,* 150).

36. On Saadiah's early years, see Malter, *Saadia Gaon,* 33–59.

37. For an account of the calendar controversy, see ibid., 69–87; see also Katz, *Divine Law,* 132–36.

38. See Baron, citing communities in Syria and Egypt where some Jews observed Palestinian rites and others followed Babylonian rites (*The Jewish Community,* 1:167).

39. An account of the controversy is related in *Seder Olam Zuta* (Neubauer, *Medieval Jewish Chronicles,* 2:80).

40. Saadiah Gaon, *Sefer Hayerushot* (Muller ed.).

41. When Ginzberg labels the succession to be gaon as "quasi-hereditary" and Grossman describes it as inheritance "with a notable degree of flexibility" in the order of inheritance, their qualified descriptions gloss over the fundamental differences between inheritance of office, on the one hand, and the pattern of succession in effect among the Babylonian geonim, on the other. The differences are more pronounced than the similarities. Graetz was closer to the mark when he wrote, "The members of the college generally bequeathed their offices to their sons, but the office of president [gaon] was not hereditary" (*History of the Jews,* 3:97). Even this statement may overstate the role of inheritance in filling the lower positions.

42. The interlude between father and son in the case of the geonim differed from the gap in time that sometimes occurs in the Torah's order of inheritance when the heir to office is a minor at his father's death. Then the heir's elevation is deferred until he reaches majority (bar mitzvah, age thirteen). Thus Maimonides ruled regarding monarchy: "If he left a son who is a minor, the kingdom is held for him until he grows up, as Jehoiada acted in the case of Joash" (*Mishneh Torah,* Kings and Wars 1:7 [A. Hershman trans., 208]). By contrast, among the geonim the interregnum did not end when the heir reached majority. For example, Saadiah's son Dosa was a minor when his father died in 942, either seven years old (if Dosa was born in 935) or twelve years old (if he was born in 930). He waited seven decades after his father's death to become gaon in 1013. In the interim three individuals from other families occupied the post.

43. *Tosefta, Sheqalim* 2:15.

44. *Sifre, Piska* 162.

45. See chap. 17, above.

46 Maimonides, *Mishneh Torah,* Kings and Wars 1:8–9.

CHAPTER 19

1. Pearl, *Rashi,* 9.
2. Baron, *The Jewish Community,* 2:23, 106–8.
3. Isaac ben Moses of Vienna, *Or Zaru'a,* no. 115.
4. Grossman, "From Father to Son," 204–16.
5. Ibid., 204–17.
6. Ibid., 216.
7. See chap. 18, above.

8. Grosssman, "From Father to Son," 208–9, 211, 213.

9. Ibid., 216.

10. Ibid.

11. See chap. 17, above.

12. Ibid., 219–20. Grossman suggests that accounts of opposition to the leading families might have been suppressed by the scholars who wrote the works that have come down to us, since they were the progeny of the leading families.

13. Saperstein publishes a passage he attributes to Rabbi Isaac ben Yedaiah (southern France, 13th c.) that contains a critique of the practice of sons inheriting their fathers' positions when they are not qualified for office ("Earliest Commentary," 283). Grossman reads the critique as applying to inheritance of spiritual as well as communal leadership ("From Father to Son," 219n93). However, it is not clear that the writer was aiming at spiritual leadership. The titles that concern him are *nasi* and *nagid,* which can denote temporal as well as spiritual governance. Nor does he object to inheritance of office per se; he objects to behaving like the Gentile nations and installing the heir *regardless of his fitness for the post.* Saperstein describes the contents of the passage as "an excoriation of those who use the title *nasi* for men unworthy of honor or responsibility, whose only claim is that their father or grandfather bore the title before them. . . . Our passage attacks the entrenched leadership structure of many Jewish communities through a reasoned critique of hereditary transfer of official positions, and particularly the title *nasi*" ("Earliest Commentary," 283–84).

14. Hazan, *Hekrei Lev, Orah Hayyim,* part 1, no. 15. *Hekrei Lev* explains the difference of opinion as a dispute among *Rishonim* on whether it is permissible to derive two halakhot from a single biblical verse. The verse is Deuteronomy 17:20, which contains the words *bekerev yisra'el,* "in the midst of Israel," and the two halakhot are (1) the rule of inheritance for religious posts and (2) the rule that requires anointing a king whose succession is disputed. Authorities answering the question in the affirmative derive both rules from the verse. Those answering in the negative derive only the rule that concerns anointing a king and hence lack the rule of inheritance of religious posts. Hazan himself decides the matter in favor of the inheritance of rabbinic posts, resolving the problem he raised by demonstrating how the two rules can be derived by taking each word in the phrase *bekerev yisra'el* separately as a basis for one of the rules (*Hekrei Lev, Orah Hayyim,* part 1, no. 15).

15. Maimonides, *Mishneh Torah, Hilkhot Melakhim* 1:7 and *Hilkhot Kelei Hamikdash* 4:20.

16. Rashba, *Responsa,* no. 300.

17. Commandment no. 497. *Sefer Hahinukh* appeared anonymously in the thirteenth century. It is often attributed to Rabbi Aaron Halevi of Barcelona.

18. A. Hershman, trans., *Mishneh Torah, Hilkhot Melakhim* 1:7, 208. Joseph Karo cites the midrash in *Sifre* as the source for this rule (*Kesef Mishnah, Hilkhot Melakhim* 1:7).

19. Lewittes, trans., *Mishneh Torah, Hilkhot Kelei Hamikdash* 4:20. In *The Book of Temple Service,* 57–58.

20. Ibid., 4:21.

21. See Grossman, "From Father to Son," 190n3.

22. Hazan, *Hekrei Lev, Orah Hayyim,* part 1, no. 15. Hoenig cites the passage in *Hilkhot Melakhim* as the primary source for the rule that rabbinic posts descend by inheritance ("Filial Succession," 18). It is interesting to note that Maimonides' son, Abraham (1186–1237), was appointed *nagid* of Egyptian Jewry after his father's death, and was succeeded in the post by his grandson, David ben Abraham Maimuni (1222–1300), and great-grandson, Abraham ben David Maimuni (1246–1316).

23. Zafrani, *Les Juifs du Maroc,* 124–25.

24. Deshen, *The Mellah Society*, 71.
25. See Gerber, *Jewish Society in Fez*, 83–84; see also Deshen for a family's hereditary right to write marriage contracts in Elbaz (*Mellah Society*, 72).
26. Schwarzfuchs, *Concise History*, 73.
27. Deshen, *Mellah Society*, 82–84.
28. Zafrani, *Les Juifs du Maroc*, 124.
29. Deshen, *Mellah Society*, 73.
30. Maharsham, *Da'at Torah, Yoreh De'ah, Hilkhot Shehitah* 1:81.
31. Hazan, *Hekrei Lev, Orah Hayyim*, part 1, no. 20.
32. Hatam Sofer, *Responsa, Orah Hayyim*, no. 12.
33. See chap. 15, sec. 1, above.
34. Rivash, *Responsa*, no. 271.
35. Rema, *Shulhan Arukh, Yoreh De'ah* 245:22.
36. Elijah ben Salomon Zalman of Vilna, "*Be'ur Hagra,*" *Yoreh De'ah* 245:22, par. 38, citing (1) *Sifre, Piska* 162 ("*bekerev yisra'el*—anyone who is in the midst of Israel, his son will fill his place"); (2) *Tosefta, Sheqalim* 2:15 ("Whoever takes precedence in inheritance takes precedence in positions of authority, so long as he follows the custom of his forefathers"); and (3) *Ketubbot* 103b ("Simeon my son [shall be] *hakham*, Gamaliel my son [shall be] *nasi*").
37. Radbaz, *Responsa* (1882 ed.), no. 953; Moses Schick (*Maharam Shik*), *Responsa, Yoreh De'ah*, no. 22; see also Isaac ben Moses of Vienna, *Or Zaru'a*, no. 115.
38. For a good discussion of this point, see the opinion of the rabbinical court in "*A*" *v. Selection Board for the Ashkenazic Chief Rabbi of City "B" and the Religious Council of City "B,*" 11 P.D.R. 97 (5738), at 100–106; see also Weinberg, *Al Devar Yerusha be-Rabbanut*, 493–94 (citing *Minhat Yehi'el, Beit Yitzhak,* and *Maharsham*).
39. Rema, *Shulhan Arukh, Yoreh De'ah* 245:22; see also Tenenbaum, *Divrei Malkhiel*, part 4, no. 82 (to qualify as successor, heir must be a scholar but need not be as great as his father). That the heir must be qualified for the post in order to inherit it is derived from *Sifra, Tsav*, chap. 5, par. 2 ("When he fills his father's place he has priority over all others, but if he does not fill his father's place, let another come and serve in his stead") and from the circumstances related in the Talmud, regarding the succession of Gamaliel to the post of nasi upon the death of his father, Rabbi Judah (*Ketubbot* 103b).
40. See, for example, Amarillo, *Sefer D'var Moshe, Orah Hayyim, Hilkhot Shatz*, no. 1.
41. Abraham ben Mordecai Halevi, *Ginat Veradim, Yoreh De'ah* 3:7 (attributing this view to the Maharashdam); but see Amarillo, *Sefer D'var Moshe, Orah Hayyim, Hilkhot Shatz*, no. 1 (stating this is view of *Ginat Veradim* only, whereas Maharashdam denies inheritance applies to keter Torah at all).
42. See the discussion of this point by the rabbinical court judges in *Religious Council of Tel Aviv-Yaffo v. Rabbi "A,"* 10 P.D.R. 38 (5732), at 54 ("And no one disputes and holds that where a learned sage dies and leaves an ignorant son [the son inherits], for we do not appoint him and the rule of inheritance lapses as to him").
43. For example, Hazan, *Hekrei Lev, Orah Hayyim*, part 1, no. 15 ("The inheritance of positions is nothing but a preference").
44. *Yoreh De'ah* 245:22.
45. Compare Algazi, *Simhat Yom Tov*, no. 6 (rule is from the Torah, citing *Sifre, Parshat Shoftim*) with Grumbiner, *Magen Avraham, Orah Hayyim* 53:25 (rule is a rabbinic enactment, based on custom dating from the time of Hillel). Algazi concedes that the rule is not expressly stated in the Torah but derived by way of midrash.
46. Abraham ben Mordecai Halevi, *Ginat Veradim, Yoreh De'ah* 3:8.

47. Maimonides, *Mishneh Torah, Hilkhot Melakhim* 1:7.
48. Abraham ben Mordecai Halevi, *Ginat Veradim, Yoreh De'ah* 3:8.
49. Amarillo, *Sefer D'var Moshe*, no. 1; Bornstein, *Avnei Netzer, Yoreh De'ah*, no. 312, sec. 39.
50. Hazan, *Hekrei Lev, Orah Hayyim*, part 1, no. 18.
51. This is the view of the rabbinical court judges in "*A" v. Selection Board for the Ashkenazic Chief Rabbi of City "B" and the Religious Council of City "B,"* 11 P.D.R. 97 (5738), at 107.
52. Ibid.
53. Algazi, *Simhat Yom Tov*, no. 6.
54. Hatam Sofer, *Responsa*, vol. 1, *Orah Hayyim*, no. 12.
55 Ibid., *Orah Hayyim*, no. 13.
56. Ibid.; see Cohen, "*La succession*," 150–68. Hoenig's discussion of the Hatam Sofer's views must be read with caution, for he apparently misunderstood his change of position. He states that Rabbi Sofer came to acknowledge the son's priority in ancient times, when the rabbinic vocation was sacred, but not at present, when the rabbi is subservient to the community's needs (Hoenig, "Filial Succession," 20). In fact, this reverses the Hatam Sofer's final position on the matter.
57. *Maharam Shik, Responsa, Yoreh De'ah* 228. For a discussion of the Hatam Sofer's change of heart and the reasons for it, see Vais, *Rabbanut Ukehila*, 150–54.
58. Hatam Sofer, *Responsa, Orah Hayyim*, no. 13.
59. Ibid.
60. Vais, *Rabbanut Ukehila*, 150.

Chapter 20

1. *Avot* 4:5.
2. *Nedarim* 37a.
3. Maimonides, *Commentary on the Mishnah, Avot* 4:7 (Kapah ed., 288–91); see also Maimonides, *Mishneh Torah, Hilkhot Talmud Torah*, chaps. 1–3.
4. Hatam Sofer, *Responsa*, vol. 6, *Hoshen Mishpat*, no. 21.
5. Schick, *Responsa, Yoreh De'ah*, no. 228.
6. Hazan, *Hekrei Lev, Orah Hayyim*, part 1, no. 20 (citing *Mordecai*); Bornstein, *Avnei Netzer, Yoreh De'ah*, no. 312; Maharsham, *Responsa*, vol. 4, no. 53. In the prohibition against selling rabbinic positions, it is plausible to see a delayed condemnation of a practice common toward the end of the Second Temple period when quite frequently the high priest's post was transferred by sale. The incumbent changed as often as once a year, defeating the rule of inheritance. Compare Alon, who states that the families of the high priests regarded the office as their property that they could sell or lease (*Jews, Judaism*, 65–68).
7. For example, *Rashi, Horayot* 11b, commenting on Deut. 17:20, wrote, "This indicates it [the monarchy] is an inheritance for them, like a father's estate that passes to his sons"; and Maimonides ruled, "The one who preceded in inheriting the property of the deceased also preceded in inheriting his office," based on *Tosefta, Sheqalim* 2:15 (*Mishneh Torah, Hilkhot Kelei Hamikdash* 4:20).
8. Hazan, *Hekrei Lev, Orah Hayyim*, part 1, no. 15.
9. Medini, *Sedei Hemed, Hazakah Bemitzvot*, sec. 7, par. 61.
10. Algazi, *Simhat Yom Tov*, no. 6.
11 Hazan, *Hekrei Lev, Orah Hayyim*, part 1, no. 16.
12. "*A" v. Selection Board for the Ashkenazic Chief Rabbi in City "B,"* 11 P.D.R. 97 (5735).
13. Ibid.

14. Ibid.

15. Tecoresh, "*Yerusha be-Misrah Tzeburit*," 96–101. The post at issue was not described in any detail but it was not a rabbinic position nor did the incumbent occupy a position of communal leadership. In an interesting portion of his paper, Rabbi Tecoresh, a member of the Chief Rabbinate of Israel, expressed the view that a daughter might inherit such a post and transfer it to her husband, "for it is the common practice of mankind to seek the assistance of relatives" (ibid., 98).

16. See Reiss, *B'inyan Yerushat Hezkat Rabbanut*, 10–11.

Chapter 21

1. See Kirschenbaum, "*Mara de-Atra*," 38–39, for the factors that in the modern era dispelled the notion that the local rabbi rules his locality as its sole authority of Jewish law.

2. Ibid., 38.

3. See Hazan, *Hekrei Lev, Orah Hayyim*, part 1, no. 15; Maharashdam, *Da'at Torah, Yoreh De'ah Hilkhot Shehitah* 1:81; and Tecoresh, "*Yerusha Be-Misrah Tzeburit*," 100–101.

4. Y. Epstein, *Arukh Hashulhan, Yoreh Deah* 245:28 (emphasis added).

5. Ibid.

6. Rabbi Israel Meir Hakohen Kagan (*Hafetz Hayyim*, 1838–1933), *Mishnah Berurah, Hilkhot Berakhot* 53:83.

7. See also Judah Ashkenazi of Tiktin, "*Be'er Hataev*," in Kagan, *Mishnah Berurah, Hilkhot Berakhot* 53:83: "It is an important [legal] principle regarding all appointments that the son has priority, *except* appointments in the realm of the Torah crown (*keter Torah*) where sons do *not* have priority, although starting with the time of Hillel it has been customary to give the sons priority" (emphasis added).

8. See the discussion in Schwarzfuchs, *Concise History*, 133.

9. Freedman, "Fundamental Problems," 137–40.

10. See discussion of this point in Hoenig, "Filial Succession," 16–17.

11. Ibid.; see also Weinberg, "*Al Davar Yerusha Berabbanut*," 496. The Baal Shem Tov was succeeded by his pupil, Rabbi Dov Baer, who was succeeded in turn by his disciples, Rabbis Levi Yitzhak of Berditchev, Shneur Zalman of Ladi, and two brothers Zischa and Elimelech of Lizensk, each of whom gave rise to his own strain of *Hasidut*.

12. *Religious Council of Tel Aviv-Yaffo v. Rabbi "A,"* 10 P.D.R. 38 (5735).

13. Ibid. at 50–61 (majority opinion by Rabbi Mordecai Elijah and concurring opinion by Rabbi Eliezar Goldschmidt).

14. Ibid., 59.

15. Ibid., 51, 59.

16. Ibid., 42–50 (citing *Yoma* 72b, *Maharashdam, Magen Avraham*, and *Hatam Sofer*).

17. Ibid.

18. Ibid., 59–60.

19. Ibid., 60–61.

20. 11 P.D.R. 97 (5738). The case was heard before a three-judge panel of Rabbis S. Karelitz, M. Solti, and Y. Meshorer. Rabbi Solti passed away during the deliberations, and the parties agreed to accept the judgment of the remaining two (ibid., 115). The reported opinion is unsigned. There is no mention by the judges here of the Rabbinical High Court's opinion in the *Rabbi "A"* case, decided three years earlier, an omission we may attribute to the lack of a doctrine of binding precedent in Jewish law. See Elon, *Principles of Jewish Law*, 115–17. Each judge has a personal obligation to address the legal questions in a case according to his own lights and

apply his legal conclusions to the facts presented as he deems proper. Still, wholly apart from the issue of the bindingness of precedents, one may question whether failing to acknowledge a decision rendered three years earlier by judges in the same court system dealing with the same legal issues and sources is a sound way to develop a coherent jurisprudence on this or any other issue before the rabbinical courts.

21. 11 P.D.R. 99.
22. See chap. 19, above.
23. 11 P.D.R. 100.
24. Ibid.
25. Ibid.
26. Schick, *Responsa, Yoreh De'ah*, no. 228.
27. 11 P.D.R. 100.
28. See chap. 19, above.
29. 11 P.D.R. 114–15.
30. Ibid., 115.

Epilogue

1. Heb. *bittul zeman*. On the religious strictures against "wasting time" and the tendency to promote Torah study at the expense of other activities, see Katz, *Tradition and Crisis*, 136–37.

2. Rabbis who were especially devoted to Torah studies might elect to serve in small Jewish communities where public responsibilities were light, maximizing the time available for private study and reflection.

3. Mishnah, *Pe'ah* 1:1.

4. Rabbi Jacob ben Asher, *Arba'ah Turim (Tur), Orah Hayim* 53 (citing the *Rashba*). The reference here is to cantors.

BIBLIOGRAPHY

Where a Hebrew work has an English title page, the English title is given followed by the Hebrew title. When a work gives the Hebrew year as the publication date, the Hebrew year is stated unless the title page also gives the English year. Authors with traditional Hebrew names, such as Jacob ben Asher and Abraham ibn Daud, are alphabetized under their first names. Rabbinic titles (rabbi, *rabbenu*) are omitted. In the case of traditional authorities, rabbinic acronyms follow the author's name.

Aaron Halevi of Barcelona. *Sefer Hahinukh Al Taryag Mitzvot*. Jerusalem: Eshkol, n.d.
Aberbach, Moshe. *Labor, Crafts and Commerce in Ancient Israel*. Jerusalem: Magnus, 1994.
Abrabanel [Abravanel], Isaac. *Nahalat Avot: Abrabanel on Pirkei Avot*. Compiled and translated by A. Chill. New York: Sepher-Hermon Press, 1991.
———. *Perush al Hatorah*. 3 vols. Tel Aviv: Hapo'el Hamizrahi, 5724.
Abraham ben Mordecai Halevi. *Ginat Veradim*. Constantinople, 1716.
Abraham ibn Daud. *The Book of Tradition (Sefer Ha-Qabbalah)*. Translated by Gerson D. Cohen. Philadelphia: Jewish Publication Society of America, 1967.
Abrahams, Israel. *Hebrew Ethical Wills*. 2 vols. Philadelphia: Jewish Publication Society of America, 1948.
Abramsky, C. "The Crisis of Authority within European Jewry in the Eighteenth Century." In *Studies in Jewish Religious and Intellectual History*, edited by Siegfried Stein and Raphael Loewe. University: University of Alabama Press, 1979.
Adelman, Howard E. "Leon Modena: The Autobiography and the Man." In *The Autobiography of a Seventeenth-Century Venetian Rabbi: Leon Modena's Life of Judah*, translated and edited by Mark R. Cohen. Princeton, N.J.: Princeton University Press, 1988.
Agus, Irving. *The Heroic Age of Franco-German Jewry*. New York: Yeshiva University Press, 1969.
Algazi, Yom Tov ben Israel Jacob. *Simhat Yom Tov*. Salonika, 1794.
Alon, G. *Jews, Judaism and the Classical World*. Translated by I. Abrahams. Jerusalem: Magnes Press, 1977.
Amarillo, Hayyim. *Sefer D'var Moshe*. Salonika, 1742.
Asher ben Yehiel [*Rosh*]. *Perush Harosh*. Commentary printed in Talmud Bavli.
Assaf, Simha. *Lekorot Harabbanut (B'ashkenaz Polania V'lita)*. In Simha Assaf, *B'ohalei Ya'akov*. Jerusalem: Mosad Harav Kook, 5703.
———. "Responsa of R. Azriel Dayyena" [in Hebrew]. *Kiryat Sefer* 15 (1938–39): 113–19.
Assaf, Simha, and Joshua Berend. "Gaon, Geonim." *Encyclopedia Hebraica* 10 (5716): 131–37.
The Babylonian Talmud. Edited by I. Epstein. 35 vols. London: Soncino Press, 1935–52.
Bacharach, Yair Hayyim [*Havvot Ya'ir*]. *She'elot Uteshuvot* (Responsa). Jerusalem, 5733.
Bacher, W. "Gaon." *Jewish Encyclopedia*. 5 (1903): 567–72.
Baer, Y. F. "The Origins of Jewish Communal Organization in the Middle Ages." *Binah: Studies in Jewish History* 1, 59–82. New York: Praeger, 1989.
Bah. See Sirkes, Joel.
Baron, Salo W. *The Jewish Community: Its History and Structure to the American Revolution*. 3 vols. Philadelphia: Jewish Publication Society of America, 1942.
———. *A Social and Religious History of the Jews*. 2nd ed. 18 vols. New York: Columbia University Press, 1952–83.

Bashan, Eliezer. "Exilarch." In *Encyclopedia Judaica* 6 (1971): 1023–34.
Baumgarten, Albert I. "The Politics of Reconciliation: The Education of Rabbi Judah the Prince." In *Jewish and Christian Self-Definition,* edited by E. P. Sanders, A. I. Baumgarten, and Alan Mendelson. Vol. 2, *Aspects of Judaism in the Graeco-Roman Period.* Philadelphia: Fortress Press, 1981.
Beer, Moshe. "The Hereditary Principle in Jewish Leadership" [in Hebrew]. *Bar-Ilan Annual* 13 (1976): 149–57.
Ben-Sasson, Haim Hillel. *Hagut Vehanhagah.* Jerusalem: Mosad Bialik, 5719.
———, ed. *History of the Jewish People.* Cambridge, Mass.: Harvard University Press, 1976.
Benveniste, Hayyim. *Knesset Hagedolah.* 3 vols. Bnei Brak, Israel: Tiferet Torah, 1987.
Blackman, Philip, trans. *Mishnayoth.* 6 vols. New York: Judaica Press, 1964.
Bleich, J. David. *Contemporary Halakhic Problems.* 3 vols. Hoboken, N.J.: Ktav, 1977–89.
Bomzer, Herbert W. *The Kolel in America.* New York: Shengold, 1985.
Bonfil, Robert. *Rabbis and Jewish Communities in Renaissance Italy.* Translated by J. Chipman. New York: Oxford University Press, 1990.
Bornstein, Abraham. *Avnei Netzer.* 4 vols. New York: A. I. Friedman, n.d.
Breuer, Mordechai. *The Rabbinate in Ashkenaz during the Middle Ages* [in Hebrew]. Jerusalem: Historical Society of Israel, 1976.
Bright, John. *A History of Israel.* London: SCM Press, 1960.
Brody, Robert. *The Geonim of Babylonia and the Shaping of Medieval Jewish Culture.* New Haven, Conn.: Yale University Press, 1998.
Carlebach, Elisheva. *Pursuit of Heresy: Rabbi Moses Hagiz and the Sabbatian Controversy.* New York: Columbia University Press, 1990.
Carlton, Dennis W., and Avi Weiss. "The Economics of Religion, Jewish Survival and Jewish Attitudes toward Competition in Torah Education." *Journal of Legal Studies* 30 (2001): 253–75.
Cohen, Gerson D. "The Reconstruction of Gaonic History." Introduction to *Texts and Studies in Jewish History and Literature* by Jacob Mann. New York: Ktav, 1972.
Cohen, Mark R., trans. and ed. *The Autobiography of a Seventeenth-Century Venetian Rabbi: Leon Modena's Life of Judah.* Princeton, N.J.: Princeton University Press, 1988.
Cohen, Stuart A. "Keter as a Political Symbol: Origins and Implications." *Jewish Political Studies Review* 1 (1989): 39–62.
———. "La succession à un office public dans la loi rabbinique: Remarques de Moche Sofer sur les trois ketarim." *Pardes* 1 (1985): 150–68.
———. *The Three Crowns: Structures of Communal Politics in Early Rabbinic Jewry.* Cambridge: Cambridge University Press, 1990.
Colon, Joseph ben Solomon [*Maharik*]. *She'elot Uteshuvot* (Responsa), edited by S. B. Deutsch. Jerusalem: Oraysoh Press, 1987.
Danby, Herbert, trans. *Mishnah.* Oxford: Clarendon Press, 1933.
Daube, David. *Sons and Strangers.* Boston: Institute of Jewish Law, Boston University, 1984.
David ben Hayyim Hakohen of Corfu [*Radakh*]. *She'elot Uteshuvot* (Responsa). Salonika, 1803.
David ibn Abi Zimra [*Radbaz*]. *She'elot Uteshuvot* (Responsa). 2 vols. 1882; Bnei Brak, Israel: Heichal Hasefer, 1971.
Davis, Natalie Zemon. "Fame and Secrecy: Leon Modena's *Life* as an Early Modern Autobiography." In *The Autobiography of a Seventeenth-Century Venetian Rabbi: Leon Modena's Life of Judah,* translated and edited by Mark R. Cohen. Princeton, N.J.: Princeton University Press, 1988.

Deshen, Shlomo. *The Mellah Society: Jewish Communal Life in Sherifan Morocco*. Chicago: University of Chicago Press, 1989.
Dresner, Samuel H. *Levi Yitzhak of Berdichev*. New York: Hartmore House, 1974.
Ehrenreich, H. I. "Heker Beshe'elat Yerushat Haminuyim Be'yisrael." *Otzar Hahayyim* 4 (5688): 11–16.
Elijah ben Hayyim of Constantinople [*Ranah*]. *She'elot Uteshuvot* (Responsa). Jerusalem, 1959.
Elijah ben Salomon Zalman [Vilna Gaon]. *Be'ur Hagra*. Commentary in Joseph Karo, *Shulhan Arukh*. New York: M. P. Press, 1975.
Elon, Menahem, ed. *The Principles of Jewish Law*. Jerusalem: Keter, 1975.
———. "The Sources and Nature of Jewish Law and Its Application in the State of Israel, Part I." *Israel Law Review* 2 (1967): 515–65.
Encyclopedia Hebraica (Ha'encyclopedi'ah Ha'ivrit). 32 vols. Jerusalem and Tel Aviv: Encyclopedia, 5709–42.
Encyclopaedia Judaica. 16 vols. Jerusalem: Keter, 1971.
Encyclopedia Talmudit. See *Talmudic Encyclopedia*.
Epstein, I. *The Responsa of Rabbi Simon b. Zemah Duran*. London: Oxford University Press, 1930.
Epstein, Yehiel Michal. *Arukh Hashulhan*. 8 vols. Israel, n.d.
Etkes, Emanuel. "The Relationship between Talmud Scholarship and the Institution of the Rabbinate in Nineteenth-Century Lithuanian Jewry." In *Scholars and Scholarship*, edited by Leo Landman. New York: Yeshiva University Press, 1990.
———, [Immanuel]. *The Gaon of Vilna: The Man and His Image*. Translated by Jeffrey M. Green. Berkeley: University of California Press, 2002.
Falk, Joshua [*Sma*]. *Sefer Me'irat Eina'im*. Commentary in Karo, *Shulhan Arukh*.
Feinstein, Moses. *Iggerot Moshe*. 6 vols. New York: Moriah, 1959.
Feuchtwanger, O. *Righteous Lives*. New York: Block, 1965.
Finkelstein, Louis. *Jewish Self-Government in the Middle Ages*. New York: Jewish Theological Seminary of America, 1924.
Freedman, Menahem. "Fundamental Problems in the Congregational Rabbinate in Modern Society" [in Hebrew]. In *The Jewish Spiritual Leadership in Our Times*, edited by Ella Belfer. Ramat Gan: Bar-Ilan University, 1982.
Fuenn, S. J. *Kiri'ah Na'amanah: Korot Adat Yisra'el Be'ir Vilna*. Vilna, 1915.
Galinski, Myer. *Pursue Justice: The Administration of Justice in Ancient Israel*. London: Nechidim, 1983.
Gammie, John G., and Leo G. Perdue, eds. *The Sage in Israel and the Ancient Near East*. Winona Lake, Ind.: Eisenbrauns, 1990.
Gerber, Jane S. *Jewish Society in Fez, 1450–1700*. Leiden: E. J. Brill, 1980.
Ginzberg, Louis. *Geonica*. 2nd ed. New York: Hermon, 1968.
———. *Students, Scholars and Saints*. Philadelphia: Jewish Publication Society of America, 1928.
Goitein, S. *A Mediterranean Society*. 5 vols. Berkeley: University of California Press, 1967–88.
Goldberg, Hillel. *Between Berlin and Slobodka: Jewish Transition Figures from Eastern Europe*. Hoboken, N.J.: Ktav, 1989.
Goldin, Judah, trans. *The Fathers according to Rabbi Nathan*. New Haven, Conn.: Yale University Press, 1955.
Goldman, Israel M. *The Life and Times of Rabbi David Ibn Abi Zimra*. New York: Jewish Theological Seminary of America, 1970.
Goodblatt, Morris S. *Jewish Life in Turkey in the XVIth Century: As Reflected in the Legal Writings of Samuel De Medina*. New York: Jewish Theological Seminary of America, 1952.

Goode, Alexander. "The Exilarchate in the Eastern Caliphate, 637–1258." *Jewish Quarterly Review, New Series* 31 (1941): 149–69.
Goody, Jack, ed. *Succession to High Office*. Cambridge Papers in Social Anthropology 4. Cambridge: Cambridge University Press, 1966.
Graetz, Heinrich. *History of the Jews*. 6 vols. Philadelphia: Jewish Publication Society of America, 1894.
Grant, Michael. *Jews in the Roman World*. Reprint; New York: Barnes and Noble Books, 1995.
Greenberg, Simon. "Jewish Educational Institutions." In *The Jews: Their History, Culture and Religion*, vol. 2, edited by Louis Finkelstein. 3rd ed. New York: Harper and Brothers, 1960.
Greenspahn, Frederick. *When Brothers Dwell Together*. New York: Oxford University Press, 1994.
Groner, Tsvi. *The Legal Methodology of Hai Gaon*. Chico, Calif.: Scholars Press, 1985.
Grossman, Abraham. "From Father to Son: The Inheritance of the Spiritual Leadership of the Jewish Communities in the Early Middle Ages" [in Hebrew]. *Zion* 50 (1985): 189–220.
———. "Social Structure and Intellectual Creativity in Medieval Jewish Communities (Eighth to Twelfth Centuries)." In *Studies in Medieval Jewish History and Literature* 3, edited by I. Twersky and J. M. Harris. Cambridge, Mass.: Harvard University Center for Jewish Studies, 2000.
Gumbiner, Abraham. *Magen Avraham*. Commentary. Printed in Karo, *Shulham Arukh*.
Guttman, Alexander. *Studies in Rabbinic Judaism*. New York: Ktav, 1976.
Hafetz Hayyim. See Kagan, Israel Meir.
Hatam Sofer. See Sofer, Moses.
Havvot Ya'ir. See Bacharach, Yair Hayyim.
Hazan, Joseph ben Hayyim. *Hekrei Lev*. 13 vols. Jerusalem: Hartman Institute, 1998.
Heiman, D., ed. *Yalkut Shimoni Al Hatorah*. Jerusalem: Mosad Harav Kook, 1986.
Heller, Yom Tov Lippman. *Tosafot Yom Tov*. Commentary. Printed in the Mishnah.
Hershman, M. *Rabbi Isaac Ben Sheshet Perfet and His Times*. New York: Jewish Theological Seminary of America, 1943.
Hertz, J. H., ed. *Pentateuch and Haftorahs*. 2nd ed. London: Soncino Press, 1993.
Hitti, Philip K. *History of the Arabs*. 10th ed. New York: St. Martin's Press, 1970.
Hoenig, Sidney B. "Filial Succession in the Rabbinate." *Gratz College Annual of Jewish Studies* 1 (1972): 14–22.
Holy Scriptures according to the Masoretic Text. Philadelphia: Jewish Publication Society of America, 1917.
Hyamson, M., trans. *Mishneh Torah: The Book of Knowledge by Maimonides*. Jerusalem: Feldheim, 1981.
Isaac ben Moses of Vienna. *Or Zaru'a*. 2 vols. Zitomar, 1862.
Isaac ben Sheshet Perfet [*Rivash*]. *She'elot Uteshuvot Ben Sheshet* (Responsa of Ben Sheshet). New York: Merkaz Haseforim, 1974.
Isserlein, Israel. *Terumat Hadeshen: Pesakim u-Ketavim*. Bnei Brak, Israel: 5731.
Isserles, Moses [Rema]. *Glosses*. Printed in Karo, *Shulhan Arukh*.
———. *She'elot Uteshuvot Harema*. Edited by Asher Ziv. Jerusalem: Hemed, 1970.
Jacob ben Asher. *Arba'ah Turim* (also *Tur*). 7 vols. Jerusalem: Offset Press Esther, 5732.
Jewish Encyclopedia. 12 vols. New York: Funk and Wagnalls, 1901–5.
Joseph ben Meir Halevi ibn Migas [*Ri Migas*]. *She'elot Uteshuvot* (Responsa). Jerusalem, 5751.
Joseph ben Moses Mitrani [*Mahari Trani*]. *She'elot Uteshuvot* (Responsa). Furth: Y. Petshviyo, 1768.

BIBLIOGRAPHY 159

Judah Ashkenazi of Tiktin. *Be'er Hataev.* Commentary in Kagan, *Mishnah Berurah.*

Kagan, Israel Meir Hakohen [*Hafetz Hayyim*]. *Mishnah Berurah.* 6 vols. New York: A. I. Friedman, 1964.

Karo, Joseph. *Beit Yosef.* Commentary. Printed in Jacob ben Asher, *Arba'ah Turim.*

———. *Kesef Mishnah.* Commentary. Printed in Maimonides, *Mishneh Torah.*

———. *Shulhan Arukh.* 10 vols. New York: M. P. Press, 1975.

Katz, Jacob. *Divine Law in Human Hands: Case Studies in Halakhic Flexibility.* Jerusalem: Magnes Press, 1998.

———. *Tradition and Crisis: Jewish Society at the End of the Middle Ages.* Translated by Bernard Dov Cooperman. New York: New York University Press, 1993.

Kirsch, G. *Jews in Medieval Germany.* New York: Ktav, 1970.

Kirschenbaum, Aaron. "*Mara de-Atra:* A Brief Sketch." *Tradition* 27, no. 4 (1993): 35–40.

Kober, Adolf. "Documents Selected from the Pinkas of Friedberg, a Former Free City in Western Germany." *Proceedings of the American Academy for Jewish Research,* 17 (1949): 19–59.

Kook, Abraham Isaac Hakohen. "Hasagat Gevul Berabbanut." *Techumin* 5 (5744): 285–86.

———. *Mishpat Hakohen.* Jerusalem, 1937.

Krauss, Simcha. "Hasagath Gvul." *Journal of Halacha and Contemporary Society* 19 (1995): 5–29.

Leiter, Samuel. "Worthiness, Acclamation, Appointment: Some Rabbinic Terms." *Proceedings of the American Academy for Jewish Research,* 41–42 (1974): 137–68.

Lewittes, M, trans. *The Code of Maimonides: Book Eight—The Book of Temple Service.* New Haven, Conn.: Yale University Press, 1957.

Levine, Lee I. *The Rabbinic Class of Roman Palestine in Late Antiquity.* New York: Jewish Theological Seminary of America, 1989.

Lichtenstein, Aharon. "The Israeli Chief Rabbinate: A Current Halakhic Perspective." *Tradition* 26, no. 4 (1992): 26–38.

Maalin, Nehemiah. "Binyan Meshihat Veyerushat Melekh." *Hapardes* 30 (5716): 8–10.

Mabit. See Moses Mitrani.

Magen Avraham. See Gumbiner, Abraham.

Maharam Padua. See Meir ben Isaac Katzenellenbogen.

Maharam Shik. See Schick, Moses ben Joseph.

Maharashdam. See Samuel ben Moses De Medina.

Maharik. See Colon, Joseph ben Solomon.

Mahari Mintz. See Mintz, Judah.

Mahari Trani. See Joseph ben Moses Mitrani.

Maharsham. See Schwadron, Shalom Mordecai Hakohen.

Maharyu. See Weil, Jacob ben Judah.

Maimonides, Moses [*Rambam*]. *The Code of Maimonides: Book Fourteen—The Book of Judges.* Translated by Abraham M. Hershman. New Haven, Conn.: Yale University Press, 1977.

———. *The Commandments: Sefer Ha-Mitzvoth of Maimonides.* Translated by C. Chavel. 2 vols. London: Soncino Press, 1967.

———. *Mishneh Torah* (also *Hayad Hahazakah*). 6 vols. Jerusalem: Pardes, 1955.

———. *Mishnah Im Perush Rabbenu Moshe Ben Maimon* (Commentary on the Mishnah). 6 vols. Edited by Josef Kafah. Jerusalem: Mosad Harav Kook, 5727.

Maller, Julius. "The Role of Education in Jewish History." In *The Jews: Their History, Culture and Religion,* vol. 2, edited by Louis Finkelstein. 3rd ed. New York: Harper and Brothers, 1960.

Malter, Henry. *Saadia Gaon: His Life and Works.* Philadelphia: Jewish Publication Society of America, 1921.

Marcus, Ivan G. *Piety and Society: The Jewish Pietists of Medieval Germany.* Leiden: E. J. Brill, 1981.

Margolis, Max L., and Alexander Marx. *A History of the Jewish People.* Philadelphia: Jewish Publication Society of America, 1927.

Marx, Alexander. "Glimpses of the Life of an Italian Rabbi of the First Half of the Sixteenth Century (David ibn Yahya)." *Hebrew Union College Annual,* 1 (1924): 605–15.

———. "The Removal of Rabbi Josef of Arles from the Rabbinate and His Reinstatement" [in Hebrew]. *Tarbitz* 8 (1937): 171–84.

Medini, Hayyim Hezekiah. *Sedei Hemed Hashalem.* 10 vols. New York: Abraham Isaac Friedman, 5732.

Meir ben Isaac Katzenellenbogen [*Maharam Padua*]. *She'elot Uteshuvot* (Responsa). Cracow, 5642; Jerusalem, 5740.

Meyer, Michael A. *Without Wissenschaft There Is No Judaism.* Braun Lectures in the History of the Jews in Prussia, vol. 11. Tel Aviv: Bar-Ilan University, 2004.

Midrash Rabbah: Exodus. Translated by S. Lehrman. London: Soncino Press, 1983.

Midrash Rabbah: Leviticus. Translated by J. Israelstam. London: Soncino Press, 1983.

Midrash Rabbah: Numbers. Translated by J. Slotki. London: Soncino Press 1983.

Midrash Tanhuma Hashalem. 2 vols. Jerusalem: Tifereth Press, 5748.

Minkin, Jacob S. *The World of Moses Maimonides.* New York: T. Yoseloff, 1957.

Mintz, Judah [*Mahari Mintz*]. *She'elot Uteshuvot* (Responsa). Cracow, 5642; Jerusalem, 5740.

Mishnah. 3 vols. Jerusalem: Eshkol, 5738.

Mordecai ben Hillel. *Sefer Mordecai.* Commentary. Printed in editions of the Talmud. See *Talmud Bavli.*

Moses Mitrani [*Mabit*]. *She'elot Uteshuvot* (Responsa). Israel, 5734.

Naaman, Pinhas. "Hakamat Melekh Vehorashat Hamalukha Beyisra'el." *Bet Mikra* 41 (1970): 189–201.

Nariyah, Moses Zvi. "Serrarah al Ha-Tzibur." *Shevilin* 29–30 (5737): 128–29.

Nathanson, Joseph. *Shoel U-Masheev.* Jerusalem, 5733.

Neubauer, A. D., ed. *Medieval Jewish Chronicles and Chronological Notes.* 2 vols. Oxford: Clarendon Press, 1887.

Neusner, J., trans. *Talmud of the Land of Israel.* Vol. 23, *Nedarim.* Chicago: University of Chicago Press, 1985.

Obadiah of Bertinoro. Commentary on the Mishnah. In *Mishnah.* 3 vols. Jerusalem: Eshkol, 5738.

Passamaneck, Stephen M. "Towards Sunrise in the East, 1300–1565." In *An Introduction to the History and Sources of Jewish Law,* edited by N. S. Hecht et al. New York: Oxford University Press, 1996.

Pearl, Chaim. *Rashi.* New York: Grove Press, 1988.

Pesikta De-Rab Kahana. Translated by W. G. Braude and Israel J. Kapstein. Philadelphia: Jewish Publication Society of America, 1975.

Piskei Din Shel Batei Hadin Rabani'im Beyisra'el. 19 vols. Tel Aviv: Gideon, 1949–95.

Polish, David. *Give Us a King: Legal-Religious Sources of Jewish Sovereignty.* Hoboken, N.J.: Ktav, 1989.

Porter, J. Roy. "The Succession of Joshua." In *Proclamation and Presence,* edited by J. L. Durham and J. R. Porter. Richmond, Va.: John Knox Press, 1970.

Rabinowich, Nosson D., trans. *Iggeres of Rav Sherira Gaon.* Jerusalem: Moznaim Press, 1988.

Rabinowitz, Louis I. *The Herem Hayyishub.* London: E. Goldstone, 1945.

Rabinowitz-Teomin, Benjamin. "*Ma'alin Bekodesh.*" In *The Leo Jung Jubilee Volume,* edited by Menahem Kasher, Norman Lamm, and Leonard Rosenfeld. New York: Jewish Center, 1962.

Radakh. See David ben Hayyim Hakohen of Corfu.

Radbaz. See David ibn Abi Zimra.

Rakover, N. *Modern Applications of Jewish Law.* 2 vols. Jerusalem: Jewish Heritage Society, 1992.

Rambam. See Maimonides, Moses.

Ranah. See Elijah ben Hayyim of Constantinople.

Rashba. See Solomon ben Abraham ibn Adret.

Rashi. See Solomon ben Isaac.

Reiss, Shneur Zusha. "*B'inyan Yerushat Hezkat Rabanut,*" *Ha-Maor* 5 (5714): 10–11.

Rema. See Isserles, Moses.

Reviv, Hanoch. *The Elders in Ancient Israel.* Jerusalem: Magnes Press, 1989.

Rheins, Richard. "The Professionalization of the Rabbinate in the Talmud and the Halakhic Commentaries of Rambam and Karo." In *Rabbinic-Lay Relations in Jewish Law,* edited by Walter Jacob and Moshe Zemer. Tel Aviv: Rodef Shalom Press, 1993.

Ri Migas. See Joseph ben Meir Halevi ibn Migas.

Ritva. See Yom Tov ben Abraham Ishbili.

Rivash. See Isaac ben Sheshet Perfet.

Rosensweig, Bernard. "The Emergence of the Professional Rabbinate in Ashkenazic Jewry." *Tradition* 11, no. 3 (1970): 22–30.

Rosh. See Asher ben Yehiel.

Roth, Jeffrey I. "Inheriting the Crown in Jewish Law: The Question of Rabbinic Succession." In *Jewish Law Association Studies 10: The London Conference Volume,* edited by E. A. Goldman. Atlanta, Ga.: Scholars Press, 1997.

———. "Responding to Dissent in Jewish Law: Suppression versus Self-Restraint." *Rutgers Law Review* 40 (1987): 31–99.

———. "Three Aspects of the Rabbinate: Compensation, Competition and Tenure." *Drake Law Review* 45 (1997): 569–624.

Saadiah Gaon. *Sefer Hayerushot.* Edited by J. Miller. Paris, 1897.

Samuel ben Moses De Medina [*Maharashdam*]. *She'elot Uteshuvot* (Responsa). Israel, 1980.

Saperstein, Marc. "The Earliest Commentary on the *Midrash Rabbah.*" In *Studies in Medieval Jewish History and Literature,* edited by Isadore Twersky. Cambridge, Mass.: Harvard University Press, 1979.

———. *Jewish Preaching, 1200–1800: An Anthology.* New Haven, Conn.: Yale University Press, 1989.

Schacter, Jacob S. "History and Memory of Self: The Autobiography of Rabbi Jacob Emden." In *Jewish History and Jewish Memory: Essays in Honor of Yosef Hayim Yerushalmi,* edited by E. Carlebach, J. M. Efron, and D. N. Myers. Hanover, N.H.: University Press of New England for Brandeis University Press, 1998.

Schick, Moses ben Joseph [*Maharam Shik*]. *She'elot Uteshuvot* (Responsa). 2 vols. Jerusalem: Admon, 1980.

Scholem, Gershom G. *Major Trends in Jewish Mysticism.* New York: Schocken Books, 1954.

Schwadron, Shalom Mordecai Hakohen [*Maharsham*]. *She'elot Uteshuvot* (Responsa). 6 vols. Jerusalem, 5734.

Schwarzfuchs, Simon. *A Concise History of the Rabbinate.* Oxford: Blackwell Publishers, 1993.

Shabbetai ben Meir Hakohen [*Shakh*]. *Siftei Kohen.* Commentary. Printed in Karo, *Shulhan Arukh.*

Shakh. See Shabbetai ben Meir Hakohen.
Shilo, S. "Circumvention of the Law in Talmudic Literature" [in Hebrew]. *Shenaton Hamishpat Haivri* 8 (5741): 309–55.
Sicker, Martin. *The Judaic State: A Study in Rabbinic Political Theory.* New York: Praeger, 1988.
Sifra. Edited by Louis Finkelstein. 3 vols. New York: Jewish Theological Seminary of America, 1983.
Sifre. Translated by Reuven Hammer. New Haven, Conn.: Yale University Press, 1986.
Silver, Daniel Jeremy. "Moses Our Teacher Was a King." *Jewish Law Annual* 1 (1978): 123–32.
Simon ben Zemah Duran [*Tashbetz*]. *Sefer Hatashbetz.* Amsterdam: N. H. Levi, 1738.
Sirkes, Joel [*Bah*]. *She'elot Uteshuvot Bayit Hadash.* Frankfurt, 1697.
Sma. See Falk, Joshua.
Sofer, Moses [*Hatam Sofer*]. *She'elot Uteshuvot* (Responsa). 3 vols. Jerusalem: Makor, 1969.
Solomon ben Abraham ibn Adret [*Rashba*]. *She'elot Uteshuvot* (Responsa). 6 vols. Jerusalem: Tiferet Torah, 1988.
Solomon ben Isaac [*Rashi*]. Commentary. Printed in the Talmud. See *Talmud Bavli.*
Soloveitchik, Haym. "Religious Law and Change: The Medieval Ashkenazic Example." *AJS Review* 12 (1987): 205–21.
Solti, Bezalel. "*Behirat Rabbanim.*" *Torah she-Baal Peh* 20 (5739): 26–32.
Stampfer, S. *Heyeshivah Halita'it Behithavutah.* Jerusalem: Merkaz Zalman Shazar, 1995.
Stillman, Norman A. "Aspects of Jewish Life in Islamic Spain." In *Aspects of Jewish Culture in the Middle Ages,* edited by Paul E. Szarmach. Albany: State University of New York Press, 1979.
Strack, Hermann L. *Introduction to the Talmud and Midrash.* Philadelphia: Jewish Publication Society of America, 1931.
Talmud Bavli. 20 vols. New York: Hoza'at Me'orot, 1959.
Talmud of the Land of Israel. Vol. 23, *Nedarim.* Translated by J. Neusner. Chicago: University of Chicago Press, 1985.
Talmud Yerushalmi. 7 vols. Jerusalem 5735.
Talmudic Encyclopedia [in Hebrew]. Edited by Meyer Berlin (Bar-Ilan) and S. J. Zevin. 25 vols. Jerusalem: Yad Harav Herzog, 1987–2002.
Tama, Diogene M. *Transactions of the Parisian Sanhedrim.* London: Charles Taylor, 1807.
Tamari, Meir. *With All Your Possessions: Jewish Ethics and Economic Life.* New York: Free Press, 1987.
Tanakh: A New Translation of the Holy Scriptures according to the Traditional Hebrew Text. Philadelphia: Jewish Publication Society of America, 1985.
Tashbetz. See Simon ben Zemah Duran.
Tecoresh, Catriel F. "*Yerusha be-Misrah Tzeburit.*" *Shevilin* 31–32 (5739): 96–101.
Tenenbaum, Malkhiel. *Divrei Malkhiel.* 7 vols. Jerusalem: Mosad Harav Kook, 1976.
Teshuvot Hageonim. Edited by Abraham E. Harkavy. 2 vols. Berlin, 5647.
Tosefta. Edited by Moses S. Zuckermandel. New ed. Jerusalem: Wahrman Books, 1974.
Tosefta: Moed. Translated by J. Neusner. Hoboken, N.J.: Ktav, 1981.
Tuchman, Barbara W. *A Distant Mirror: The Calamitous Fourteenth Century.* New York: Knopf, 1978.
Twersky, Isadore. *Introduction to the Code of Maimonides (Mishneh Torah).* New Haven, Conn.: Yale University Press, 1980.
———. *Rabad of Posquières.* Cambridge, Mass.: Harvard University Press, 1962.

Urbach, Ephraim E. *The Sages: Their Concepts and Beliefs.* Translated by I. Abrahams. 2 vols. Jerusalem: Magnes Press, 1975.

Vais, Yaakov. *Rabbanut Ukehila Bemishnat Maran Hahatam Sofer Zal.* Jerusalem: Yaakov Vais, 1987.

Vilna Gaon. *See* Elijah ben Salomon Zalman.

Weil, Jacob ben Judah [*Maharyu*]. *She'elot Uteshuvot* (Responsa). Jerusalem, 5719.

Weinberg, Ephraim. "Al Davar Yerusha Berabbanut." *Hatorah Vehamedina* 9–10 (5718–19): 491–98.

Weinfeld, Moshe. "The Transition from Tribal Republic to Monarchy in Ancient Israel and Its Impression on Jewish Political History." In *Kinship and Consent: The Jewish Political Tradition and Its Contemporary Uses,* edited by David J. Elazar. Ramat Gan: Turtledove, 1981.

Wengrove, Charles, trans. *Sefer haHinnuch: The Book of [Mitzvah] Education.* 5 vols. New York: Feldheim, 1978.

Werblowsky, R. J. Zwi. *Rabbi Joseph Karo: Lawyer and Mystic.* London: Oxford University Press, 1962.

Whitelam, Keith. *The Just King: Monarchical Judicial Authority in Ancient Israel.* Sheffield: University of Sheffield, 1979.

Wilensky, Mordecai L. "The Polemic of Rabbi David of Makow against Hasidism." *Proceedings of the American Academy for Jewish Research,* 25 (1956): 137–56.

Yalkut Shimoni. 2 vols. Jerusalem, 5740.

Yom Tov ben Abraham Ishbili [*Ritva*]. *Hidushei Ha-Ritva.* 3 vols. Jerusalem, 1980.

Zafrani, Haim. *Les Juifs du Maroc.* Paris: Paul Geuthner, 1972.

Zborowski, Mark, and Elizabeth Herzog. *Life Is with People: The Culture of the Shtetl.* New York: Schocken Books, 1952.

Zeitlin, Solomon. "The Opposition to the Spiritual Leaders Appointed by the Government." *Jewish Quarterly Review* 31 (1940): 287–300.

Zemer, Arik Isaac. *Rabbi Hayyim ben Bezalel of Friedberg: Brother of Maharal of Prague* [in Hebrew]. Jerusalem: Mosad Harav Kook, 1987.

Zimmer, Eric. *Harmony and Discord.* New York: New York University Press, 1970.

———. "R. David b. Isaac of Fulda: The Trials and Tribulations of a 16th Century German Rabbi." *Jewish Social Studies* 45 (1983): 217–31.

INDEX

Aaron, 85, 89, 93, 101
Aaron ben Meir, 99–100
Aaron Halevi of Barcelona, 150n17
Abihu, 85, 89
Abraham ben David of Posquières, 30
Abraham ibn Daud, 11–12
Abu Jafar, 10
academic tenure, 59–60
Africa, 10, 23, 42, 104–5
Aharonim, 88, 109–11, 117, 120
Alfasi, Isaac, 104, 106
Algazi, Yom Tov, 80, 110
Algiers, 23
Aleppo, 99
Alkabetz, Solomon, 110
Alsheikh, Moses, 110
Altona, 64
appointment, of rabbis, 37–38; consent to, 60–62, 104, 109, 102–21, 123, 138n17, 142n4, 146n38
Arama, Isaac, 61
Arba'ah Turim, 17, 106, 108, 124
Artaxerxes, 126n33
Arukh Hashulhan, 51, 117
Asher ben Yehiel, 16–18, 106, 128n14, 131n23
Ashi, Rav, 92; his successors, 146n35
Ashkenazim, 15, 27, 42–43, 60, 78, 80–81, 105, 109, 141n4, 142n4
assistant, appointment of, 107–8
Astruc, Isaac, 78
autobiography, rabbinic, 17, 30, 138n10
av beth din, 97–99, 132n30, 148n26, 148nn28–29
Avot. See *Ethics of the Fathers*

Babylonia, 10–11, 69, 92, 94–102, 104
Bacharach, Yair Hayyim, 87
Baghdad, 10, 11, 96, 99, 147n14
Barcelona, 15
Beit Yosef, 106, 198
Benveniste, Hayyim, 75

Berlin, 64
Bezalel, 61
Black Death, 70, 140n13
Bologna, 139n11
bribes, 8
Bruna, Israel, 38, 43–44
Brünn (Brno), 38

Calatayud, 33
calendar, 23, 99–101
cantors, 29, 34, 75–76, 107–8, 117; fund for support of, 15–16; temporary, 141n10
Capsali, Moses, 64
Castile, 28
Catholic Church, 140n13
change of circumstances, 27–28, 79, 113
change in Jewish law, 26, 122–23
chaplains, 116
charity, 13,18, 25, 30, 43, 76, 128n14
Charles V, King of France, 77–78
chief rabbi, 29, 77–78, 108, 120–21; Moses Sofer's view of, 111, 121
Chief Rabbinate, of Israel, 118–21, 153n15
circumcisers, ritual, 107
Cohn, Emil, 64
Colon, Joseph, 64
contract, breach of, 127n14; of cantors, 107–8; disincentives in, 33; employment, 74; of Judah ben Asher, 18, 129n25; marriage, 151n25; of rabbis, 29, 73–76, 116, 118, 131n26, 132n30, 142n24; termination of, 73
Cordova, 11, 12
countergaon, 99, 149n33
court Jews, 105
courts, jurisdiction of, 80; location of, 50, 56. *See also* judges; litigation
Cracow, 111, 135n18
crowns, of monarchy, 91, 94–95, 101, 105–6, 119, 146n2; of pride, 129n39; of priesthood, 91, 106; three crowns, 63, 87, 93, 145n21; of Torah, 38, 87, 91, 93, 94–95, 101, 104, 106–7, 119, 120, 123, 153n7

customs, as law, 25, 130n21; change of, 119; good and bad, 72; various, 50, 72–73, 75–76, 108, 109, 117, 142n32, 145n21, 151n45, 153n7
Cyrus, 142n4

Damascus, 147n14
daughters, dowries of, 19, 22, 31; and inheritance, 107, 114, 153n15; marriage to scholars, 8
David ben Hayyim of Corfu, 70–71
David ben Isaac of Fulda, 60
David ben Zakkai, 95, 100
David ibn Abi Zimra, 61
David ibn Yahya, 39–40, 53
David, King of Israel, 68, 89, 91, 93, 95, 101, 145n22
De Medina, Samuel ben Moses, 87–88, 124
divorce, 7, 32, 87, 133n52; bill of, 29; fees for, 29, 49, 131n25
Dosa, son of Saadiah Gaon, 147n18, 149n42
dowry, 19, 22, 29, 31
Duran, Simon ben Zemah, criticism of Maimonides, 23–27; life, 23; salary, 23

Edels, Israel, 30
Egypt, 10, 12, 23, 99, 147n14, 149n35, 149n38, 150n22
Elazar ben Azariah, 66, 73
Eleazar, son of Aaron, 89
elections of rabbis, 37, 133n1
elementary education, 53–54. *See also* schoolteachers
Eliezer of Bohemia, 15–16, 22
Elijah ben Hayyim, 79
Elijah ben Salomon Zalman, Vilna Gaon, 109
Elijah, Mordecai, 119
Emancipation, 41, 43, 116, 134n16
England, 42
Epstein, Yehiel, 51, 75, 117
equity, 72
Eretz Israel, 10, 91, 94, 99–100, 101, 104, 146n2
eruvin, 53, 119
Ethics of the Fathers, 21, 92, 112, 129nn38–39
Europe, 72, 103–5, 140n10

excommunication, 33, 78, 79, 140n10
exilarch, 10, 94–95, 98, 99, 101, 146n6, 146n9, 147n10, 147n11, 147n13
Eybeschutz, Jonathan, 64
Ezra, 126n33, 142n4

Falk, Joshua, 30
fees, after father's death, 114–15; invalidate verdicts, 5–6; for rabbinic services, 29, 38–40, 49–51, 60; for schoolteachers, 8, 54; for Torah scholars, 48. *See also* suspension fee
fee for trouble (*sekhar tirha*), 9
festivals, 27, 75; Hanukah, 139n24, New Year, 100; Passover, 99–100; Purim, 15; Simhat Torah, 15; Yom Kippur, 65
fiscal appointees, 75
France, 17, 29, 42, 77–78, 104–5, 108, 142n4, 150n13
freedom of movement, 41–44, 46
Friedberg, 29
functions of rabbis, 25, 31, 48–49, 53, 76, 86, 111, 116, 119

Gabes. *See* Kabis
gadol ha-dor, 111
Gamaliel, Rabban: removal from office, 66–67, 73, 75; and Rabbi Joshua, 6–7
Gamaliel, son of Judah Hanasi, 91, 151n39
Gamaliel VI, 94
gambling, 30–31, 132n39
gaon, as a title, 104. *See also* Geonim
Geonim, 10, 12, 112; succession in Eretz Israel, 94; succession in Babylonia, 94–102, 104–5; their law summaries, 69; their legal traditions, 95
Germany, 17, 42, 78, 104–5, 128n14, 129n46
Gershom of Mainz, 42, 48
Gideon, 85
gifts, to Judah ben Asher, 18; to judge, 8; to priests and Levites, 16; of rabbinic posts, 113; to scholar, 24, 30, 53
Goldschmidt, Eliezer, 119
Graetz, Heinrich, 78
Great Sanhedrin, 85–86, 141n12

Hai Gaon, son of Nahshon, 96
Hai Gaon, son of Sherira, 99

Halevi, Meir. *See* Meir Halevi
Hamburg, 132n30
hasagat gevul, 38, 48, 50, 113, 135n20
Hasidei Ashkenaz, 15, 129n46
Hasidim, 64, 118
Hasmoneans, 91
haver, 29, 136n18
Hazan, Joseph ben Hayyim, 91–92, 105–6, 108, 150n14
heder, 54, 136n10
hefker, 93, 113
Hekrei Lev. See Hazan, Joseph ben Hayyim
Herod, 91
Hezekiah ben David, 99, 147n14
hiddur mitzvah, 75
hierarchy, rabbinic, 121
high priest, 24, 61–62, 63–64, 65, 68, 73; in Second Temple, 152n6; substitute, 65, 73, 141n12; succession of, 86, 91, 106, 108, 113
Hillel, 6, 7, 24, 66, 91, 105, 109, 112, 129n39, 130n8, 145n21, 145n23
hillul ha-Shem, 12, 115
holiness, 65–67, 72, 75–76, 78, 80, 81, 139n21
Holocaust, 116
honors, of scholars, 143n9; in the synagogue, 45
hora'ath sha'ah, 86
Huna ("Huna I"), 13–14, 42, 45
Huna ben Rav Joshua ("Huna II"), 42
Hungary, 15, 111

imported rabbis, 59, 79, 87
insolvency, of rabbis, 31
investments, 7, 13, 17–18, 20–21; rabbinic posts as, 32
Iran, 10, 95
Iraq, 10, 95
Isaac ben Moses of Vienna, 128n1
Isaac ben Yedaiah, 150n13
Isserlein, Israel, 38–40, 41, 43, 46, 48, 49–51, 72, 93, 124
Isserles, Moses, 61, 73, 135n18; on rabbinic competition, 46–52; on rabbinic inheritance, 109–11, 117; on removal of rabbis, 68, 142n32
Israel, State of, 107, 116, 124; rabbinical courts of, 118–21; rabbis in, 117–21, 131n6

Israeli, Saul, 119, 124
Istanbul, 64
Italy, 28, 41, 42, 104, 125n4

Jacob ben Asher, 17, 106, 108
Jamnia. *See* Yavneh
Jerusalem, 85, 99
Joseph of Arles, 139n11
Johanan ben Matathiah, 78
Joseph, Rabbi, 45, 68, 92
Joseph ben Ulam, 65
Joseph ibn Migas, 69, 104
Joshua, 145n7; ordained by Moses, 5; successor of Moses, 89–90
Joshua, Rabbi: and Rabban Gamaliel, 6–7, 66, 73
jubilee, 74
Judah ben Asher, 16–22, 33; on gambling, 132n39
Judah ben Samuel Hahasid, 15, 129n46
Judah Hanasi, 90–91, 109, 145n22, 151n39
judges, 5–6, 8–10, 13–14, 17, 70, 85–86, 107; and precedent, 153n20; rabbis as, 87–88, 116; in the Talmudic era, 27. *See also* courts
Judges, biblical, 85–86, 90, 143nn2–4, 145n23
Judaism, 16, 65

Kabis, 104
Kagan, Israel Meir Hakohen, 117
Kairawan, 104, 105
kallah month, 11
Karaites, 12, 91
Karna, 8–9; Maimonides' view of, 13–14
Karo, Joseph, 106, 109, 128n38, 135n18; criticism of Maimonides, 24–26; rulings on competition, 42, 46, 52
Khurasan, 95
king, 61, 63, 75, 86, 101, 106–8, 110–11, 149n42; abdication of, 143n9; anointing of, 91, 106, 150n14; rabbis as, 86, 117, 144n18; succession of, 86, 106–7, 113. *See also* crown, of monarchy
kolel, 32, 133nn50–51
Kook, Abraham Isaac, 65
Korah, 72
Kovno, 32, 33

168　Index

Land of Israel. *See* Eretz Israel
law of the land is law, 37, 78
lay leaders, 25, 30, 53, 61, 64, 70, 79, 103, 148n32
leadership, 7, 17, 25, 74, 85, 89–90, 93–94, 98, 103–5, 107, 117, 132n46, 141n4, 141n19, 150n13; consent to, 60–62
Levi Isaac of Berdichev, 64, 153n11
Levites, 16, 93, 126n33
Lithuania, 28, 133n69, 134n4, 136n18
litigation, 7, 29–30, 32, 87, 133n52; fees for, 29–30
loans, 17–20, 32
Loeb, Asher, 29, 33, 132n30
lost property, 7, 13
Lucena, 104

Magdeburg, 103–4
Maimonides, Moses, 23, 28, 31, 112, 122; criticism by Duran, 23–26; criticism by Karo, 24–26; on work and study, 7; rulings: on competition, 42, 46, 52; on gambling, 132n39; on inheritance, 106–7, 110, 120, 149n42; on teaching Torah gratis, 12–14; his successors as *nagid*, 150n22. *See also Mishneh Torah*
Mainz, 104–5
manuscripts, 69, 103
Mar, son of Rav Ashi, 92, 146n35
mara d'atra, 86, 153n1
marketplace, of ideas, 47; Maimonides' view, 13; scholars in, 26; scholars' priority, 7–8, 29, 43
marriage, 7, 8, 28, 87; fees for, 29, 47, 49; to a relative, 129n26
Matathiah ben Joseph, 77–78
matchmaking, 29, 31
Meir Halevi, 78, 108, 142n4
Meir of Padua, 40
Meir of Rothenburg, 17
Metz, 29, 33, 125n4
midrash, 24, 68, 86, 89–93, 101, 108–10
minors, and succession, 107, 110, 114, 149n42
miracle of appointment, 68
Mishnah, 26, 54, 61, 75, 90, 112
Mishnah Berurah, 117

Mishneh Torah, 24, 106–7, 120. *See also* Maimonides, Moses
mitzvah, 24, 80
Modena, Leon, 30–31, 53, 136n18
moneylending, 28, 43
monopolies, 29, 131n21
Morocco, 107
Moses, 85; blesses the Israelites, 92; farewell address, 6; on fees for teaching, 6, 26, 112, 127n29; as king, 90; ordains Joshua, 5; and Korah, 72; presents Bezalel, 61; as rabbi, 5; and his sons, 89–90, 143n4, 145n23
Moses ben Hanokh, 11
Moses ben Hasdai Taku, 103, 134n15
Moses ben Joseph Mitrani, 80
Moses ben Maimon. *See* Maimonides
moving expenses, 33

Nadab, 85, 89
Nahshon Gaon, 96
Naples, 39–40, 53
Napoleon, 37
Narbonne, 104–5
nasi, 66, 75, 91, 96, 101, 105, 109, 141n12, 145n21; his office abolished, 94; supports scholars, 7
Nathan Habavli, 146n6, 148n26
Nehemiah, 142n4
Novaredok, 33, 131n6

Obadiah of Bertinoro, 29, 127n29
ordination, 5, 53, 55, 72, 112, 125n3, 133n54, 136n18; purchase of, 70; as a wedding present, 32
Or Zaru'a, 39, 128n1, 129n46

Padova, 125n4
Padua, 40, 41
Palestine, 132n50. *See also* Eretz Israel
Paris, 37
Patriarch. *See nasi*
pawnbroking, 28
peace, for the sake of, 50, 59, 126n33
pension, 18, 19
Perfet, Isaac ben Sheshet, 33, 78, 108
Petah Tikvah, 120

piety, 8, 26, 106
pirates, 11, 39
Pirke Avot. See *Ethics of the Fathers*
pogroms, 1648–49, 134n16
Poland, 15, 29, 30, 72, 134n4, 140n12
Ponivezh, 33
power of the purse, 60, 77
poverty, 131n7, 136n13
Poznan, 74
prayer, 16, 19, 75, 107
precedent, in Jewish law, 153n20
president. See *nasi*
pride, 129n39
priest anointed for war, 85–86, 90, 106
priests, 7, 9, 16, 93; tax exemption for, 8, 123n33. *See also* crown, of priesthood
printers, 28–29, 31
property, inheritance of, 113–14, 152n7; of priests, 126n33; high priesthood as, 152n6; rabbinic posts as, 113, 123
prophets, 85–86
public opinion, 26, 31, 73, 77–81, 90, 100, 123, 132n46
public service, 72, 111, 122, 154n2
Pumbeditha, 10, 92, 95–99, 127n6, 147n14, 149n33

qualifications, for judges, 86; of heir, 151n39; for high priest, 24; lack of, 89, 147n13, 151n39; for priest anointed for war, 85; for rabbinate, 55, 60, 69, 109, 118–19, 120, 123

Rabbinical High Court of Jerusalem, 118, 153n20
Rashi, 25, 54, 89, 92, 103–4; on leadership, 74
refugees, 41, 44, 54, 107, 134n16
Regensburg, 38–39, 41, 43, 46, 48, 49
Reiss, Schneur Zusha, 114
removal from office, 55, 59, 64–66, 68–69, 73, 77–81, 138n23, 141n10; of cantors, 75
renunciation, 79, 143n9
Resh galuta. See exilarch
resignation, 33, 149n33
retirement, 65, 118
Riga, 34

Rishonim, 150n13; on inheritance, 105–9, 112
Russia, 15, 134n4

Saadiah ben Joseph Gaon, 99–101, 147n18, 149n35
Sabbath, 27, 37, 54, 66, 75, 100, 118–19, 131n14
Sabbetai Zevi, 64
safek d'oraita, 110
Salanter, Israel, 32
sale, of high priesthood, 152n6; of rabbinic posts, 32, 70, 113; by the government, 32, 37–38
Salonika, 61
Samuel ben Avigdor, 139n12
Saragossa, 33
Sarfati, Jacob, 61
Sarfati, Judah, 61
Saul, King of Israel, 68
Saul ben Rabbi Heschel, 144n20
Savoy, 78
Schick, Moses, 111, 113, 143n4, 145n23
schoolteachers, compared to rabbis, 53, 137n19; competition among, 45–46, 52–56, 136n12; fees for, 8, 24, 127n29; Maimonides' view of, 13; poverty of, 136n13; rabbis as, 28, 40; tax exemption for, 136n3
Schwadron, Shalom, 50, 108
scribes, 28, 31, 40, 81, 107; scribe of the academy, 97, 148n25
Sefer Hahinukh, 106, 107; authorship of, 150n17
Sefer Hayerushot, 100
seminaries, rabbinical, 5, 10, 116, 125n4; students in, 31, 60
Sephardim, 27, 42–43, 60, 78, 80–81, 109
serarah, 107
sermons, 27, 32, 59, 66, 131n14, 131n25, 137n6
Seville, 18
Shabbetai Hakohen, 49
Shammai, 7, 125n20
Sherira Gaon, 25, 99, 147n14, 149n35
shipura, 25
shofar, 25
shtetl, 136n13

Shulhan Arukh, 34, 48, 49, 109, 135n18
Sifre, 90–91, 101, 106, 109, 150n18
silence, 5, 129n38
Simeon, son of Judah Hanasi, 91
slaughterers, ritual, 29, 107, 108, 117
slavery, 11, 39, 74, 125n25, 141n19, 143n9
social status, of rabbis, 31
Sofer, Moses, 50–51, 90–91, 105, 108–11, 113, 119, 124, 140n7, 142n32, 152n56
Sofer, Shimon, 111
Solomon ben Yeruham, 145n27
Solomon ibn Adret, 17, 106–8
sons, of Aaron, 85, 89; of cantor, 107–8; of Judah ben Asher, 19, 22; of Judges, 85; of Moses, 89–90, 143n4; of prophets, 85; of scholars, 92, 146n34
Spain, 11–12, 16–17, 23, 42, 103–5, 107, 128n14, 131n8
specialization, by rabbis, 116–17
Spector, Isaac Elhanan, 33, 34
Spira, Menahem, 29, 132n30
stipends, 25, 30, 32, 133n51, 148nn26–27
strikes, rabbinic, 60, 131n6
students, 7, 8, 43, 125n25; attitude toward rabbinate, 31; as rabbinic authorities, 38
Sura, 10, 92, 95–100, 127n6, 146n35, 147n14, 147n18
suspension fee, 9, 27–28, 32, 131n4; and Duran's salary, 23; in Italy, 28; Maimonides' view, 13–14
synagogues, 16, 45, 53, 79; directors of, 116, 142n24; income from, 138n12
synods, rabbinic, 28, 32, 37, 53, 64, 78, 139n11
Syria, 149n38

Tabernacle, 61, 89–90
Talmud, 6, 10, 24–25, 69, 91, 109, 112, 123; on competition, 42, 45; copies of, 126n2; era of, 12, 25, 95; introduced to Spain, 11; jurisprudence of, 55, 60, 65–66, 70, 74, 94; on sons of sages, 92; suspension fee in, 27; text of, 126n2, 128n36; three crowns in, 93
Tam, Jacob, 43
taxation, as an abuse, 15, 32; by geonim, 95; exemption for: priests, 126n33, scholars, 7–8, 29, 39, 43, 125n22, 126n33, 134n19, 134n21, 135n19, schoolteachers, 136n3; Maimonides' view of, 13; resisters, 135n21
Tecoresh, Catriel F., 114
Temple of Jerusalem, 9, 16, 24–25, 65–66, 93, 126n33; destruction of, 63, 126n33; treasury of, 9
Tenenbaum, Malkhiel, 60, 81
tent of meeting, 89
Theodosius II, Roman emperor, 94
tithes, 8, 16; by Asher ben Yehiel, 128n14; by Judah ben Asher, 18–19
titles, rabbinic: 5, 26, 72; gaon, 10, 127n5, 147n14; *haver,* 29, 136n18; *morenu ha-rav,* 125n3; *nagid* and *nasi,* 150n13; rabbi, *rav,* 5. See also *av beth din*
Toledo, Spain, 16, 22, 33
Torah, blessing over, 92; devotion to, 12, 26, 122–23; knowledge of, 47–48; love of, 5; obligation to study, 69; provides a living, 24; study of, 5, 92–93; study of and labor, 25, 112, 130n22; and succession, 89; as a trade, 26
Tosafot, 61–62
Tosefta, 91, 109
trade protection, 42, 47
trades, of rabbis, 28; of refugees, 41; of sages, 6, 24; and Torah study, 25
Troyes, 103–4
Tur. See *Arba'ah Turim*

Ukba, 95
Ukraine, 70
United States, 32, 133n51

Valladolid, 28
Venice, 30, 135n18, 136n18
Vilna, 139n12
Vilna Gaon. *See* Elijah ben Salomon Zalman
visiting rabbi, 45–47

waste, of time, 122, 154n1; gambling as, 132n39
wealth, 6, 7, 8, 13, 15, 20–22, 24, 30, 113
Weil, Jacob, 38, 39–40, 41, 43, 46, 50–51
Worms, 104–5

Yavneh, 6, 66
Yehiel, Rabbi, 129n46
Yossi, rabbi in the Talmud, 92

Zadok Gaon, 96
Zadok, Rabbi, 6, 21, 26, 47, 112
Zemah ben Shahin, 100
Zionism, 64